Building the Skills for Economic Growth
and Competitiveness in Sri Lanka

DIRECTIONS IN DEVELOPMENT
Human Development

Building the Skills for Economic Growth and Competitiveness in Sri Lanka

Halil Dundar, Benoît Millot, Yevgeniya Savchenko, Harsha Aturupane, and Tilkaratne A. Piyasiri

THE WORLD BANK
Washington, D.C.

ISBN (paper): 978-1-4648-0158-7
ISBN (electronic): 978-1-4648-0159-4
DOI: 10.1596/978-1-4648-0158-7

Cover photo: © Luxshmanan Nadaraja, World Bank/Sri Lanka Photo Collection. Used with permission. Further permission required for reuse.
Cover design: Debra Naylor, Naylor Design

Library of Congress Cataloging-in-Publication Data

Dundar, Halil.
Building the skills for economic growth and competitiveness in Sri Lanka / Halil Dundar, Benoît Millot, Yevgeniya Savchenko, Harsha Aturupane, and Tilkaratne A. Piyasiri.
     pages cm. — (Directions in development)
   Includes bibliographical references.
ISBN 978-1-4648-0158-7 (alk. paper) — ISBN 978-1-4648-0159-4 (ebk)
   1. Vocational education—Sri Lanka. 2. Vocational qualifications—Sri Lanka. 3. Labor market—Sri Lanka. 4. Economic development—Sri Lanka. I. World Bank. II. Title.
   LC1047.S72D86 2014
   370.113095493—dc23   2013048723

Contents

Boxes

Figures

Tables

Foreword

Despite internal conflict and the global financial crisis, Sri Lanka has made remarkable progress in the past decade, enjoying healthy economic growth and substantially reducing poverty. Moreover, Sri Lankans are the best-educated people in South Asia: the country has a 98 percent literacy rate, widespread access, high completion rates in both primary and secondary education, and gender parity in general education.

Economic growth and structural changes in the economy, however, make skills development imperative as Sri Lanka implements its development plan—the *Mahinda Chintana* (MC)—to become a regional hub in strategic economic areas. An effective skills development system will help diversify the economy, improve labor productivity and competitiveness, give the country the flexibility it needs to compete effectively in the global economy, and further reduce poverty. As Sri Lanka moves from a factor-driven to an efficiency-driven economy, its workforce is shrinking even as demand for skills—especially advanced technical and soft skills—is rising.

Recognizing how important skills are to raising inclusive and sustainable growth, the Government of Sri Lanka has put skills development at the center of the MC and several other national development programs. A number of initiatives have already been launched. For example, the Tertiary and Vocational Education Commission has been established as the apex agency, the National Vocational Qualification Framework has been developed, colleges of technology have been expanded to educate midlevel technicians and professionals, and the University of Vocational Technology has been opened.

Yet the education and training system still cannot meet skills demands effectively, and youth unemployment is becoming a serious problem. Skills shortages and mismatches are widespread, and firms with undereducated employees and a shortage of skilled labor are less productive. Sri Lanka has been slow to expand technical and vocational education and training (TVET) and tertiary education. Responsibility for TVET is fragmented, the system is supply-driven, there is a shortage of reliable information on labor market skills demand and supply, employers are sidelined, and the resources invested are not linked to performance.

The MC recognizes the severity of the skills constraint and highlights the importance of investing in workforce skills to raise both productivity and competitiveness. This report analyzes skills demand and supply in Sri Lanka and scrutinizes how skills are formed, the factors shaping skills demand, and the responsiveness of the system. Finally, it offers suggestions for how skills development can be improved so that Sri Lanka can meet its economic growth and poverty reduction goals.

Jesko Hentschel
Director, Human Development
South Asia Region
The World Bank

Acknowledgments

The research on which this book is based was conducted by a team led by Halil Dundar, under the general direction of Amit Dar, Education Sector Manager, and Michal Rutkowski and his successor, Jesko Hentschel, Human Development Sector Directors for the South Asia Region. The core team consisted of Benoît Millot, Yevgeniya Savchenko, Harsha Aturupane, and Tilkaratne A. Piyasiri.

The book draws on background papers by Nisha Arunatilake and Samanthi Bandara (cost and financing of vocational and technical education in Sri Lanka), Hugo Blunch (skills demand and firm-based training), and Jee-Peng Tan and Brent Parton (an assessment of workforce development policies). Shalika Subasinghe provided organizational and administrative support for the design and implementation of the skills measurement surveys and preparation of the report.

The team also benefited from the advice and comments of a number of individuals at critical points in the report's preparation, notably Hong Tan, Sunil Chandrasiri, Oni Lusk-Stover, Jee-Peng Tan, Ernesto Caudro, and Gaminie Sunasinghe. Jinendra Kothalawala (Nielsen Company Sri Lanka) and Valerie Evans helped with designing, piloting, and implementing the skills measurement surveys. The peer reviewers for the report were Ximena Del Carpio and Alexandria Valerio. The report also benefited from valuable advice and comments provided by Maria Laura Sanchez Puerta, George Joseph, and Robert Chase. The team worked closely with government counterparts during preparation of the report. The team gratefully acknowledges comments and assistance from Dr. B. Batagoda, Ministry of Finance and Planning; Professor D. S. Wijeyesekera, Tertiary and Vocational Education Commission; and Mr. A. R. Desapriya, Ministry of Youth Affairs and Skills Development. Many individuals from the Ministry of Youth Affairs and Skills Development and the Ministry of Finance and Planning also participated in and provided extremely useful insights at consultations and dissemination events.

None of the above bears any responsibility for the analyses and findings of this report. The authors alone assume full responsibility for its conclusions.

The team also gratefully acknowledges financial support from the Skills Measurement Multi-Donor Trust Fund and the Rapid Social Response Multi-Donor Trust Fund for the design and conduct of the skills measurement surveys and from the Canadian International Development Agency (CIDA) for the preparation of background reports.

Kalpana Kaul assisted with the editing of background papers. Anne Grant did an excellent job of editing and preparing the manuscript for publication. We are grateful to Anita Fernando and Alejandro Welch for their assistance on administrative issues. Finally, we also thank the World Bank's Publishing and Knowledge Division, in particular Rumit Pancholi, for efficient management of the publication process.

About the Authors

Halil Dundar is a lead education specialist at the World Bank. He is currently leading the Bank's operational and analytical work on tertiary education in Pakistan and skills development in Sri Lanka. Previously, he managed the Bank's operational and analytical work on education in Azerbaijan, Ethiopia, and Nigeria. Before joining the Bank, he worked as a research associate in the Office of Planning and Analysis at the University of Minnesota and subsequently held the position of assistant professor of education policy at the Middle East Technical University in Ankara, Turkey, and served as a policy advisor to the Turkish Ministry of Education. He has published numerous journal articles and book chapters on education finance, productivity, and quality improvement issues. Mr. Dundar holds a PhD in education from the University of Minnesota, with a concentration in the economics of higher education.

Benoît Millot is a former lead education economist at the World Bank, where he specialized in education finance and higher education issues in several regions, having led the Bank's operational and analytical work on tertiary education. He holds a PhD in the economics of education from the University of Dijon, France. Before joining the Bank, he was a research director at the Institute for Research on Economics of Education in Dijon.

Yevgeniya Savchenko is a consultant at the World Bank with specialization in education, human capital development, labor markets, and enterprise behavior. She holds a PhD in economics from Georgetown University.

Harsha Aturupane is a lead education specialist at the World Bank. He is the Human Development Coordinator for Sri Lanka and the Maldives. He currently manages the Bank's analytical and operational work on education in Sri Lanka and the Maldives and on higher education in Afghanistan. He has a PhD and MPhil in economics from the University of Cambridge. Before joining the Bank, he was senior lecturer in economics at the University of Colombo, Sri Lanka.

Tilkaratne A. Piyasiri is vice chancellor of the University of Vocational Technology in Sri Lanka. He specializes in technical and vocational education training issues with extensive experience in Sri Lanka, leading the government's advisory committee on the preparation of the national skills development plan. Before joining the university in 2012, he was the director general of Sri Lanka's Tertiary and Vocational Education Commission. He earned a PhD in mechanical engineering from the University of Newcastle upon Tyne, United Kingdom.

Acronyms

ADB	Asian Development Bank
ATI	Advanced Technological Institute
ATPA	Accredited Training Providers Association
BCW	basic competencies to work
CBT	competency-based training
CCPI	Colombo Consumer Price Index
CETRAC	Construction Equipment Training Centre
CGTTI	Ceylon-German Technical Training Institute
CIMA	Chartered Institute of Management Accountants
CIMO	Integral Quality and Modernization Program, Mexico
COT	College of Technology
CVET	continuing vocational education and training
DCS	Department of Census and Statistics
DNP	Department of National Planning
DTET	Department of Technical Education and Training
EPZ	export processing zones
ESDFP	Education Sector Development Framework and Programme
ET&R	Education, Training and Research Unit
FC	Finance Commission
FCCISL	Federation of Chambers of Commerce and Industry of Sri Lanka
FDI	foreign direct investment
GCE	General Certificate of Education
GDP	gross domestic product
GNI	gross national income
HEI	higher educational institution
HRD	human resource development
HRDF	Human Resource Development Fund, Singapore
IAU	Internal Audit Unit
ICT	information and communications technology

ICTAD	Institute for Construction Training and Development
ICTRL	International Center for the Training of Rural Leaders
IDA	International Development Association
ILA	individual learning accounts
INGRIN	Institute of Printing and Graphics
ISCED	International Standard Classification of Education
IT	information technology
IVET	initial vocational education and training
KPP	*Kursus Para Profesi*
LFS	Labor Force Survey
LIC	low-income country
LMIC	lower-middle-income country
M&E	monitoring and evaluation
MC	*Mahinda Chintana*, Sri Lanka's economic development plan
MFP	Ministry of Finance and Planning
MIC	middle-income country
MIS	management information system
MoAG	Ministry of Agriculture
MoCESHCA	Ministry of Construction, Engineering Services, Housing and Common Amenities
MoE	Ministry of Education
MoED	Ministry of Economic Development
MoH	Ministry of Health
MoHE	Ministry of Higher Education
MTEF	medium-term expenditure framework
MYASD	Ministry of Youth Affairs and Skills Development
NAITA	National Apprentice and Industrial Training Authority
NASVI	National Alliance of Street Vendors in India
NCS	National Competency Standards
NEC	National Education Commission
NGO	nongovernmental organization
NHREP	National Human Resources and Employment Policy
NIBM	National Institute of Business Management
NVQ	National Vocational Qualification
NYSC	National Youth Services Council
OECD	Organisation for Economic Co-operation and Development
OJT	on-the-job training
OPA	Organization of Professional Associations
OTC	Operator Training Centre

PIP	Public Investment Program
PPP	public-private partnership
PSDC	Penang Skills Development Centre
RPL	recognition of prior learning
SABER	World Bank System Approach for Better Education Results Framework for Workforce Development
SDF	skills development fund
SDFL	Skills Development Fund Ltd.
SENAI	National Industrial Apprenticeship Service, Brazil
SEPI	Self Employment Promotion Initiative
SLBFE	Sri Lanka Bureau of Foreign Employment
SLIATE	Sri Lanka Institute of Advanced Technological Education
SLIOP	Sri Lanka Institute of Printing
SLITHM	Sri Lanka Institute of Tourism and Hotel Management
SLQF	Sri Lanka Qualifications Framework
SSC	Sector Skills Council
STEP	Skills Toward Employment and Productivity
TCTI	Technology and Computer Training Institute
TVEC	Tertiary and Vocational Education Commission
TVET	technical and vocational education and training
UCEP	Underprivileged Children's Education Program, Bangladesh
UGC	University Grants Commission
UIS	UNESCO Institute of Statistics
UMIC	upper-middle-income country
UNESCO	United Nations Educational, Scientific, and Cultural Organization
UNIVOTEC	University of Vocational Technology
VET	vocational education and training
VTA	Vocational Training Authority of Sri Lanka
VTT	Vocational Training Tax, Tunisia
WfD	workforce development

Overview

Introduction

As in the rest of the world (ADB 2008; McKinsey 2012; OECD 2012; UNESCO 2012), demand for job-specific skills is growing in Sri Lanka, which intends to become a more competitive, middle-income country (MIC). As its economy has grown, the composition of its gross domestic product (GDP) has begun moving from agriculture to higher-value-added industry and services, where jobs as machine operators, technicians, craftspeople, sales personnel, professionals, and managers require specialized training.

Sustaining economic growth is at the heart of the government's development plan, the *Mahinda Chintana* (MC). Its ambitious vision rests on Sri Lanka becoming a maritime, aviation, commercial, energy, and knowledge hub for Asia. To continue achieving the government's goal of annual real GDP growth of at least 8 percent well into the future and to make Sri Lanka a hub in those five strategic areas will require a highly skilled workforce. Unfortunately, at present,

- although Sri Lankans spend more time in the education system than neighbors in South Asia, employers are questioning the system's quality and its relevance; and
- major skills shortages and mismatches undermine productivity and thus growth.

Skills development is a cumulative life cycle process that begins during early childhood development and continues through general and tertiary education, technical and vocational education and training (TVET), and on-the-job training (OJT). The knowledge base on skills produced by the general and higher education sectors in Sri Lanka is deep (see, for example, World Bank 2005, 2009, 2011). However, the TVET policy debate[1] has not been informed by rigorous evidence-based studies of the incidence, determinants, and effects of TVET on how different groups, especially youth and females, perform in the labor market.

To design a responsive reform agenda, policy makers need to thoroughly understand both demand-side pressures for skills and constraints on skills supply.

To identify constraints on effective skills development and offer policy options for addressing gaps, this study asks:

- What is the demand for skills in Sri Lanka? What characterizes skills gaps and mismatches?
- What skills do Sri Lanka's workers have? How do individuals with different levels of education, training, and skills fare in the labor market?
- Does the education and training system produce the skills the labor market demands? If not, why not?
- How can TVET more efficiently build the skills demanded?

Job-specific skills are supplied by formal TVET and higher education institutions, nonformal training centers (for example, firm-based), and informal training (such as apprenticeships). This report is concerned primarily with the pre-employment training provided by formal TVET[2] and the OJT provided by firms; it discusses skills formation by primary and secondary education and higher education institutions only as part of the analysis of skills demand and supply.

Investment in building job-specific technical and vocational skills is vital to economic growth and competitiveness. The complexity of competing in the global economy requires not only advanced technical and vocational skills but also a workforce that can adjust to shifts in demand. At 68th out of 144 countries in the 2012/13 Global Competitiveness Index, Sri Lanka compares favorably with the rest of South Asia but trails East Asian countries. To transition from being factor-driven to being efficiency-driven, its workforce needs skills like computer knowledge, ability to operate the latest equipment, and fluency in foreign languages to communicate with international clients.

Asked about barriers to their growth, Sri Lankan firms put the quality and supply of skilled technicians third after taxes and regulation, and financing (Dutz and O'Connell 2013). Employers around the world are demanding that new hires have both technical and "soft" skills (see, for example, di Gropello, Kruse, and Tandon 2010; di Gropello, Tan, and Tandon 2010; World Bank 2012a).

Skills are essential to reducing poverty and improving individual well-being. In Sri Lanka, for instance, workers with technical skills earn more than those without even if both have the same amount of education. Technical skills also reduce the likelihood that a worker will turn to the informal sector for work or be underemployed. However, skills do not automatically lead to jobs and growth (box O.1); skills development needs to be part of a comprehensive national strategy for economic development. As a cumulative life cycle process, it should also be part of an umbrella education strategy.

Skills formation is complex. Traditionally, skills are measured through proxy indicators, such as educational attainment or test scores. But proxies are often an inadequate basis on which to design skills development policies that can actually meet labor market needs because they do not fully capture the diversity of skills the labor market demands. Skills development[3] crosses institutional boundaries, takes place in a variety of settings, engages a highly diverse

---

Box O.1 Global Evidence: Pitfalls in Skills Building

Skills contribute significantly to economic growth and poverty alleviation. Yet factors beyond the education and training system contribute to skills shortages and mismatches, reducing the impact of workforce development programs. For example, the 2013 *World Development Report on Jobs* cautioned as follows:

> The root cause of skill shortages or mismatches might not lie with the education and training system. Shortages and mismatches may instead result from wrong signals generated by market distortions and institutional failures elsewhere in the economy. If a civil service career pays overly well, young people may study to obtain such jobs even if they need to queue for them. This can lead to the acquisition of skills that are irrelevant in the private sector and to unrealistic expectations, as was observed, for example, in the Arab Republic of Egypt. Similarly, compressed pay scales reduce the incentives to invest more in education and training. Lack of information about employment opportunities, transportation costs, or housing market failures may be the real reason why workers do not take available jobs. In all of these cases, constraints that seem to be skills-related actually reside outside the education and training system (World Bank 2013, 174–77).

If the formal economy cannot accommodate all entrants to the labor market, most of them may end up in the informal sector or become unemployed or underemployed. On the other hand, migration of skilled labor in search of better-paying jobs may be contributing to skills shortages.

---

clientele, involves multiple delivery mechanisms, and must constantly respond to changing occupational requirements.

Skills formation proceeds in stages, each building on the previous one. *Basic cognitive skills*, such as literacy and numeracy, are typically acquired in primary school. *Job-specific* skills are usually acquired in TVET or higher education or through apprenticeships and OJT. *Soft* skills may be acquired at any point, often by interactions with family members, peers, or colleagues. An efficient skills development system embraces the entire spectrum of education and training and provides opportunities for lifelong learning.

Background

Economic Growth

Sri Lanka is a lower-middle-income country (LMIC) that had per capita income of $2,836 in 2011—significantly higher than South Asia as a whole but below MIC averages (figure O.1). Its economy has enjoyed 5.3 percent average annual growth for the past decade. The cessation of armed conflict accelerated growth, which averaged 8 percent in 2010 and 2011 (World Bank 2012b). Although growth in Sri Lanka was lower than in India, since 2003 it has been higher than

Figure O.1 GDP Per Capita, Selected Countries, 2011
GDP per capita is measured in USD

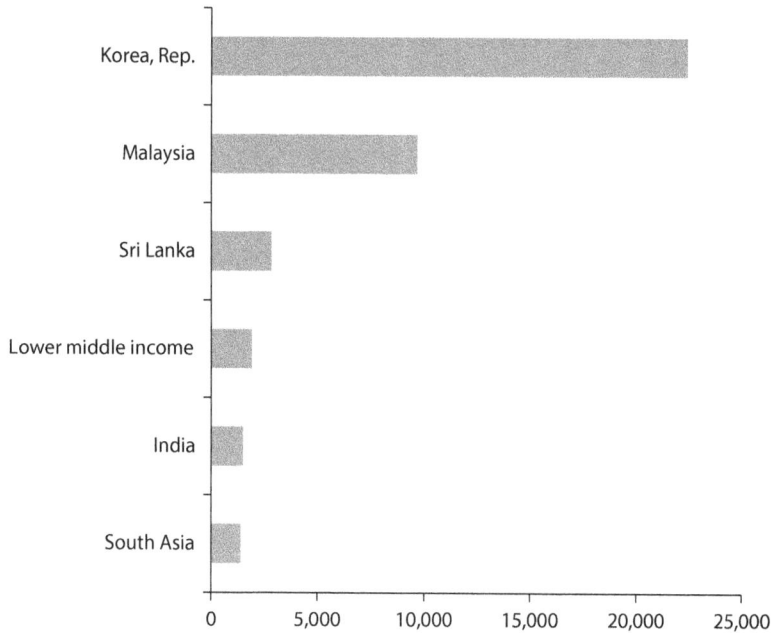

Source: World Development Indicators, World Bank 2012c.

in Malaysia or the Republic of Korea (figure O.2). The government goal is to increase GDP per capita to $4,000 by 2016.

Between 1977 and 2010, agriculture's share in GDP declined from 30.7 percent to 12.8 percent (close to Malaysia's 11 percent); the industry share stabilized at around 29.4 percent; and the services share rose from 40.6 percent to 57.8 percent (similar to Korea). The share of agriculture was lower than in South Asia as a whole (18 percent) or the average for other LMICs (17 percent). However, in Sri Lanka the share of industry in GDP is closer to that of South Asian countries and LMICs than to Korea or Malaysia.

Between 2002 and 2009–10, the poverty rate declined from 22.7 percent to 8.9 percent, more because of economic growth (56 percent) than redistribution (33 percent). However, sustaining the impressive progress in poverty reduction requires a skilled workforce and a more dynamic labor market.

Labor Market Trends

Since 1990 Sri Lanka's labor force has been growing by 2 percent a year, from 6 million in 1990 to 8.46 million in 2012. The working age population (aged 15–59) is now expected to grow more slowly, from an estimated 13.3 million in 2011 to 13.9 million in 2026, and then gradually decline. Moreover, labor force participation declined from 50.3 percent to 47.2 percent between 2000 and 2012. In comparison, participation rates in faster-growing East Asian economies are close to

Figure O.2 Real GDP Growth Rates, Selected Countries
Percent

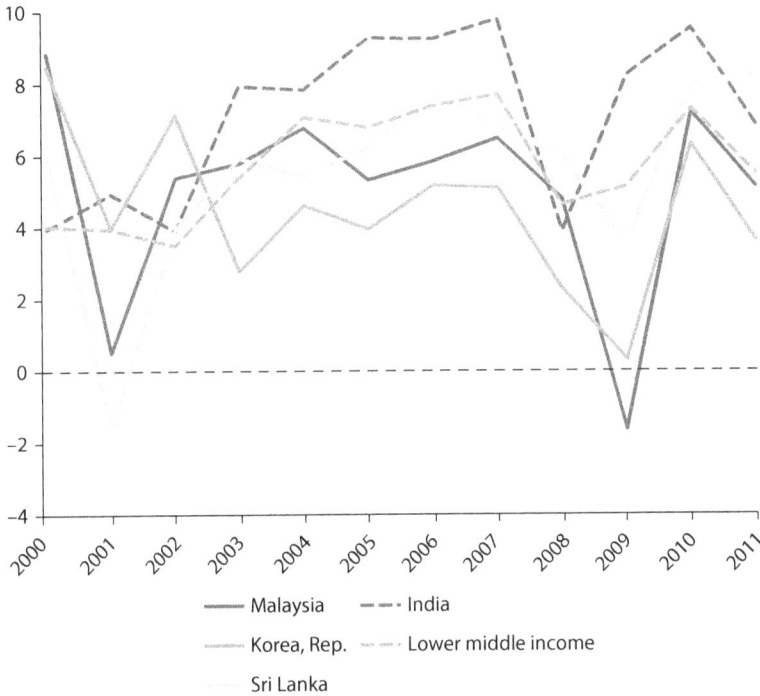

Legend:
— Malaysia   — — · India
—— Korea, Rep.   ·· — ·· Lower middle income
····· Sri Lanka

Source: World Development Indicators, World Bank 2012c.

60 percent. Meanwhile (1) Sri Lanka's population growth rate has been declining, increasing the dependency ratio; (2) more working-age adults are leaving to work abroad; and (3) the participation of women in the labor force is half that of men. As the job market tightens, to sustain economic growth Sri Lanka will need more workers with better and more relevant-job specific skills.

Though unemployment has been low at just 4.2 percent (DCS 2011), Sri Lanka has high underemployment and a large informal economy. Of respondents to the Skills Toward Employment and Productivity (STEP) survey, 59 percent were in the labor force and only 6 percent of those were unemployed in 2012. But 18 percent were underemployed[4] and 37 percent were self-employed.[5]

The low unemployment rate masks several major problems: (1) youth aged 15–29 are three times more likely to be unemployed (13 percent) than adults (4 percent), and unemployment is almost 20 percent for those aged 15–24; (2) while unemployment declines with education level for adults, almost 25 percent of young adults aged 15–29 with a bachelor's degree and above are unemployed, compared to 1 percent of adults; (3) the unemployment rate for women (10 percent) is three times higher than for men; and (4) underemployment is high, especially for women (22 percent) and rural residents (21 percent).

Underemployment of youth peaks at GCE O-level education (26 percent), after which it declines. The reasons for underemployment are not clear.

Between 1971 and 2010, agriculture's share of employment declined from 51 percent to 34 percent and the shares of industry rose from 11 percent to 25 percent and of services from 38 percent to 42 percent. Between 2000 and 2008 labor productivity, measured as output per worker, increased in the services sector from SL Rs 352,000 to SL Rs 479,000, in industry from SL Rs 312,000 to SL Rs 357,000, and in agriculture from SL Rs 100,000 to SL Rs 122,000. Since population growth is slowing, improving labor productivity will be a priority if the MC goals are to be achieved.

An estimated two-thirds of Sri Lankan workers are employed informally. Disaggregation by sector of employment shows that 87 percent of agricultural and 51 percent of nonagricultural workers are employed informally (DCS 2011). Most have little general education, having dropped out because of family poverty or a lack of schooling or training opportunities. Recognizing the dominant role of the informal sector in the economy, the government now envisions skills training for workers in this sector (SSM 2012).

Labor Force Quality

With a 98 percent literacy rate, Sri Lanka is the most educated country in South Asia. About 96 percent of its citizens have completed primary school and 87 percent secondary school, and there is gender parity in completion. But despite free education, individuals from poorer backgrounds have fewer years of education than those from richer families. While the proportion of Sri Lankans with secondary education is comparable with East Asian countries, for example Malaysia, Sri Lanka's tertiary education numbers are much lower than in East Asian countries.

Although *access* to primary and lower secondary education is impressive, *achievement* is modest. For example, a mere one-third of primary school children master language and mathematics skills. Relatively few students in tertiary education are enrolled in programs defined as national priorities, the labor market relevance of many programs is not up to date, and many graduates are idle for a considerable time before their first job (Gunatilaka, Mayer, and Vodopivec 2010).[6]

Main Findings

Skills Profiles of the Sri Lankan Labor Force

This study classifies skills into three broad categories: cognitive, technical, and noncognitive ("soft") skills. Almost all individuals with higher education (bachelor's degree or higher) use cognitive skills, but only 52 percent of those with primary and secondary education do so. Though cognitive skills are shaped mostly in primary and secondary school, one in 10 respondents to the STEP survey said that limited literacy impeded their job search or career growth. Higher cognitive skills measured by test scores are associated with a larger number of young people employed for wages outside of agriculture, and to some extent noticeably more in higher-status occupations (Lee and Newhouse 2013).

Few workers have technical skills; for example, only 16 percent of workers can use computers and only 24 percent are proficient in English. Moreover, while 28 percent of the urban population and 44 percent of higher-skilled workers use computers, only 8 percent of rural residents and lower-skilled workers do so. The trend is similar for English language skills.

Employers are increasingly demanding soft skills, such as teamwork and presentation ability, conscientiousness, and decision making. About 77 percent of workers actively use teamwork skills and 50 percent presentation skills. However, Sri Lanka's education and training system does not do much to shape soft skills. This implies an urgent need for curriculum revision.

Returns to Schooling and Skills

For the past decade in Sri Lanka returns to GCE A-levels and above have been rising (figure O.3a) and those to GCE O-levels and below have been decreasing. Between 2000 and 2012, for instance, the premium for passing GCE A-levels relative to GCE O-levels went up from 17 percent to 31 percent and the premium for a bachelor's degree and above relative to GCE A-levels increased from 35 percent to 54 percent.

The return on TVET went up from about 12 percent in 2000 to 21 percent in 2004 (figure O.3a) but by 2012 had dropped slightly, to 17 percent. In 2012 the TVET premium was 25 percent for the self-employed but only 12 percent for formal wage-earners.[7] It appears that in 2012 there were no statistically significant returns to either formal or informal apprenticeship.

Sri Lankans with technical skills like technology, computer knowledge, and English (figure O.3b) and soft skills like openness and emotional stability earn more than those without them.

Skills Shortages and Mismatches

The major drivers of skills demand in Sri Lanka are economic growth, labor migration, urbanization, expansion of primary and secondary education, and demographic change. Several of these drivers call for a better-educated and trained labor force, upgraded skills, and workers able to use new technologies and perform complex tasks efficiently.

Firms[8] in Sri Lanka are much more likely (16 percent) to identify an inadequate labor force as a major or severe constraint than firms in Pakistan (8.1 percent) or Nepal (5.9 percent). The proportion of manufacturing firms experiencing skills constraints grew from 21 percent in 2004 to 26 percent in 2011.[9] Skills constraints suppress both enterprise performance and productivity.

Sri Lanka seems to have serious mismatches in education and training supply and demand, though useful data are limited. Comparing employers' perception of skills demand with the skills available in the workforce[10] reveals serious

Figure O.3 Wage Premiums in Sri Lanka, by Education and Skill Type
Percent

a. Wage premiums, by education

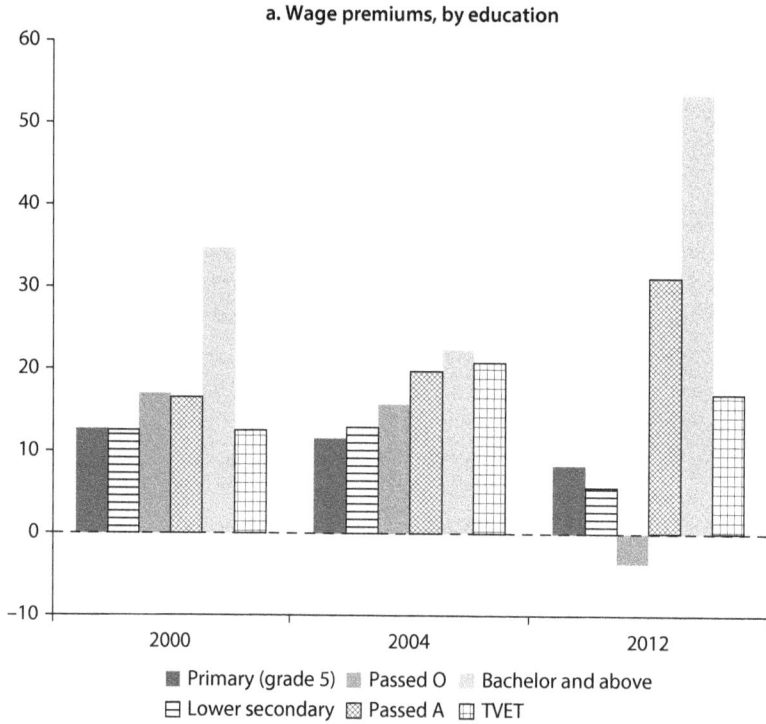

Primary (grade 5) ■ Passed O Bachelor and above
⊟ Lower secondary ▨ Passed A ⊞ TVET

b. Wage premiums, by skill type

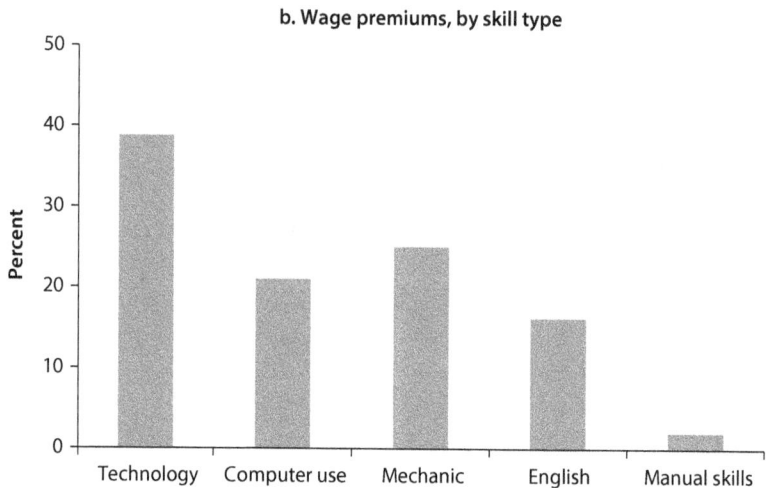

Sources: Labor Force Surveys 2000, 2004 (DCS 2010); STEP household survey 2012.
Note: The first bar for each year (Panel A) reflects the wage premium for completed primary education relative to no or incomplete primary education, and the next to the last bar the premium for completing bachelor's and above relative to passing A-levels. The last bar is the premium for TVET relative to non-TVET. The wage premiums represent differences in the coefficients of a regression of log hourly wage on basic controls (education, TVET, gender, urban, province, age, and age squared).

mismatches: while 56 percent of employers think that high-skilled workers should pass GCE A-levels, only 18 percent of the population have done so. Similarly, 70 percent of employers think that an average low-skilled worker should have passed GCE O-levels, but only 35 percent of low-skilled employees and 40 percent of the self-employed have done so. About 60 percent of employers expect average workers in a high-skilled occupation to have completed technical or vocational education and training, and 24 percent think low-skilled workers should have. Yet only 16 percent of the population has done so.

At Sri Lanka's current level of economic development, there are no substantial mismatches in low-skilled jobs between supply of and demand for cognitive skills (figure O.4a), but since foundational cognitive skills are essential for acquiring more advanced job-specific skills, building cognitive skills must be a policy priority if the country is to become efficiency-driven.

Sri Lanka does not produce enough of the job-specific technical skills employers value: 80 percent expect a higher-skilled worker to know English and 40 percent expect that of less-skilled workers. Similarly, 75 percent think an average higher-skilled worker should have computer skills and 38 percent expect the same of lower-skilled workers (figure O.4b). However, only 20 percent of Sri Lankans are fluent in English and only 15 percent can use computers. The differences are less stark in workers who are formally employed than in the informal sector.

Sri Lanka's TVET system has failed to provide the skills needed for work in fields like tourism that are vital to economic diversification and competitiveness. Meanwhile, educated Sri Lankans aged 19–25 have unemployment rates as high as 28 percent.

Many employers question the quality and relevance of TVET curricula in terms of conveying up-to-date knowledge (50 percent) or producing the kinds (54 percent) or levels (52 percent) of skills needed (figure O.5).

In Sri Lanka, a mix of factors probably contributes to skills shortages and mismatches, e.g.:

- The formal wage economy may not be generating enough jobs to accommodate all labor market entrants.
- Market distortions and institutional failures may also be giving the wrong signals for employment, resulting in unrealistic expectations about job opportunities.
- Skilled workers migrating for better-paying jobs may be contributing to skills shortages.
- The labor market does not provide enough information to guide policies related to skills demands and the provision and quality of training. Students choosing courses, institutions wanting to respond to changing demands, and policy makers all need more comprehensive information.
- Finally, TVET programs may be outdated and unresponsive to changing employer demand, with public budgets allocated without real incentives for performance.

Building the Skills for Economic Growth and Competitiveness in Sri Lanka
http://dx.doi.org/10.1596/978-1-4648-0158-7

Figure O.4 Skills Mismatches
Percent

a. Cognitive skills

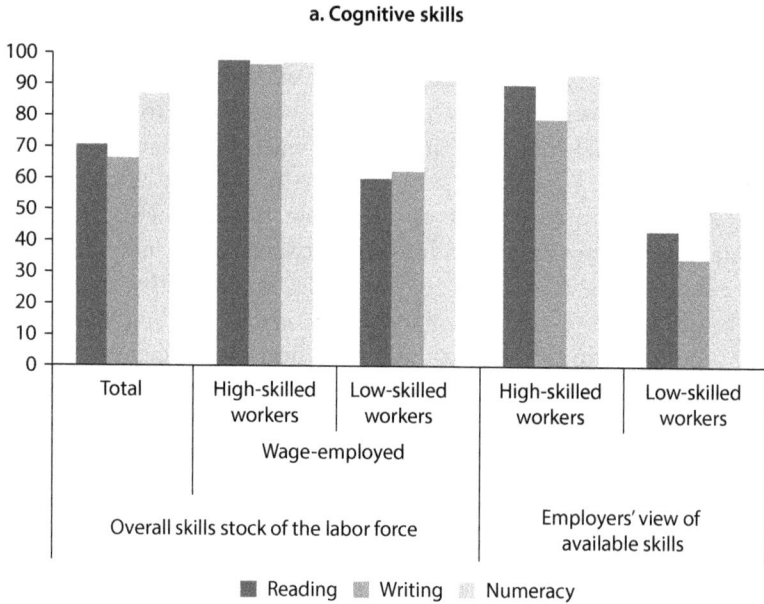

Reading Writing Numeracy

b. Technical skills

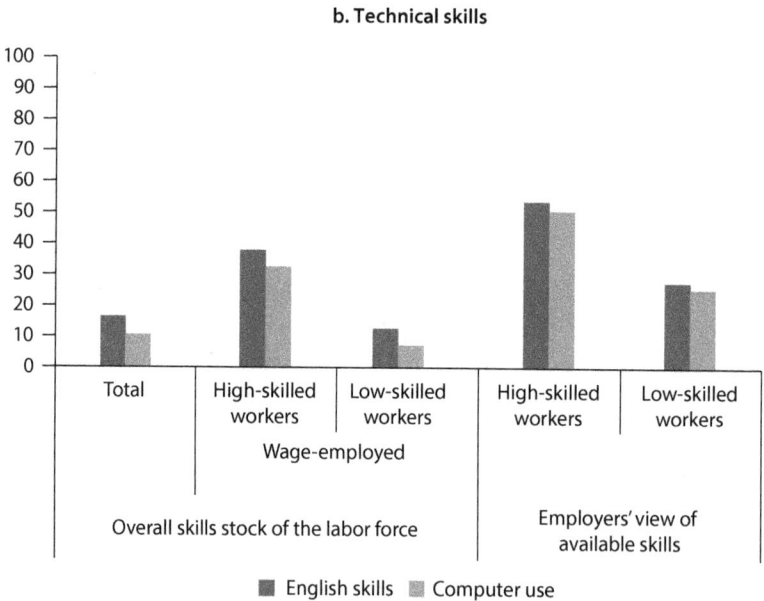

English skills Computer use

Source: Sri Lanka STEP Household Skills Measurement and Employer Surveys.
Note: Overall skills stock is measured from the STEP household survey of the population aged 15–64. Employers'
view of available skills is measured from the STEP employer survey and serves as a proxy for skills demand.

Figure O.5 Employer Perceptions of General Education, TVET, and University
Percent

The general education, TVET, and university system DO NOT...

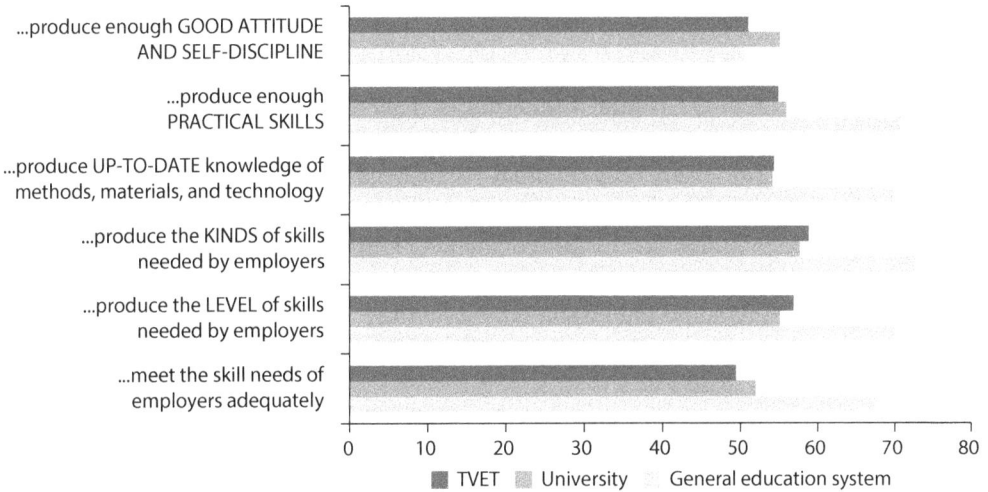

Source: Sri Lanka STEP Employers Survey.

Challenges to Formal TVET

Every year an estimated 140,000 students complete general education without having acquired job-related skills. The government sees the TVET system as having a major role in closing the gap, but Sri Lanka's goal of becoming a competitive middle-income economy may be jeopardized by the system's deficiencies in terms of organization and management effectiveness; access and equity; internal efficiency and effectiveness (for example, quality of instruction, unit costs, resource utilization); and relevance or external efficiency.

Organization and Management Effectiveness

Sri Lanka is building a coherent framework for training, but the complexity of the TVET system requires more effective coordination to deal with challenges confronting the sector like these:

• Current skills development programs are not yet well-integrated with national development priorities, which stress skills development as being vital to economic growth.
• The planning process does not regularly ascertain national and regional demand based on labor market information. Timely and accurate information about current demand for skills and available training opportunities is lacking, as are reliable forecasts of potential needs.

- To realize government skills-development policies, inter-ministerial coordination is necessary but not as yet formalized Preparation of the National Human Resources and Employment Policy (NHREP) and the proposed Inter-Ministerial Sector Coordination Committee as part of the Government's Skills Sector Development Program, would be major steps toward coordinating policies and programs at the national level.
- Because the central authorities exercise tight control, public training centers have little incentive to respond to—let alone anticipate—potential demand.
- Employers are only minimally associated with the activities of public institutions and centers; the TVET sector is heavily supply-driven, taking into account neither the skills demand of employers nor the needs of the informal sector.
- Finally, some employers have taken the initiative to upgrade staff skills but there are no government mechanisms, such as training funds, to encourage them to do so.

Access and Equity

Public institutions provide training without charge, and students are given additional, though meager, financial support. While there is gender parity in educational attainment, there are inequities in access to education and training for the poor and those living in rural areas.

Because some TVET programs are perceived as a dead-end or last-choice option, student demand for them is low, especially given the perception that those in TVET have less academic ability; negative perceptions about its financial payoff; a negative association between training and manual labor; a lack of vertical articulation; and restrictions on upward mobility.

The government is now working to increase awareness about TVET, promote it as a pathway to upward mobility, and introduce horizontal articulation. Although initiatives like the University of Vocational Technology (UNIVOTEC) have increased the profile of TVET, their effectiveness needs to be rigorously evaluated.

TVET Program Quality

The quality of what is taught varies substantially by institution. About 64 percent of employers state that the general education system is not meeting their skill needs, especially for the newer trades. They also feel that TVET graduates lack general business and management skills, which reduces their opportunities for promotion. Several factors contribute to poor TVET outcomes:

- *The poor quality of primary and secondary education* limits student achievements, lengthens the time it takes to complete training, and often necessitates bridging programs.
- *Governance and Finance arrangements* suffer because (1) the private sector is not involved adequately in skills development. (2) public institutions have little freedom to replace obsolete training courses, change curricula, and

involve the private sector in decision making so as to become more responsive to labor market demand; and (3) resources are not linked to performance.

- *Training standards and curricula* need to be updated. Competency-based training and the National Vocational Qualification (NVQ) framework could help define training standards based on occupational requirements, but NVQ implementation is still problematic.
- *The quality of instruction:* There is a shortage of qualified instructors, especially those with industrial experience; inadequate professional development opportunities drain teacher motivation and discourage retention; salaries and performance incentives are unattractive; and conditions of service are poor.
- *Instructional materials, equipment, and facilities:* Except for a few established institutions, instructional materials, equipment, and facilities are not up to par.
- *Quality assurance:* A large number of private providers are still neither registered nor accredited, and there is no mechanism to monitor and improve quality in public institutions, for example by program and institutional reviews and self-assessments.
- *Monitoring and evaluation:* There are no regular studies that track competencies achieved, and it is not possible to evaluate the outputs of TVET programs directly.

Relevance

The government has moved to make TVET programs more relevant to the labor market by establishing the Tertiary and Vocational Education Commission (TVEC)—which also has members from the private sector—and by creating the NVQ system with employer participation. Moreover, several institutions do have good links with business. However, there are continued challenges in ensuring relevance:

- The NVQ framework, though created with employer input, does not cover the full range of skills employers require.
- Though skills needs change along with changes in the economy and labor market demand, the TVET system is not designed to respond quickly.
- There is no mechanism, aside from the NVQ, through which employers can feed their skills needs into the TVET system.
- Because ministries do not coordinate, delivery of TVET programs is often not aligned with national development priorities.
- Some private training providers are more oriented to social demand than to actual labor market demand.

TVET Cost and Financing

Sources of financing. In 2012, the total financial effort for the sector amounted to about 1.5 percent of general government expenditures; the sector seems under-resourced compared to neighboring countries or other MICs.

Building the Skills for Economic Growth and Competitiveness in Sri Lanka
http://dx.doi.org/10.1596/978-1-4648-0158-7

Responsibility for public TVET is scattered among a number of ministries, making it difficult to accurately estimate its costs. Spending in constant prices by the Ministry of Youth Affairs and Skills Development (MYASD), the main source, has steadily increased over a decade. The ministries of agriculture; health; construction, engineering services, housing and common amenities; and economic development run their own training centers, at significant cost. Spending by other line ministries that provide training is minimal, as is provincial spending on TVET. Public institutions rely essentially on public funding and rarely recover their costs, despite modest fees for some audiences. They rarely seek alternative sources of revenues from productive activities because they would not be able to retain the revenues.

Management of resources. Budget allocations are arbitrarily determined and not linked to performance. Public TVET institutions are mainly financed by the national budget and are based on previous allocations, with annual inflation adjustments. A well-monitored change to a more transparent system through which an institution requests funds based on identified needs would help ensure that funds are allocated more effectively.

Where the money goes. MYASD investments in TVET are targeted at sectors identified in the MC as priorities. Development spending currently outweighs recurrent. The bulk of the MYASD budget is funneled to the operation of centers run by about 10 agencies within the ministry.

TVET unit costs in Sri Lanka are close to those observed for secondary education in South Asia but vary depending on the type of institution. Some centers operating with a small staff train many students, and many centers rely heavily on contractual instructors to maximize flexibility. Because monetary incentives are too low to attract qualified instructors, staff turnover is high. External efficiency is lower in terms of placement but relatively higher in terms of incomes for trainees who find a job after completing a course.

Strategic Priorities

To reach middle-income status, Sri Lanka is moving to capture the recent peace dividends and deal with the expiration of its demographic dividend. The current quantitative and qualitative mismatch between the supply of and demand for skilled labor threatens a critical source of growth. In particular, current TVET is not responsive to changes in employer demand, and incentives to ensure quality TVET services are not sufficient. The country needs to embark on integrated reforms like those identified in the MC and in the NHREP and incorporated into the Skills Sector Development Plan (2014–2020). But much remains to be done. The following reforms can be framed as strategic priorities and policy options.

Priority 1. The preparation and implementation of an integrated skills development strategy is essential if workers are to acquire job-specific skills.

An integrated approach to skills formation that covers the entire education and training system from early childhood through OJT is crucial. Skills formation is cumulative. Improving the quality of primary and secondary education will help build a solid foundation in literacy, numeracy, science and technology, and languages. Employees with a sound foundation are more trainable; they can learn on the job, solve problems, communicate clearly, and function well in teams. As Sri Lanka moves up the development ladder, it needs to balance the priorities of primary, secondary, and postsecondary education to meet increasingly complex education and skills requirements.

Priority 2. The quality of current TVET services needs to be improved so that it becomes both more attractive for youths and more relevant for employers.

A student's decision to acquire vocational training or technical education depends on the perceived benefits, particularly financial. In turn, monetary returns are linked to the quality of the training received. Similarly, employers' decisions to hire TVET graduates depend on whether the graduates are ready to work immediately or need more training. In short, the decisions of both workers and employers are linked to their perceptions of training quality.

To achieve Sri Lanka's MC goals, systemic curriculum reform that builds on experiences from the NVQ framework and explicitly incorporates industry-led competency-based standards is necessary to ensure that the skills students acquire in the educational system are both relevant and of high quality. Some countries successfully involve employers directly in designing training curricula (OECD 2012).

General education and TVET do not produce needed soft skills to the same degree as cognitive or technical skills. Given their importance, Sri Lanka can learn from countries that are now incorporating soft skills into youth training curricula.

Creating opportunities for the professional development of instructors and introducing performance-based incentives could enhance TVET instruction and the relevance of the skills taught to labor market needs. Teaching staff must not only be qualified in their own technical field but should also have mastered the pedagogical tools needed for efficient transmission of knowledge and practices.

Vocational centers often lack equipment that would allow trainees to practice what they are being taught. Their graduates are thus often not workplace-ready. Employers are reluctant to recruit graduates who have no hands-on experience; they prefer to hire trainable youth with a good general education whose technical skills they can build in-house on specific equipment.

Over the past decade Sri Lanka has become a regional leader in the design and implementation of the NVQ. However, it should be better implemented to build up the quality and relevance of both public and private training and facilitate transfers between streams of training and education. Moreover, its image should be enhanced so that employers recognize NVQ qualifications and private training providers have their courses accredited their courses to assure training quality.

Finally, to move the national workforce development strategy forward, it would be helpful to expand TVET to postsecondary technician and professional programs for high-skilled labor in emerging sectors. Here Sri Lanka can draw upon the Korean experience from the mid-1970s to the mid-1990s as it

Building the Skills for Economic Growth and Competitiveness in Sri Lanka
http://dx.doi.org/10.1596/978-1-4648-0158-7

transitioned from a labor-intensive factor-driven economy to a capital-intensive efficiency-driven economy.

Priority 3. As the economy moves forward, the TVET system will need to become more diversified; active engagement with employers would make the system truly demand-driven. Not only do employers know best what skills they require, they are well positioned to articulate the skills emerging technologies will call for. TVET institutions that do not respond to the needs of trainees and employers will become irrelevant. While public-sector demand for general and technical education graduates is dwindling, private-sector demand is booming. Because employers are the best source of information on skills requirements, it is important to involve them in both system direction and evaluation of system outcomes. Employers can be invited to contribute to the design of programs and curricula, staff exchanges, decisions on types of equipment needed, hosting of interns, and quality control. Their intensive participation at all TVET levels, from vocational training centers to the UNIVOTEC, could prove highly beneficial.

As Sri Lanka scales up its economy, its TVET system cannot remain where it was when the country was still a low-income country (LIC), producing only low-value-added services. More responsive regulation and innovative public-private partnerships (PPPs), as in Malaysia and elsewhere, would help leverage private provision of both pre-employment training and OJT. Currently, training by private providers is of uneven quality, but those that meet high standards can be encouraged to prosper along with public providers through efficient regulation and quality assurance efforts.

Priority 4. The effectiveness of the TVET system will depend on whether it is adequately resourced and whether the funds allocated are used efficiently. The TVET system needs enough resources so that eligible candidates, regardless of background, can access programs and acquire job-specific skills. It would be advisable to design the financing system not only to ensure adequate resources but also to improve efficiency and accountability in how they are used. For public institutions, in particular, inadequate funds are often a major problem. Although it takes more than funding alone to improve the quality and relevance of TVET programs, they cannot be effective without adequate resources.

Allocating resources for public vocational and technical institutions on the basis of performance would promote quality. When funds are allocated without clear reference to their mission and how they achieve it, institutions have no incentive to perform with even minimal efficiency, much less be innovative. Funds should be allocated based on such outcome indicators as graduation, retention, or employment rates. It is also important that allocations take into account equity concerns, in particular the underinvestment that characterizes some provinces or regions.

Diversifying their revenue sources would be a sound idea for public institutions. With the likely increase in enrollments, additional resources will be needed not just to keep up services but also to improve their quality. However, public resources are likely to remain constrained, and the needs of other sectors are not retreating. To reduce their dependence on public monies and expand their sources of revenues, public providers might use some type of equity-neutral cost-sharing as a first avenue to that objective, but generating their own funds has more potential. If incentives are built in, PPPs could both increase resources and maximize efficiency.

If public vocational and technical institutions were financially autonomous, they could retain the revenues they generate from their own activities. Vocational and technical centers and colleges have a special opportunity to charge fees for courses targeting working adults and to sell goods and services produced by training activities. They might also rent out underused facilities. Financial autonomy is the most obvious way to incentivize training centers and technical colleges to innovate to meet demand. It is also the best approach to ensure accountability for the use of public monies. Gradual devolution of administrative and financial powers from central agencies to training centers and colleges would enhance quality, efficiency, and accountability and generate capacity to adjust to changing needs.

If public providers begin to rely on self-generated funds to complement budgetary allocations, private providers might also be subsidized to some extent when they promote accumulation of human capital and workforce productivity. Among methods used elsewhere are special fiscal treatment for the purchase of training-related inputs and free or discount access to public facilities and resources. A more comprehensive solution is to introduce competitive funding open to both public and private providers, to help institutions perform better and stimulate innovation.

It would be beneficial to design mechanisms to ensure that academically eligible trainees are not barred from accessing training because of financial constraints. Though stipends and scholarships are already in use, they do not seem large enough to offset the opportunity cost of attending courses or to encourage course registration and completion. Vouchers given directly to trainees would allow them to purchase training from any eligible institution of their choice, public or private. Vouchers also stimulate competition among providers, making them more responsive to trainee demand and producing better quality at lower cost.

Priority 5. Flexible and accountable governance mechanisms are needed at all TVET levels, with their components coordinated not only with each other but also with all system stakeholders.

Since funds to support TVET will undoubtedly have to be ramped up to keep pace with rising social and economic demands for training, better governance is crucial to make TVET not only efficient but a real engine of productivity and competiveness. Though increased funding is indispensable, it will not bring radical positive changes if management of this currently supply-driven and uncoordinated sector remains centralized and inefficient. It is vital that all those active in human development, private as well as public, have permanent and stable channels of communication and consultation. An empowered skills development committee could serve that purpose, provided it is impartial, politically independent, and representative of the entire spectrum of public and private providers, employers, and financing agencies and planners.

The multiplicity of public providers and an equally substantial supply of private providers make an inter-ministerial committee another priority. While in principle the diversity of TVET providers is a good thing, it runs the risk of duplication. Closer coordination is important among all agencies involved in supplying and demanding job-specific skills, with the MYASD playing a more effective and visible role. The TVEC role could be expanded to coordinate the entire system, overseeing financing and curriculum development; supervising skills testing, certification, and accreditation; and providing information on institutional quality and effectiveness. An inter-ministerial committee headed by TVEC might address the crowding-out of private entities by public ones, excessive concentration of institutions in a few locations and programs in saturated fields, and deficits of supply where there is heavy unmet demand.

Further devolution of responsibilities to public providers would induce them to take more initiative. Although financial autonomy is indispensable for their survival, full benefits can only be reaped if it is accompanied by devolution that covers administration (such as selection of heads of institutions, hiring and firing staff) and academic matters (such as course offerings). Devolution—with mechanisms for rigorous accountability—would unleash the energy of managers and staff to respond more quickly to changing patterns of demand.

Monitoring and evaluation capacity, supported by better labor market information, is critical. Information can be generated through periodic labor market surveys, consultations, and tracking studies about skills in demand, absorption of skills, and the benefits of investment in skills. If the supply of TVET services is to match demand both quantitatively and qualitatively, information has to flow in both directions. Yet the data that policy-makers need to deal with employment issues and educational and training authorities need to plan, organize, and put programs into operation are not readily available. One useful policy initiative might be to build up a labor market information system that can effectively assess, estimate, and monitor demand, and employment opportunities. Here again it would be useful to reinforce the role of TVEC.

To change the perception that TVET leads to low-status jobs, in addition to improving the quality of the services themselves, campaigns to communicate the benefits of TVET are needed. Career guidance and student centers in secondary schools, supported by perceptible signals from employers, would support this effort.

An integrated skills development strategy and a roadmap to implement it are essential. The MC recognizes the importance of education and training to achieve the government's ambitious development goals to become a competitive middle-income country. Building on the vision and strategic directions of the MC, the government has recently adopted a sector-wide, medium-term program to transform Sri Lanka's TVET sector into an effective skills development system. The buy-in of stakeholders, including employers, will be greatly enhanced if implementation is coordinated effectively and it is based on a solid foundation of relliable information. The advisory committee suggested could be entrusted with drafting the strategy, but high-level political commitment and a far-flung consultative process are necessary to heighten its chances of success.

Priority 6. The needs of the informal sector should be specifically targeted.

The self-employed and informal employers often do not see the rationale for investing in the vocational skills that could help raise productivity and incomes. Unskilled informal workers can be trained through cost-effective skills-upgrading programs. The government should create an environment that supports private providers through (1) regulation and policy incentives; (2) curriculum development, training of trainers, and competence-based skills testing; and (3) stimulating investment through tax incentives or financial support. Increasingly, other countries are addressing the skills needs of the informal sector.

It would be important to revise how the apprenticeship system operates and to understand how to make it more effective in providing both formal and informal job-specific skills. Although in Sri Lanka apprenticeship does not yield high returns in terms of either employment opportunities or earnings, other countries have demonstrated that a well-organized apprenticeship system can be highly beneficial to both employers and trainees. The TVEC and the National Apprentice and Industrial Training Authority (NAITA) could facilitate its rejuvenation.

Priority 7. It would be beneficial to evaluate and specifically address the needs of companies regarding enterprise-based training.

Despite its huge potential, the unique value of enterprise-based training has not been fully exploited in Sri Lanka. While in-service training may have gained momentum in recent years, formal school-based training is still emphasized even though most skills are acquired on the job. Companies might be willing to expand the resources available for building workforce skills if they are offered incentives like training funds or levies. For instance, the current training fund could be restructured to provide continuous and reliable support to firms providing in-service training. Such funds have proved successful in both OECD and developing countries. Though the Sri Lanka Skills Development Fund (SDF) was established as part of the TVEC Act to collect training levies, it has never been fully functional.

Reviving the SDF would require building significant administrative capacity. It might first be piloted in the tourism sector. Rapid development there could have a transformative effect on the entire economy. Skills requirements in tourism likely will be massive and are relatively easy to forecast. Before reviving the SDF, it would be important to (1) complete a careful feasibility study; (2) ensure full partnership with employers; and (3) undertake in-depth capacity-building. It is crucial that employers perceive a training fund financed through levies not just as an additional fiscal burden but as a genuine instrument for building staff skills. That is another reason why employers need to be explicitly involved in structuring a reinvigorated Sri Lankan SDF from the early stages. Experience also suggests that taxes to finance training funds should not be imposed on payrolls, since that tends to make employers reluctant to recruit new staff.

Notes

1. Several studies were financed by the Asian Development Bank (ADB) in preparation for ADB-financed TVET projects (for example, Association of Canadian Community Colleges 2004).

2. While recognizing the importance of training in the informal sector, this report does not deal with it because there is not enough information available.

3. In this study, which focuses on TVET skills development, "technical" refers to occupations in the technician category that are usually prepared at the postsecondary level, and "vocational" mid-level or traditional occupations for semiskilled and skilled workers. TVET here covers education and training delivered at secondary, postsecondary, and first-stage (non-degree) tertiary levels within the formal education system and informal TVET outside the education system.

4. The Sri Lanka Labor Force Survey (LFS) defines underemployment as working less than 35 hours a week and willing to work longer for the same pay rate. *Note*: the LFS shows underemployment in 2011 at the much lower rate of 2.8 percent.

5. In this study "self-employment" is used as a proxy for informal employment.

6. The recent National Strategy issued by the Ministry of Higher Education emphasizes graduate employability

7. The TVET premium in the informal sector was statistically significant at 12 percent. The low significance level could be explained by relatively small sample sizes.

8. Firms in both the manufacturing and service sectors are included.

9. Because services firms were not covered by the 2004 Enterprise Survey, they were excluded from the calculations that compared changes in skills constraints in Sri Lanka over time.

10. The standard approach is to compare an individual's education to educational requirements of either specific jobs or occupations, using one of three methods: self-assessment, job analysis, or realized matches (Leuven and Oosterbeek 2011). Given the data available, the realized matches approach was used here.

Bibliography

ADB (Asian Development Bank). 2008. *Education and Skills*. Manila: ADB.

Ashton, D., and F. Green. 1996. *Education, Training and the Global Economy*. Cheltenham, UK.: Edward Elgar.

Association of Canadian Community Colleges. 2004. *Sri Lanka: Proposed Human Resource Investment Project*. Manila: ADB.

DCS (Department of Census and Statistics). 2010. *Quarterly Labour Force Surveys 1991–2010*. Colombo.

———. 2011. *Sri Lanka Labor Force Survey—Annual Report 2011*. http://www.statistics .gov.lk/samplesurvey/LFS%20Annual%20Report_2011.pdf.

di Gropello, E., A. Kruse, and P. Tandon. 2010. *Skills for the Labor Market in Indonesia: Trends in Demand, Gaps, and Supply*. Human Development Department, World Bank, Washington, DC.

di Gropello, E., H. Tan, and P. Tandon. 2010. *Skills for the Labor Market in the Philippines*. Human Development Department, World Bank, Washington, DC.

Dutz, M. A., and S. D. O'Connell. 2013. "Productivity, Innovation and Growth in Sri Lanka: An Empirical Investigation." World Bank Policy Research Working Paper 6354, World Bank, Washington, DC.

Gunatilaka, R., M. Mayer, and M. Vodopivec. 2010. *The Challenge of Youth Employment in Sri Lanka*. World Bank: Washington, DC.

Lee, J., and D. Newhouse. 2013. "Cognitive Skills and Youth Labor Market Outcomes." Background Paper for *World Development Review* 2013, World Bank, Washington, DC.

Leuven, E., and H. Oosterbeek. 2011. "Overeducation and Mismatch in the Labor Market." In *Handbook of the Economics of Education*, eds. E.A. Hanushek, S.J. Machin, and L. Woessmann. Amsterdam: North-Holland, Elsevier.

McKinsey Center for Government. 2012. "Education to Employment: Designing a System that Works." McKinsey and Company. http://mckinseyonsociety.com/downloads /reports/Education/Education-to-Employment_FINAL.pdf.

MoE (Ministry of Education, Sri Lanka). 2011. "Sri Lanka Education Information 2011." http://www.moe.gov.lk/web/images/stories/statistic/sri_lanka_education_information _2011.pdf.

MFP (Ministry of Finance and Planning). 2010. *Mahinda Chintana*. http://www.treasury .gov.lk/publications/mahindaChintanaVision-2010full-eng.pdfc.

OECD (Organisation for Economic Co-operation and Development). 2012. *Better Skills, Better Jobs, Better Lives: A Strategic Approach to Skills Policies*. Paris: OECD Publishing.

SSM (Secretariat for Senior Ministers). 2012. *The National Human Resources and Employment Policy for Sri Lanka*. Secretariat for Senior Ministers. Colombo: Government of Sri Lanka.

TVEC (Tertiary and Vocational Education Commission). 2011. *Labor Market Information Bulletin 2011*. Colombo.

———. 2012a. *Corporate Plan 2012–16*. http://www.tvec.gov.lk/pr/images/Corporate _Plan%202012-2016-edited.pdf.

———. 2012b. *National Vocational Qualifications Framework*. http://www.tvec.gov.lk/pdf /NVQ_Framework.pdf.

UNESCO (United Nations Educational, Scientific and Cultural Organization). 2012. *Youth and Skills: Putting Education to Work*. EFA Global Monitoring Report. Paris: UNESCO Publishing.

World Bank. 2001. *Bangladesh: Education Sector Review*. Washington, DC: World Bank.

———. 2005. *Treasures of the Education System in Sri Lanka*. Human Development Unit, South Asia Region, World Bank, Washington, DC.

———. 2009. *The Towers of Learning: Higher Education in Sri Lanka*. Human Development Unit, South Asia Region, World Bank, Washington, DC.

———. 2010. *Stepping Up Skills for More Jobs and Higher Productivity*. Washington, DC: World Bank.

———. 2011. *Transforming School Education in Sri Lanka: From Cut Stones to Polished Jewels*. Human Development Unit, South Asia Region, World Bank, Washington, DC.

———. 2012a. *More and Better Jobs in South Asia*. Washington, DC: World Bank.

———. 2012b. "Sri Lanka Economic Update." Poverty Reduction and Economic Management Unit, South Asia Region, World Bank, Washington, DC.

———. 2012c. *World Development Indicators*. Washington, DC: World Bank.

———. 2013. *Jobs. World Development Report*. Washington, DC: World Bank.

CHAPTER 1

Introduction

With the demand for job-specific skills growing across the world, skills development has assumed great importance (see, for example, ADB 2008; McKinsey 2012; OECD 2012; World Bank 2010). For Sri Lanka, building job-relevant skills will be a major concern as it transitions to an efficiency-driven economy that will support a more competitive middle-income country. For the past decade, the demand for skilled labor has been increasing as a result of economic growth and structural changes in the economy. Growth has been accompanied by a shift in the composition of gross domestic product (GDP) away from agriculture to the higher-value-added industrial and service sectors. Jobs in those sectors—as machine operators, technicians, craftspeople, sales personnel, professionals, and managers—require different skills and more education and training than those in an agriculture-dominated economy.

Sustaining high economic growth is at the heart of the Government of Sri Lanka's development plan, the *Mahinda Chintana* (MC). Its ambitious vision rests on Sri Lanka becoming a maritime, aviation, commercial, energy, and knowledge hub that will link East and West. In the medium term the government expects to invest as much as 33–35 percent of GDP to support private investment. It is projected that (1) exports will grow at twice the rate of real GDP; (2) earnings from tourism will quadruple; (3) remittances from skilled emigrant workers will double; (4) the share of rural employment will decline from about two-thirds to half; and (5) the share of the population living in urban areas will increase from one-quarter to one-third. Other industries identified as promising besides tourism are construction, furniture, transport, and food and beverage—each of which has unique skills demands.

To achieve this vision—and the government's ambition of sustaining real GDP growth rates of at least 8 percent annually well into the future—will require a skilled workforce. However, there are concerns about how effectively Sri Lanka's education and training system can produce an adequate supply of the skills required: (1) although Sri Lankans have higher education attainment than their neighbors in South Asia, employers in the country are critical of the quality and relevance of what they are learning; and (2) there are major skills shortages and mismatches that affect both the country's economic growth and the productivity of the private sector, especially in export-oriented businesses.

A comprehensive understanding of skills demands, the skills profile of the workforce, and the skills development system is essential for designing policies that effectively address Sri Lanka's skills challenges. The knowledge base on general and higher education in Sri Lanka is deep, thanks in large part to a series of World Bank studies (see, for example, World Bank 2005, 2009, 2011). The same, however, cannot be said for technical and vocational education and training (TVET).[1] The policy debate has not been supported by rigorous evidence-based studies on the incidence, determinants, and effects of TVET on the labor market performance of different demographic groups—especially youth and females—with varying levels of schooling.

The main objective of this study is to examine skills demand and supply in order to identify major problems and possible policy options for building skills more effectively and efficiently. Therefore it asks:

- What is the demand for skills? What are the nature and the extent of skills gaps and mismatches?
- What skills do Sri Lankan workers already have? How do individuals with different levels of education, training, and skills fare in the labor market?
- Does the education and training system produce the skills demanded by the labor market? If not, why not?
- What will make TVET more efficient in building the needed skills?

The study uses multiple data sources to examine skills demand and supply, focusing primarily on TVET. This chapter sets out the context, rationale, and framework for looking at skills development in Sri Lanka.

The Economic and Labor Market Context

The Sri Lankan economy has enjoyed healthy 5.3 percent average growth for the past decade. Sri Lanka is a lower-middle-income country (LMIC) with per capita GDP of US$2,835 in 2011—significantly higher than that of the South Asia region as a whole but considerably behind the average for middle-income countries (MICs). The cessation of armed conflict in the country accelerated growth, which averaged 8 percent in 2010 and 2011; this was one of the fastest growth rates in South Asia, spurred largely by private sector demand (World Bank 2012c). Even though the Sri Lankan economy grew more slowly than India's over the past decade, it did better than Malaysia or the Republic of Korea. The government's goal is to increase GDP per capita to US$4,000 by 2016. This will require sustained economic growth of about 8 percent a year.

Over the past decade Sri Lanka's economy has changed considerably; it is no longer agriculture-based. The resultant structural changes in the economy are reflected in the composition of GDP, which has shifted from agriculture to manufacturing and services. Between 1977 and 2010, agriculture's share of GDP declined from 31 percent to 13 percent, industry's share stabilized at around 29 percent, and the share of services grew from 41 percent to 58 percent. The 13 percent agriculture share (figure 1.1) is close to Malaysia's (11 percent) and lower than South Asia as a whole (18 percent) and other LMICs (17 percent). Moreover, the share of services is similar to Korea's. However, the industry share is closer to those of South Asian countries and LMICs than to Korea or Malaysia.

Equity-led growth in Sri Lanka has substantially reduced poverty. Between 2002 and 2009/10, the headcount poverty rate declined from about 23 percent to 9 percent. The decline in poverty has been quite general, with urban poverty dropping from 7.9 percent to 5.3 percent, rural poverty from 24.7 percent to 9.4 percent, and estate poverty from 30 percent to 11.4 percent (World Bank 2012c). The government is committed to sustaining equity-led growth and decreasing the poverty rate to 4.2 percent by 2016 (MFP 2010). However, sustaining the recent impressive progress will depend on both a more dynamic labor market that produces better-quality jobs and on a skilled workforce.

Despite the country's healthy growth, foreign direct investment (FDI) in Sri Lanka has traditionally been very low, averaging only 1.3 percent of GDP annually for 2000–10 and stagnating at 1 percent since 2009. In 1977 Sri Lanka became the first economy in South Asia to open up to trade liberalization; after the mid-1980s trade rapidly expanded. As a share of GDP it peaked at 89 percent in 2000, with apparel and tea the leading exports. However, after 2000, trade steadily declined to only 49 percent of GDP in 2009. When the armed conflict ended, trade began to recover and in 2011 it constituted 60 percent of GDP. The MC envisions expanding Sri Lankan exports from US$8 billion in 2010 to US$18 billion in 2016.

Figure 1.1 Shares of Agriculture, Services, and Industry in GDP, 2010
Percent

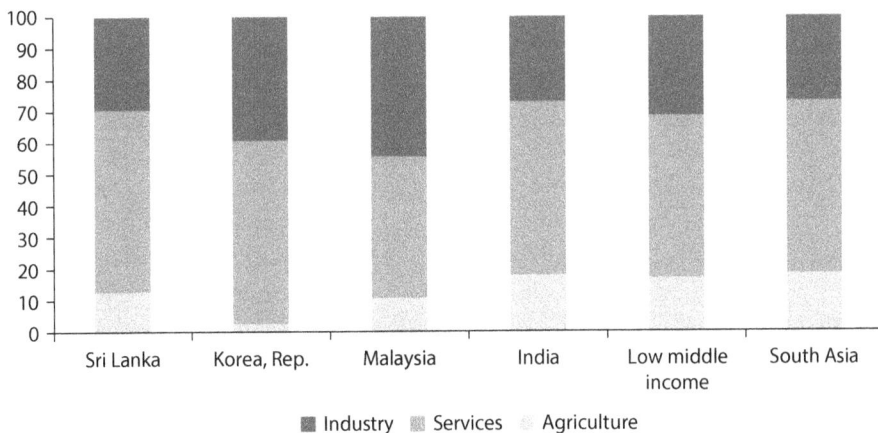

Source: World Bank 2012e.

Building the Skills for Economic Growth and Competitiveness in Sri Lanka
http://dx.doi.org/10.1596/978-1-4648-0158-7

Figure 1.2 Structural Changes in Employment, Sri Lanka
Percent

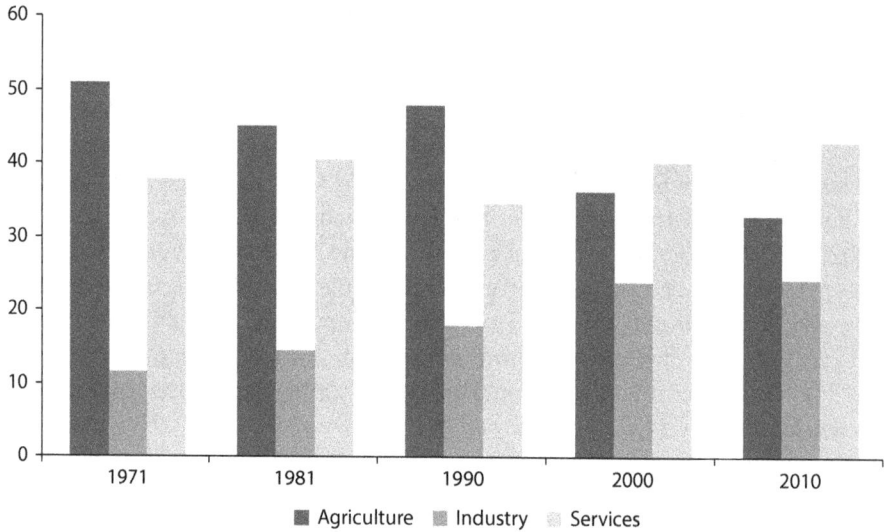

Sources: DCS 1953–81; Quarterly Labor Force Surveys 1991, 2000, and 2010 (DCS 2010).

The structural change in the Sri Lankan economy has shifted employment from agriculture to industry and services. Between 1971 and 2010, the share of agriculture in employment declined from 51 percent to 34 percent. The industry share rose from 11 percent to 25 percent and the services share from 38 percent to 42 percent (figure 1.2). As services and manufacturing grow, so does demand for a more skilled labor force.

Sri Lanka has made substantial progress in bringing down unemployment, but many youth and women still have no work. Unemployment fell from 9 percent in 2000 to 4.2 percent in 2011 (DCS 2011), but at 13 percent in 2012 the unemployment rate for youth (ages 15–29) is three times higher than the rate for adults (ages 30–64), and youth constitute more than half of all those who are unemployed (Gunatilaka, Mayer, and Vodopivec 2010). Unemployment is particularly high, almost 20 percent, for those aged 15–24. In addition, while unemployment declines with the amount of education for adults, it rises for youth. For example, almost 25 percent of Sri Lankans aged 15–29 with a bachelor's or higher degree are unemployed, compared to 1 percent of those who are older (figure 1.3). Finally, the unemployment rate for women (10 percent) is more than three times that for men (3 percent) (STEP [Skills Toward Employment and Productivity] Household Skills Measurement survey).

Despite low unemployment in Sri Lanka, in 2012 underemployment[2] is high (18 percent), especially for women (22 percent) and rural residents (21 percent). Underemployment of youth peaks at GCE O-level education (26 percent), after which it declines. The reasons for underemployment are not clear.

In the last decade, employment in Sri Lanka's informal sector has been an estimated 62 percent. Most informal workers have less general education than

Figure 1.3 Unemployment, by Age and Education
Percent

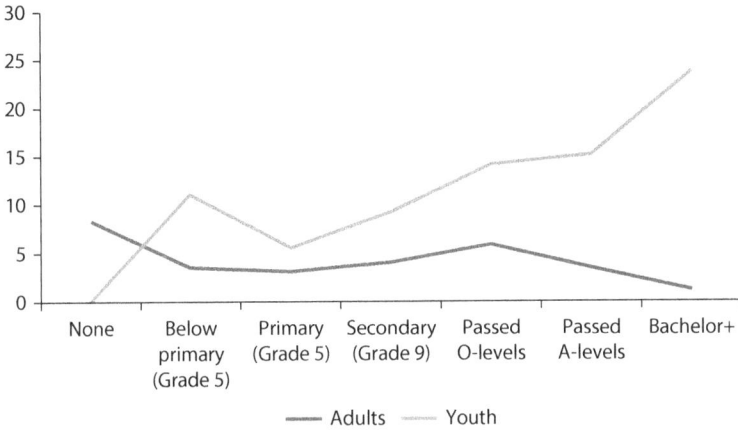

Source: STEP Household Skills Measurement survey.

formal workers. Many have had to drop out of the school system for such reasons as family poverty or a lack of training opportunities after completing primary or GCE O-level education. Yet the current skills development system is not geared to meeting the training needs of informal workers. Creating opportunities for them to acquire needed skills is therefore vital to increase their productivity. The government recognizes the problem and has plans for skills training programs for informal workers (SSM 2012).

The National Human Resources and Employment Policy (SSM 2012) estimates that more than a million Sri Lankans—about 12 percent of the labor force—are employed abroad, and annual departures of migrants have risen, from 182,188 people in 2000 to 266,445 in 2010 (SLBFE 2010). The annual outflow of workers exceeds the number of jobs created at home. In 2010 about 42 percent of the migrants left to work as housemaids. However, while most early migrants were unskilled, recent trends show increasing demand for skilled Sri Lankan workers.

Sri Lanka is the most educated country in South Asia, with a 98 percent literacy rate and widespread access to both primary and secondary education (figure 1.4). It is also characterized by high completion rates (96 percent for primary and 87 percent for secondary), and there is gender parity in completion. Nevertheless, although education is free, Sri Lankans from poorer backgrounds have fewer years of education than those who are richer. The proportion of Sri Lankans with secondary education is comparable to Malaysia but much lower than Korea. In terms of tertiary education, Sri Lanka's numbers are similar to the rest of South Asia (in 2010 only about 4 percent of the population aged 15–64 had completed tertiary education), but substantially lower than in Malaysia (15 percent) and Korea (40 percent), both of which have been investing heavily in TVET and tertiary education for more than three decades.

Figure 1.4 Educational Attainment in Sri Lanka, India, Malaysia, and the Republic of Korea
Percent

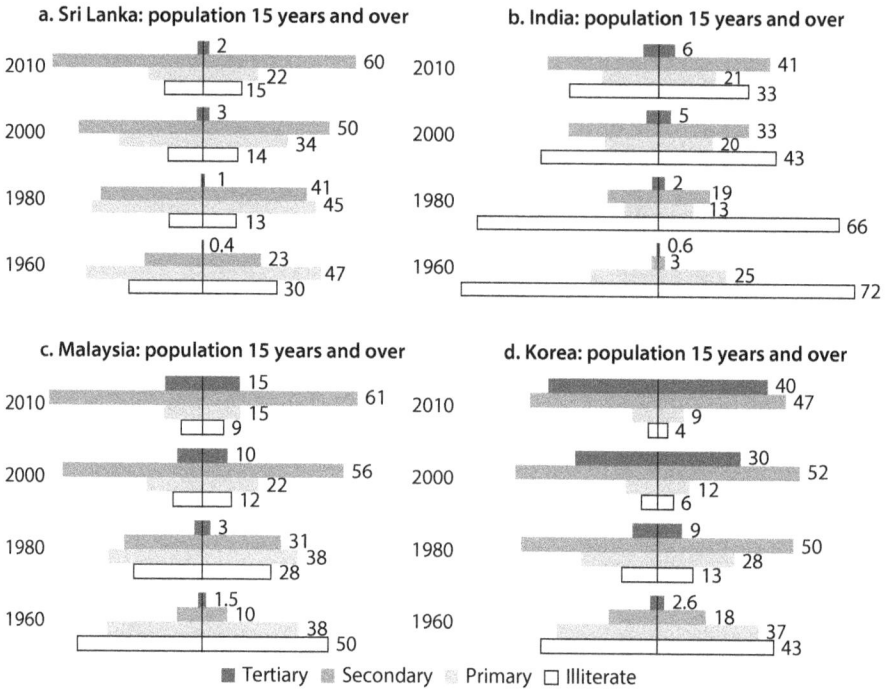

a. Sri Lanka: population 15 years and over

b. India: population 15 years and over

c. Malaysia: population 15 years and over

d. Korea: population 15 years and over

■ Tertiary   Secondary   Primary □ Illiterate

Sources: Barro and Lee 2012; Riboud, Savchenko and Tan 2007.

Despite impressive results in expanding access to primary and secondary education, Sri Lanka is confronted with large and increasing skills deficits. It would significantly benefit from investing in building job-specific technical and vocational skills to ensure economic growth and competitiveness and alleviate poverty.

Skills for Growth and Competitiveness

The complex demands of a competitive global economy require advanced skills and the ability of workers to adjust not only to domestic shifts in demand but also to what is happening in the global economy and labor market (see box 1.1 for the case of Korea). If a country is to become competitive, especially in the production of high-value-added goods and services, the overwhelming evidence is that it must invest significantly in education and training (Ashton and Green 1996). A well-designed and managed TVET system can support economic growth and competitiveness by producing a skilled and readily trainable workforce.

Most workers in Sri Lanka do not have the advanced technical skills demanded by an economy that would grow as the MC envisages. Although 16 percent of workers have completed TVET, 73 percent have acquired few, if any, job-relevant skills through *any* training program, formal or informal. Both the relevance of current programs and the employability of TVET and higher education graduates

Box 1.1 The Republic of Korea: How Economic Development Changed Investment in Skills Development

Skills needs and policies for skills development depend on the stage of economic development of a country and its future goals. The Sri Lankan economy is transitioning from being factor-driven and labor-intensive to being efficiency-driven (Schwab and Sala-i-Martin 2012). Korea experienced a similar transition between the mid-1970s and the mid-1990s (figure B1.1). As the period began the Korean economy was labor-intensive, most workers were low-skilled, and policies emphasized simple vocational (ADB 2012) and basic on-the-job training. As the economy grew more sophisticated and more capital-intensive, the need arose for better-skilled workers. The focus shifted to the acquisition of more advanced technical skills, which led to the expansion of junior technical colleges. In addition, workplace training was mandated, with an emphasis on expanding skills. Since the mid-1990s the Korean economy has moved on to become innovation-driven and knowledge-based. Skills requirements and policies have shifted from producing technicians to producing engineers and scientists; and with active industry cooperation, university education has expanded to accommodate the demand for more sophisticated skills, and firms have committed to lifelong competency development.

Figure B1.1 Changes in the TVET Sector in the Republic of Korea by Economic Development

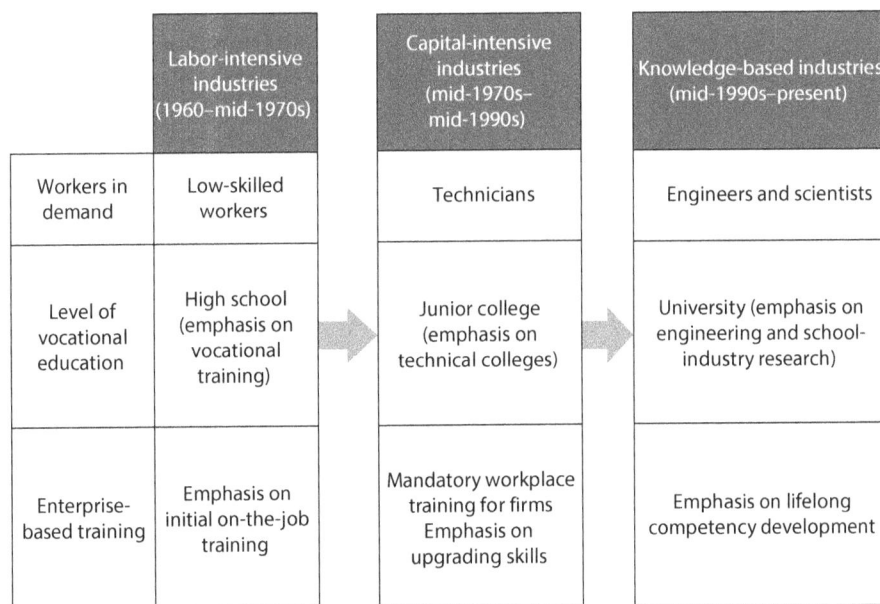

	Labor-intensive industries (1960–mid-1970s)	Capital-intensive industries (mid-1970s–mid-1990s)	Knowledge-based industries (mid-1990s–present)
Workers in demand	Low-skilled workers	Technicians	Engineers and scientists
Level of vocational education	High school (emphasis on vocational training)	Junior college (emphasis on technical colleges)	University (emphasis on engineering and school-industry research)
Enterprise-based training	Emphasis on initial on-the-job training	Mandatory workplace training for firms Emphasis on upgrading skills	Emphasis on lifelong competency development

Source: ADB 2012, adapted from Kwon 2011.
Note: TVET = technical and vocational education and training.

are minimal. Very few students are enrolled in programs defined as national priorities, and it takes many graduates a considerable time to get a job (Gunatilaka, Mayer, and Vodopivec 2010).

Ranked 68 out of 144 countries in the 2012/13 Global Competitiveness Index, Sri Lanka compares favorably with the rest of South Asia but trails East Asian countries. Becoming efficiency-driven requires concentration on production processes and product quality, which in turn requires such skills as computer knowledge, the ability to operate sophisticated equipment, and proficiency in a foreign language to communicate with international clients. Sri Lanka ranks above other South Asian countries on the quality of math and science and the availability of research and training but again trails Korea and Malaysia (table 1.1). Consequently, strategic investment in higher education and training is of critical importance.

Skills for Firm Productivity

Employers in Sri Lanka have identified the quality and supply of skilled technicians as the third-leading constraint on company growth, after concerns about power supply and taxes (Dutz and O'Connell 2013). Moreover, studies of productivity have found that access to skills (formal training programs in enterprises) is positively correlated with firm output and value-added (Dutz and O'Connell 2013). Many studies corroborate that globally employers are demanding both technical and soft (social) skills from new hires and that a shortage of workers with such skills often depresses production (di Gropello, Kruse, and Tandon 2011; di Gropello, Tan, and Tandon 2010; World Bank 2010, 2012d). Sri Lanka is not an exception—46 percent of employers in Sri Lanka indicated that job-specific skills are the single most important factor in deciding whether to retain a low-skilled worker and 38 percent said the same of high-skilled[3] workers. And Sri Lankan firms subject to skills constraints are less productive.

Skills for Poverty Reduction

Technical and vocational skills are essential both to reduce poverty and to improve personal well-being. There is international evidence that cognitive, social, and technical skills affect wage premiums and earnings (Glewwe, Huang, and Park 2011; Hanushek and Wößmann 2009; Urzúa 2008) and employment and occupation status (Borghans, ter Wel, and Weinberg 2008; Hanushek and

Table 1.1 Higher Education and Training, Selected Indicators

	Country rank	
	Quality of math and science	Availability of research and training
Korea, Rep.	8	31
Malaysia	20	17
India	30	59
Sri Lanka	69	63
Pakistan	88	102
Bangladesh	113	137

Source: Schwab and Sala-i-Martin 2012.

Wößmann 2009; Heckman, Stixrud, and Urzúa 2006; Urzúa 2008). Similarly, even after accounting for amount of education, in Sri Lanka individuals with technical and soft skills earn more than those who lack them. Technical skills also make it more likely that a worker will participate in the formal economy and be fully employed.

Skills for All

Despite Sri Lanka's success with strategies for achieving universal basic education, every year about 140,000 youth enter the labor market having completed no more than general secondary education and lacking job-specific technical and vocational skills (SSM 2012). This intensifies pressure for expansion of postsecondary education and training, including TVET. Though policymakers are concerned about *skills development for all*, as yet there is no strategy to achieve this goal.

While a skilled workforce is necessary for growth and for alleviating poverty, skills do not automatically lead to jobs and growth. Skills development needs to be part of a comprehensive economic development strategy, and job creation and skills development should be pursued together. Furthermore, skills development should be part of a lifelong education and training strategy because it is a cumulative life cycle process.

Approach, Methodology, and Data Sources

Conceptual Framework for Skills Demand and Supply

A worker's skills set consists of cognitive, soft (noncognitive), and job-specific skills (box 1.2), which are shaped in different ways. Skills formation is a cumulative process that proceeds in stages, each building on the previous one (figure 1.5). Skills development through formal education is most intense in childhood and adolescence. A solid foundation in such basic cognitive skills as literacy and numeracy, typically provided through primary school, is critical to successful post-primary education, including acquisition of job-specific skills, which are usually acquired through TVET or a higher education institution, apprenticeship, or on-the-job training (OJT). Soft skills may be learned at any point, not only in the education and training system but also by interacting with family members, peers, or colleagues. An efficient skills development system embraces all levels of education and training—from early childhood education through to university and TVET—and provides opportunities for lifelong learning of all types of skills.

Skills development crosses institutional boundaries, can be taught in a variety of settings, engages a highly diverse clientele, is delivered in a variety of ways, and responds to constantly changing job requirements. The challenge is to better understand these complexities and design policies that meet the growing demand for skills. The World Bank STEP framework illustrates skills formation throughout the life cycle and how to design systems to build the skills that enhance productivity and growth.

Box 1.2 Skill Types

The World Bank Skills Toward Employment and Productivity (STEP) Framework sets out three broad categories of worker skills:

(1) *Cognitive skills* are defined as the "ability to understand complex ideas, to adapt effectively to the environment, to learn from experience, to engage in various forms of reasoning, to overcome obstacles by taking thought" (Sanchez-Puerta *et al.* 2012). The STEP surveys measure cognitive skills as self-reported numeracy, reading, and writing.

(2) *Noncognitive skills* are defined as domains that are not directly associated with intelligence (cognition). They are also referred to as soft skills, personality traits, and behavioral or socio-emotional skills. The STEP surveys measure numerous dimensions of noncognitive skills, for example, the Big Five personality traits—extraversion, conscientiousness, openness, emotional stability, and agreeableness—long-term perseverance, decision-making skills, and teamwork and presentation skills.

(3) *Technical skills* are defined as specialized skills that are relevant for performing the tasks involved in a specific job. These are the necessary conditions for increasing productivity and fostering economic growth. The STEP surveys use the following measures of technical skills: technology use, computer use, mechanical use, machinery use, English language, ability to work autonomously, and manual labor skills.

Source: Sanchez-Puerta *et al.* 2012.

Figure 1.5 Skills Formation across the Worker Life Cycle

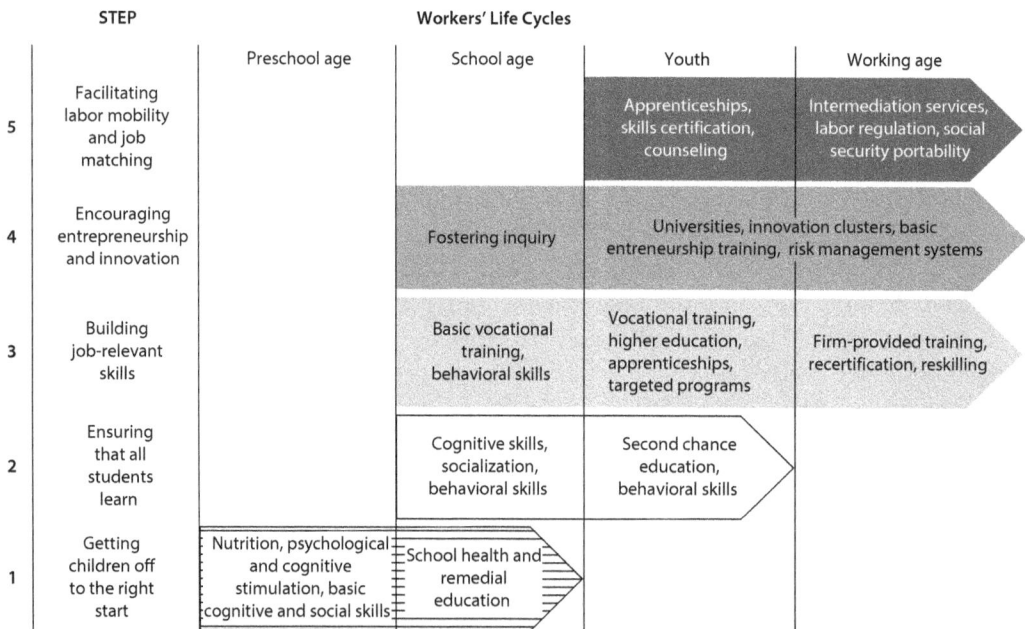

Source: World Bank 2010.
Note: STEP = Skills Toward Employment and Productivity.

An efficient skills development process requires deep understanding of both demand-side pressures on skills development and constraints on supplying skills that meet labor market demands. Figure 1.6 presents a conceptual framework for the skills market; its main feature is simultaneous consideration of how demand and supply sides interact to produce skills-matching. Skills demand in Sri Lanka is characterized by multiple players, public, private, and foreign. The demand for skills is affected by changes in the economy (because of, for example, economic growth, globalization, and technological changes); urbanization and migration; expansion of primary and secondary education; demographic changes in labor market entrants; and Sri Lanka's medium- and long-term development goals.

On the supply side, job-relevant skills are supplied by formal TVET and higher education institutions, non-formal training centers, such as firm-based, and informal training, such as traditional apprenticeship (box 1.3). Skills supply is determined by the availability, quality, and relevance of education and training programs and by policy interventions into the system, such as availability of resources, financing mechanisms, management and governance of the sector, private provision, quality assurance mechanisms, certification, and accreditation.

A major challenge for a skills development system is to ensure a good match between skills supply and demand. Effective matching can promote national growth and competitiveness, business productivity, and worker well-being. Ineffective matching can depress productivity and competitiveness and increase un- and underemployment. Information, coordination, and relationships are critical to effective skills matching: (1) Information-sharing is crucial to ensure that the education and training system produces the skills demanded by the

Figure 1.6 Conceptual Framework for Skills Demand and Supply

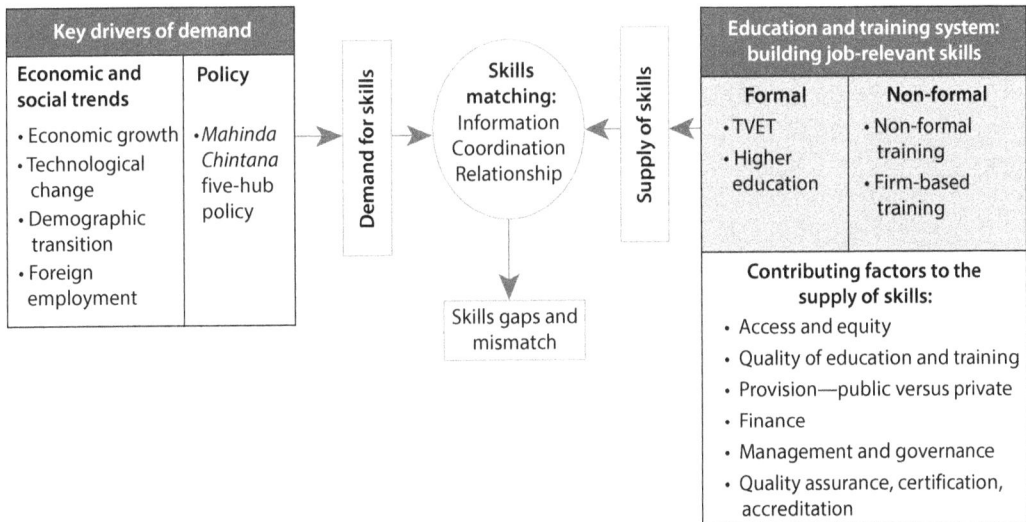

Source: Adapted from Tan *et al.* 2012.
Note: TVET = technical and vocational education and training.

Building the Skills for Economic Growth and Competitiveness in Sri Lanka
http://dx.doi.org/10.1596/978-1-4648-0158-7

Box 1.3 Definition of Training

Formal education and training usually end with accredited or certified outcomes. *Non-formal training* is structured learning outside the formal education and training system, both within and outside the workplace, and does not result in an accredited qualification. *Informal training*, which is less organized, usually takes place in the workplace—such as learning by doing and guided by an experienced worker.

TVET refers to a range of instruments for job preparation at different levels of the education and training system. *Vocational* refers to mid-level traditional trade occupations for semi-skilled and skilled workers. *Technical* refers to occupations in the technician category, usually offered at the postsecondary level. TVET, as considered in this study, includes education and training delivered at the secondary, postsecondary, and non-degree tertiary levels within the formal education system as well as non-formal training outside the education system.

Source: ADB 2008, 83.

labor market. (2) Those demanding and those supplying must coordinate closely—for example, employers would benefit from giving training institutions feedback about their skills requirements, and adjusting training programs to the skills needs of the market would enhance the labor market outcomes of TVET graduates. (3) A close relationship between those on the demand side and those on the supply side, for example, employer participation in curriculum design and trainees receiving enterprise-based as well as classroom training, would make skills-matching more efficient.

While acknowledging the importance of higher education and non-formal and informal training in the supply of job-specific skills, this report is concerned primarily with what happens in TVET and firm-based training. It does not address job-specific skills development in higher education since the World Bank (2009) has already carried out an extensive review of higher education in Sri Lanka. It is also important to note that the report considers the TVET sector at the aggregate level and in general does not differentiate skills development by provider or agency, such as the Department of Technical Education and Training or the Vocational Education Authority.

Based on this conceptual framework, chapter 2 describes the general education and training system in Sri Lanka, especially the TVET sector. Chapter 3 examines the main drivers of skills demand and skills mismatches and gaps in Sri Lanka. Chapter 4 studies the relationship between education, training, and labor market outcomes, including skills already available in the workforce. Chapters 5 and 6 analyze factors affecting the skills supply system, such as cost, financing, and governance (chapter 5) and private sector provision (chapter 6). Chapter 7 briefly reviews firm-based training in Sri Lanka based on evidence from the employer survey. Chapter 8 assesses workforce development policies in Sri Lanka based on the World Bank's Systems Approach for Better Education

Results (SABER) framework. Finally, chapter 9 provides the summary of main findings and outlines possibilities for the way forward in skills development in Sri Lanka.

Data Sources and Limitations

The study draws on numerous sources of data:

* Sri Lanka Labour Force Survey (LFS) data, 1992–2008, are used to investigate changes in training over time and the effects of training on earnings and labor market outcomes, and to examine how labor market outcomes vary over time and for different regions and demographic groups.
* The 2004 and 2010 Enterprise Surveys are a source of data for formal enterprises in Sri Lanka.
* Two national skills measurement surveys, of households and employers, were carried out with the government as part of a World Bank-financed multicountry study (box 1.4).
* The study draws on data from the Ministry of Youth Affairs and Skills Development (MYASD) and the Ministry of Finance and Planning (MFP) on characteristics of students and graduates, number and qualifications of teaching staff, enrollment by field of study, indicators of performance such as employment placements, and the costs and financing of the system.

The study also assessed policies for the delivery of skills using the World Bank's SABER Framework for Workforce Development.

Even though the skills measurements that were designed for the STEP surveys are comparable across the countries where the surveys were administered, there are several limitations:

* The surveys give a snapshot of skills stocks and demand for skills at one point of time. However, skills demand is dynamic because employer requirements change often. Periodic skills assessments could prove useful to policy makers.
* Skills requirements vary by industry. The technical skills required in information technology (IT) are quite different from those needed in mining or gem cutting. Moreover, skill sets in the informal sector could be different from formal sector requirements. In future rounds of these surveys, it would be beneficial to design a more accurate assessment of skills requirements by sector.
* Many of the skills are based on self-reports. While some can be compared with actual skills assessments (for example, a reading test conforming to international standards was administered), others are based on subjective perceptions, such as knowledge of English.
* Finally, a major data limitation comes from a change in the LFS questionnaire. After 2004 the survey stopped asking the whole population a question on TVET attainment; now it asks only the unemployed. However, given the government focus on providing skills for all, it is very important to have information on TVET participation and the outcomes for all labor market participants.

Box 1.4 Sri Lanka Skills Measurement Surveys

To assess current skills stocks, skills formation, and skills demands in Sri Lanka, a household skills measurement and an employer survey were conducted in 2012 as part of the World Bank's multicountry analysis of the Skills Toward Employment and Productivity (STEP) initially carried out in eight developing countries (Bolivia, Colombia, Ghana, the Lao People's Democratic Republic, Sri Lanka, Vietnam, Ukraine, and China's Yunnan province). The harmonized surveys made possible cross-country comparison of skills supply and a better understanding of skills formation and the link between worker skills and productivity outcomes, as well as how demand for skills varies by country.

The employer survey[a] was conducted on a national random sample of about 600 formal businesses of different sizes in key sectors. It collected information about skills and competencies needed by different firms, the relevance of skills currently available in the labor market, the nature of skills gaps and mismatches, and the education and skill endowments of recent hires and graduates from different schools and public and private TVET institutions.

The household measurement survey was conducted on a national sample of 3,000 households, of which about 40 percent were urban and 60 percent rural. The largest group of households were in the Western province (38 percent), followed by Central (11 percent), Southern (10 percent), North Western (10 percent), Eastern (8 percent), Sabaragamuwa (8 percent), and Uva, Northern, and North Central (5 percent each). From each household, one representative aged between 15 and 64 was randomly selected for a detailed individual interview and literacy testing. The eight modules of the survey elicit detailed information on education, training, different types of skills (cognitive, noncognitive, and technical), basic demographic and household information, and information on family background, employment, and wages. Average household size was 4.1 members. Women represented about 60 percent of the individuals surveyed. Youth, defined as individuals aged 15–29, comprised 28 percent and adults aged 30–64 comprised 72 percent. The average age was 38 years; average education was about 9.6 years.

a. While the household data can be compared across different countries that participated in STEP surveys, the employer data are not directly comparable due to differences in the sampling frameworks and the sectors surveyed.

Another data limitation this report encountered was the lack of streamlined information on costs and financing of the TVET system, which is crucial for understanding how efficient it is and estimating the potential costs and benefits of providing skills for all. The TVET system is complex. Numerous government entities have some responsibility for TVET activities, and assignment of responsibilities to different ministries has changed as government TVET portfolios were reshuffled several times over the past 20 years. Moreover, TVET activities are often not recorded as a separate line item in budget documents. In the private sector, the reporting methods are not uniform. Moreover, it is hard to get information on training providers that are not registered with the TVEC. TVET institutions serve a variety of clients, from school leavers to mid-career employees, and course formats are organized to suit particular needs. Estimating unit costs in such a heterogeneous sector is thus problematic. Unlike in primary education, averages say little.

Notes

1. Several studies were carried out in preparation for TVET projects financed by the Asian Development Bank (example, Association of Canadian Community Colleges 2004).

2. Underemployment is defined as in the Sri Lanka LFS: people who work less than 35 hours a week and would like to work more for the same pay rate.

3. Based on the STEP employer survey, *high-skilled workers* (type A) are those who work as managers, professionals, technicians, and associate professionals; *low-skilled workers* (type B) are mainly employed as clerical support, service workers, sales staff, skilled agriculture, forestry and fishery workers, crafts and related trades workers, plant and machine operators, and assemblers (i.e., in basic occupations).

Bibliography

ADB (Asian Development Bank). 2008. *Education and Skills*. Manila: ADB.

———. 2012. *Innovative Strategies in Technical and Vocational Education and Training for Accelerated Human Resource Development in South Asia*. Manila: ADB.

Ashton, D., and F. Greene. 1996. *Education, Training and the Global Economy*. Cheltenham, U.K.: Edward Elgar.

Association of Canadian Community Colleges. 2004. *Sri Lanka: Proposed Human Resource Investment Project*. Manila: ADB.

Barro, R., and J-W. Lee. 2012. "A New Data Set of Educational Attainment in the World, 1950–2010." NBER Working Paper 15902, National Bureau of Economic Research, Cambridge, MA.

Borghans, L., B. ter Wel, and B. A. Weinberg. 2008. "Interpersonal Styles and Labor Market Outcomes." *Journal of Human Resources* 43 (4): 815–58.

DCS (Department of Census and Statistics). 2010. *Quarterly Labour Force Surveys 1991–2010*. Colombo, Sri Lanka.

———. 2011. *Sri Lanka Labor Force Survey–Annual Report 2011*. Department of Census and Statistics, Sri Lanka. http://www.statistics.gov.lk/samplesurvey/LFS%20 Annual%20Report_2011.pdf.

di Gropello, E., with A. Kruse and P. Tandon. 2011. *Skills for the Labor Market in Indonesia: Trends in Demand, Gaps, and Supply*. Washington, DC: World Bank.

di Gropello, E., with H. Tan and P. Tandon. 2010. *Skills for the Labor Market in the Philippines*. Washington, DC: World Bank.

Dutz, M. A., and S. D. O'Connell. 2013. "Productivity, Innovation and Growth in Sri Lanka: An Empirical Investigation." World Bank Policy Research Working Paper 6354, World Bank, Washington, DC.

Glewwe, P., Q. Huang, and A. Park. 2011. "Cognitive Skills, Non-Cognitive Skills, and the Employment and Wages of Young Adults in Rural China." Paper presented at the annual meeting of the Agricultural and Applied Economics Association, Pittsburgh, PA, July 24–26.

Gunatilaka, R., M. Mayer, and M. Vodopivec. 2010. *The Challenge of Youth Employment in Sri Lanka*. Washington, DC: World Bank.

Hanushek, E., and L. Wößmann. 2009. "Do Better Schools Lead to More Growth? Cognitive Skills, Economic Outcomes, and Causation." NBER Working Paper 14633, National Bureau of Economic Research, Cambridge, MA.

Heckman, J., J. Stixrud, and S. Urzúa. 2006. "The Effects of Cognitive and Noncognitive Abilities on Labor Market Outcomes and Social Behavior." *Journal of Labor Economics* 24 (3): 411–82.

Kwon, D-B. 2011. "TVET in Korea: History of Challenges and Responses and the Future. Korean Research Institute for Vocational Education and Training." Presentation at the World Bank, February 24.

McKinsey Center for Government. 2012. "Education to Employment: Designing a System that Works." McKinsey and Company. http://mckinseyonsociety.com/downloads /reports/Education/Education-to-Employment_FINAL.pdf.

MoE (Ministry of Education, Sri Lanka). 2011. "Sri Lanka Education Information 2011." MoE, Colombo, Sri Lanka. http://www.moe.gov.lk/web/images/stories /statistic/sri_lanka_education_information_2011.pdf.

MFP (Ministry of Finance and Planning). 2010. *Mahinda Chintana*. MOF, Colombo, Sri Lanka. http://www.treasury.gov.lk/publications/mahindaChintanaVision-2010full -eng.pdf.

OECD (Organisation for Economic Co-operation and Development). 2012. *Better Skills, Better Jobs, Better Lives: A Strategic Approach to Skills Policies*. Paris: OECD Publishing.

Riboud, M., Y. Savchenko, and H. Tan. 2007. *The Knowledge Economy, Education and Training in South Asia*. Human Development Department, World Bank, Washington, DC.

Sanchez Puerta, M. L., A. Valerio, G. Pierre, and S. Urzúa. 2012. "STEP Skills Survey Data Analysis Methodology Note." Draft, Social Protection and Labor Department, World Bank, Washington, DC.

Schwab, K., and X. Sala-i-Martin. 2012. *Global Competitiveness Report 2012–13*. Geneva, Switzerland: World Economic Forum.

SLBFE (Sri Lanka Bureau of Foreign Employment). 2010. *Annual Statistical Report of Foreign Employment 2010*. Colombo: SLBFE.

SSM (Secretariat for Senior Ministers). 2012. *The National Human Resources and Employment Policy for Sri Lanka*. Secretariat for Senior Ministers. Colombo: Government of Sri Lanka.

Tan, H. 2012. "Sri Lanka: Education, Training and Labor Market Outcomes." Background paper for Sri Lanka Skills Development Report, World Bank, Washington, DC.

Tan, J-P., K. H. Lee, A. Valerio, and R. McGough. 2012. *What Matters in Workforce Development: An Analytical Framework for the Pilot Phase*. Washington, DC, World Bank. http://siteresources.worldbank.org/EDUCATION/Resources/278200 -1290520949227/7575842-1336502112143/SABER_WfD_Framework_Paper _9-07-12.pdf.

TVEC (Tertiary and Vocational Education Commission). 2012a. "Corporate Plan 2012–16." Colombo. http://www.tvec.gov.lk/pr/images/Corporate_Plan%202012-2016 -edited.pdf.

———. 2012b. *National Vocational Qualifications Framework*. Colombo: TVEC. http://www.tvec.gov.lk/pdf/NVQ_Framework.pdf.

Urzúa, S. 2008. "Racial Labor Market Gaps: The Role of Abilities and Schooling Choices." *Journal of Human Resources* 43 (4): 919–71.

World Bank. 2005. *Treasures of the Education System in Sri Lanka*. Human Development Unit, South Asia Region, World Bank, Washington, DC.

———. 2009. *The Towers of Learning: Higher Education in Sri Lanka*. Human Development Unit, South Asia Region, World Bank, Washington, DC.

———. 2010. *Stepping Up Skills for More Jobs and Higher Productivity*. Washington, DC: World Bank.

———. 2011. *Transforming School Education in Sri Lanka: From Cut Stones to Polished Jewels*. Human Development Unit, South Asia Region, World Bank, Washington, DC.

———. 2012a. *Country Partnership Strategy (FY 2013–FY 2016) for the Democratic Socialist Republic of Sri Lanka*. Report 66286-LK, Sri Lanka and Maldives Country Management Unit, South Asia Region. World Bank, International Finance Corporation, South Asia Region.

———. 2012b. *Sri Lanka Demographic Transition: Facing the Challenges of an Aging Population with Few Resources*. Report 73162-LK, Human Development Unit, South Asia Region, World Bank, Washington, DC.

———. 2012c. *Sri Lanka Economic Update*. Poverty Reduction and Economic Management Unit, South Asia Region, World Bank, Washington, DC.

———. 2012d. *More and Better Jobs in South Asia. South Asia Development Matters*. Washington, DC: World Bank.

———. 2012e. *World Development Indicators*. Washington, DC: World Bank.

CHAPTER 2

General Education and Training in Sri Lanka: An Overview

This chapter introduces the general education system in Sri Lanka; describes how the technical and vocational education and training (TVET) sector is structured; discusses TVET enrollment trends; and analyzes the efficiency and equity of the sector. This overview sets the stage for a general understanding of the factors that affect skills supply.[1] The discussion is based on official enrollment data and performance reports.

General Education. The Sri Lankan system of public education provides essentially free schooling through university (figure 2.1). General education in Sri Lanka covers[2] primary, junior secondary, and senior secondary school. Primary education consists of grades 1–5, junior secondary—grades 6–9, and senior secondary—grades 10–13. Education is compulsory until grade 9. Pre-employment training typically starts after either the GCE O-level or GCE A-level exam.

In 2011, Sri Lanka had 9,731 public primary and secondary schools. Total enrollment was about 3.9 million and there were about 220,000 teachers. Another 121,000 students were enrolled in about 98 private schools and international schools, and there were 62,000 students in the 720 state-funded *pirivena* (temple) schools (table 2.1).

Each year, about 331,000 students enter grade 1. About 97 percent of the school-age population is in primary school, and only a small number (15,600) drop out at grade 11. Students who pass the GCE O-levels—about 60 percent of those taking them in 2010, 164,000 out of 271,000 students—generally continue on to GCE A-level studies.

The Ministry of Education (MoE) manages and delivers primary and secondary education, working closely with provincial and district governments. The National Institute of Education, part of the MoE, is responsible for curricula and teacher development. The National Education Commission (NEC) advises the government on education policy.

Tertiary Education. Sri Lanka has 15 public universities, including the Open University; 8 postgraduate institutes; and 10 affiliated institutes that award

Figure 2.1 The Education and Training System in Sri Lanka

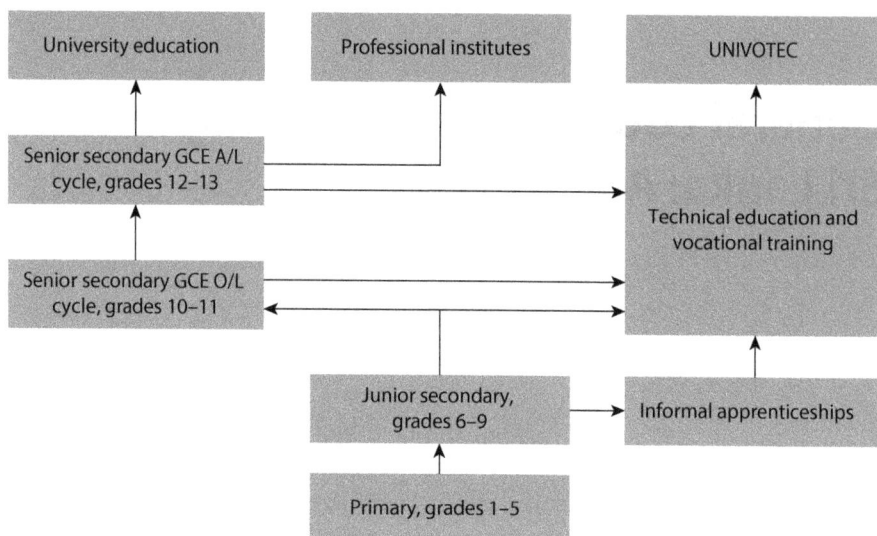

Sources: Based on World Bank 2005 and Tan 2012.

Table 2.1 Sri Lanka: General Education at a Glance

General education	2005			2011			Percentage change (2005–11)		
	Schools	Students	Staff	Schools	Students	Staff	Schools (%)	Students (%)	Staff (%)
Public schools	9,727	3,942,412	187,339	9,731	3,973,847	219,886	0	1	17
Private schools	85	105,048	4,820	98	121,764	5,810	15	16	21
Pirivena (temple schools)	652	55,279	5,465	720	6,2861	6,129	10	14	12

Sources: MoE 2005, 2011.

bachelor's degrees. Currently, about 82,000 students are enrolled in these institutions. A separate external degree program accounts for about 205,000 students. There are also a number of other public tertiary education institutions (for example, Advanced Technological Institutes, ATIs), and private institutions are mushrooming, often without any official recognition. Estimated enrollment in these institutions, both public and private, is about 46,000 students. Finally, some 10,000 students are enrolled in universities overseas. The Sri Lanka Institute of Advanced Technological Education (SLIATE) manages 12 ATIs that award higher national diplomas and constitute one of the few links between general education and TVET.

The Ministry of Higher Education (MoHE) is responsible for management and coordination of higher education and formulates policies for the sector. The University Grants Commission (UGC) is responsible for allocating funds to higher educational institutions (HEIs), maintaining academic standards, and regulating the administration of and admissions to HEIs through the Quality Assurance and Accreditation Council.

Technical and Vocational Education. One of the goals in the *Mahinda Chintana* (MC) is to provide skills for the whole population. After completing general education, students may enter the labor force (without job-specific skills), continue on to university studies, or enroll in vocational or technical training. The NHREP (SSM 2012) estimates that every year about 140,000 students in Sri Lanka leave general education without job-specific skills. Since the capacity of the higher education system is limited, the government envisions using TVET to close much of the country's skills gap.

About 150,000 students, 43 percent of them women, were enrolled in TVET courses in Sri Lanka's wide network of training institutions (TVEC 2011). The total number of institutions registered with the Tertiary and Vocational Education Commission (TVEC) in December 2011 was 2,269, operated by public and private institutions and nongovernmental organizations (NGOs), and institutions and training centers operated by other ministries offer specialized programs.[3] There were 318 public providers, 704 statutory board institutes, 990 private and 257 NGO training providers registered with TVEC[4] in 2011 (chapter 6). Providers functioning under the Ministry of Youth Affairs and Skills Development (MYASD) account for more than 70 percent of TVET enrollment nationally. Of all the programs listed in the TVEC training guide, only 8 percent are targeted at GCE A-level-qualified students; the rest are for GCE O-level-qualified (29 percent) and students with lesser qualifications (67 percent).

There are two main categories of private TVET providers, professional associations and private training institutions. Of the 42 members of the Organization of Professional Associations (OPA), 17 conduct programs that award certificates, diplomas, or degrees. More than 900 for-profit private institutions operate in Sri Lanka, 58 percent of them in the Western Province. All non-state training providers are expected to register with the TVEC, but some either do not register at all or fail to renew their registration. Private training providers (see chapter 6) are heavily concentrated in accounting and other commercial studies, information and communications technology (ICT), tailoring and sewing, travel, tourism, catering, and beauty services.

Many religious and voluntary NGOs offer craft training targeting unemployed youth, rural women, school leavers, and semi- or unskilled workers. They either charge only nominal fees or none at all. There is little information available about private and NGO enrollments, regional distribution, course offerings, and operations.

How the TVET Sector is Structured

Sri Lanka's public TVET system comprises 33 statutory bodies and training institutes under 15 ministries (figure 2.2). The MYASD is the main institution responsible for technical and vocational education and training.

Besides the MYASD, 14 other ministries also undertake some training; they do so through 22 subsidiary institutions. For example, the Ministry of Labor Relations provides training and retraining for both employed and unemployed

Figure 2.2 Structure of the TVET Sector, 2011

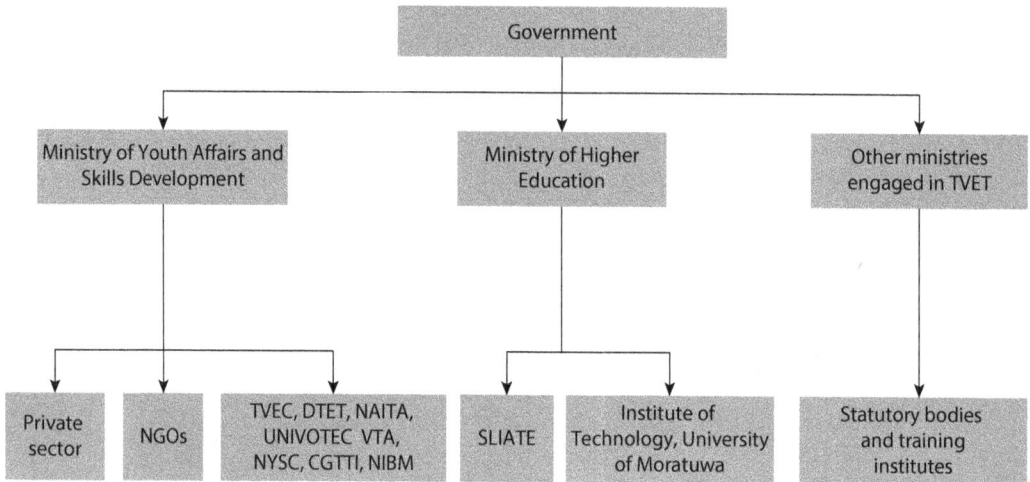

individuals. The Ministry of Rural Industries and Self-Employment Promotion advances technical and entrepreneurial skills through the Industrial Development Board. Public TVET providers cater to the training needs of 26 industry subsectors. NGOs and private providers also account for a sizable share of TVET services, although only a few are registered with the TVEC.

Ministry of Youth Affairs and Skills Development (MYASD)

Over the past decade, several reforms have restructured the organization and management of TVET within the government (box 2.1).

The MYASD discharges its responsibilities (box 2.2) through 11 training agencies, among them the Department of Technical Education and Training (DTET); the National Apprentice and Industrial Training Authority (NAITA); and the Vocational Training Authority (VTA). The University of Vocational Technology (UNIVOTEC) is charged with teacher training and curriculum development for the entire sector. The apex body of the TVET sector is the TVEC, which is part of the MYASD and which concentrates on policy formulation, coordination, planning, and direction of the TVET sector.

The MYASD is responsible for policy planning, coordination, implementation, and the development of the TVET sector in Sri Lanka. Its specific roles relate to

- *Curriculum and course materials.* Introduce and implement training courses for public and private training institutions.
- *Equity.* Extend TVET to rural areas and increase access for women, the disabled, and the poor; put in place development programs and promote self-employment opportunities for trained youth.
- *Teacher quality.* Invest intensively in building a sufficient high-quality teaching staff with both pedagogical qualifications and professional skills.

Box 2.1 Shifts in Ministerial Responsibilities for TVET

Between 2000 and 2010 the ministry chiefly responsible for TVET changed several times. In some years, institutions involved in TVET were handled by more than one ministry and in others the ministry responsible for TVET was also accountable for other activities. These variations were important considerations in constructing the data series and interpreting trends in TVET.

In 2000 and 2001, the Ministry of Vocational Training and Rural Industries was responsible for TVET. In 2002–04, responsibility moved to the Ministry for Tertiary Education and Training, which had three components: (1) the ministry itself; (2) the Department of Technical Education and Training; and (3) the Department of Contribution to the Universities and the University Grants Commission (UGC). The ministry focused primarily on vocational training and skills development. (This study takes into account spending only on the actual vocational training and technical education program. However, since 2010, when a new ministry for vocational training was formed, general administration costs have also been taken into account.) Meanwhile, throughout this period, other major TVET institutions were functioning under different ministries. For example, the Ceylon German Technical Training Institute was part of the Ministry of Transport and Ocean University was part of the Ministry of Fisheries. What the two ministries spent on these could not be obtained.

In 2005 the Ministry of Skills Development, Vocational and Technical Education was made responsible for TVET, followed in 2006–09 by the Ministry of Vocational and Technical Training. Tertiary education—Contribution to the Universities and the UGC—was within the purview of the Ministry of Education. During this time, the major function of the Ministry of Vocational and Technical Education was to implement an integrated national TVET system. In 2010, TVET was integrated into the Ministry of Youth Affairs.

- *Coordination.* Work with donor agencies to support TVET-related reform programs; develop and disseminate career and training information to students, graduates (job seekers), employers, and members of the community; and maintain international relations to attract technical and financial assistance to build up TVET.
- *Private sector participation.* Promote private participation in TVET; encourage industries and the corporate sector to fund initiation of TVET institutions.

Tertiary and Vocational Education Commission (TVEC). Since the NVQ Framework was introduced in 2005, the TVEC has been tasked with significant responsibilities as TVET regulator, facilitator, and standards setter (TVEC 2012). TVEC is thus responsible for policy formulation, planning, quality assurance, coordination, and the development of TVET in Sri Lanka. Its major programs are the following:

- **Vocational Education and Training (VET).** VET plans are prepared for growing industry sectors. A plan for a particular industry identifies staffing and training needs; assesses training supply; analyzes gaps and surpluses in demand

Box 2.2 Main Public TVET Providers

Department of Technical Education and Training (DTET). The major functions of the DTET are to direct, supervise, and coordinate the delivery of technical education programs. It operates 29 Technical Colleges and 9 Colleges of Technology (COTs), one in each province.

Vocational Training Authority (VTA). The VTA was established in 1995 to facilitate self-employment and supply last-mile skills, particularly for the informal sector, through employment-oriented short courses. VTA consists of 6 national training institutes, 22 district vocational training centers, and 237 rural vocational training centers.

VTA is tasked with operating career guidance, counseling programs, and national trade tests; carrying out research and development; helping trained youth get further training and providing employment or self-employment opportunities; providing bank loans for trained youth to start small-scale self-employment projects; and coordinating with national and international public and private entities to achieve its objectives.

National Apprentice and Industrial Training Authority (NAITA). Formal apprenticeship is the responsibility of the NAITA, established in 1990. Its main task is to impart job skills through industry-based training. It arranges on-the-job training (OJT) for university engineering undergraduates, issues National Vocational Qualification (NVQ) certificates through recognition of prior learning (RPL) for informally skilled and trained craftsman, conducts entrepreneurship development programs, interacts with industry to draw up curricula, and sets national competency standards for vocational training.

About 3,500 government and private industrial and service organizations participate; 3 national institutes and 54 regional apprenticeship-training centers operate dual apprenticeship training at the centers and in industry. NAITA pays a stipend to apprentices working for an employer to get OJT. On-site training is supplemented by full- or part-time theoretical and other instruction that is institution-based.

National Youth Services Council (NYSC). Originally within the MYASD before the restructuring, the NYSC offers basic and semi-skilled courses for craftspeople, both urban and rural.

University of Vocational Technology (UNIVOTEC). UNIVOTEC was inaugurated in 2008 to provide degree-level education for those who come through the NVQ Framework or who work in industry.

Source: TVEC 2012.

---

for and supply of skills; and introduces interventions to provide the human resources needed. VET plans are regularly updated in consultation with industry, and training providers are expected to consult the plans.

- **Quality Assurance.** Quality assurance is based on registration of providers and accreditation of courses. Over 1,500 providers are registered with the TVEC, and national training standards are prepared to provide the basis for course accreditation.
- **Labor Market Information System.** This system publishes regular bulletins that give providers signals about trends in the job market.

- **Systems Development.** Systems Development undertakes new projects to build up the TVET system. The National Skill Profile provides data on the educated skills base and the output of the TVET system; the information is useful to prospective investors as well as employers.

The establishment of TVEC in 1990 to assist the supervising ministry is part of the effort to ensure good institutional governance. Given the bureaucratic character, the civil service-oriented administration, and the capacity limitations of MYASD, TVEC is vital for realizing TVET development targets and gradually shifting the MYASD role from provision to regulation. In the past decade TVEC has made a significant contribution to better governance and coordination of the TVET sector.

The National Vocational Qualification (NVQ) Framework

The NVQ Framework was established in 2005 to support the efforts of the Sri Lanka government to build an internationally competitive workforce (table 2.2). It is central to unifying TVET. Introduction of the NVQ Framework has led to setting national skills standards in consultation with industry and national quality standards for teaching and assessment using a competency-based approach. Although the NVQ Framework has seen some success, it has not yet been fully implemented or accepted by the private sector.

In 2012 the Cabinet approved the Sri Lanka Qualification Framework (SLQF), but it has not yet been implemented. It integrates the NVQ Framework and presents flexible pathways for lateral mobility between vocational and higher education. It also provides a basis for recognizing prior learning and credit transfer (MoHE 2012).

TVET in the Provinces

TVET is largely a centralized national function; it has not been constitutionally devolved to provincial councils. TVET activities are to be found in all three lists of expenditures established by the 13th Amendment to the Constitution (Provincial Council, Concurrent, and Reserved Lists). Training centers and

Table 2.2 National Vocational Qualification Framework in Sri Lanka

Level No.	Qualification	Description
Level 1	National certificate	Recognizes the acquisition of a core entry-level skill
Level 2 Level 3 Level 4	National certificate	Recognize increasing levels of competency. Level 4 qualifications provide certification of Full National Craftsmanship.
Level 5 Level 6	Diploma	Recognize increasing competencies, from technician to management level
Level 7	Bachelor's degree or equivalent	This level includes resource planning and management processes.

Building the Skills for Economic Growth and Competitiveness in Sri Lanka
http://dx.doi.org/10.1596/978-1-4648-0158-7

technical colleges, wherever located, are planned and managed by their head offices in Colombo. However, decentralized management arrangements have been made by establishing provincial and district offices.

Because planning and management are centralized, it has not been possible to orient training to the needs of provinces, districts, and rural areas. Attempts are now being made to prepare plans based on district needs and use them to allocate human and physical resources. However, to decentralize TVET planning and management, it is necessary to build up provincial and district capacity to identify, respond to, and evaluate training needs.

Enrollment Trends

The 557 public TVET institutions offer 736 accredited courses covering 23 fields of study to earn higher national education diplomas (3- or 4-year course); diplomas (1 year); and certificates (3–6 months). The average annual student intake by registered public TVET institutes is about 125,000 (table 2.3). Half of the courses are concentrated in five fields: computer and information technology (15 percent); electrical, electronics, and telecommunications (10 percent);

Table 2.3 Student Enrollment, Completion, and Dropout, Vocational Training Institutes, 2009–2011

| | | Number of students | | | | | | |
| Name of institute | No. of centers | Enrollment | | | Completed | | Dropout number | Dropout ratio[e] |
		2009	2010	2011[b]	2009	2010	2010	2010
DTET	38	22,804	7,258[c,d]	23,140	24,817	6,802[d]	456	6
VTA	264	32,740	28,445	33,930	26,200	24,537	3,908	14
NAITA	125	31,800	27,688	33,565	17,386	24,583	3,105	11
NIBM	4	7,295	10,614	na	3,333	5,066	5,548	52
INGRIN	1	580	864	na	542	817	47	5
UNIVOTEC	1	1,401	314	996	826	123	191	61
CGTTI	2	2,746	2,768	3,570	2,004	2,062	706	26
NIFNE	8	na	1,741	2,420	na	1,601	140	8
SLIOP	1	na	874	na	na	448	426	49
NYC	36	na	11,825	14,000		7,375	4,450	38
NYSC	76	10,222[a]	11,674	13,655	9,248[a]	9,007	2,667	23
ICTRL	1	na	2,187	na	na	2,185	2	0.1
Total	557	109,588	106,252	125,276	84,356	84,606	21,646	20

Sources: a. This figure was taken from data given by TVEC.
b. This figure was obtained from the Management Information System of the DTET.
c. Intake number of DTET for the year 2010 includes both full-time and part-time students.
d. Own calculation. Dropout number refers to the subtraction of completed student number in 2010 from intake number in the same year. Dropout ratio refers to a percentage of the dropout number in 2010 with respect to the intake number in 2010. Excluding the sources referred to in (a) through (e), other figures were obtained from the Department of Census and Statistics, Ministry of Finance and Planning, *Statistical Pocket Book–2011*.
Note: na = not available.

automobile repair and maintenance (9 percent); metals and light engineering (8 percent); and visual performing arts and media (7 percent).

Although most MYASD agencies serve both full- and part-time trainees and have both National Vocational Qualification (NQV) and non-NQV programs, a few are more exclusive (table 2.4):

- UNIVOTEC runs NVQ-only programs.
- NAITA serves only full-time trainees.
- NYC runs only full-time NVQ-only programs.

Performance of the TVET Sector

Efficient Use of Resources
Retention and completion rates are the two main measures of internal efficiency. Both suggest that efficiency in the Sri Lanka TVET sector is highly variable and depends to a large extent on institution type.

Although not abysmal, dropout rates are high enough to affect internal efficiency and disrupt training center functioning. As most agencies keep a record of the number of registered students and those who complete training, dropouts can be easily assessed. In the agencies run or controlled by the MYASD, the number of trainees recruited more or less stagnated in 2004–07, peaked in 2008, and then gradually headed downward. In parallel, the number of trainees who completed a course declined at first and then rose, accompanying the surge in recruitment in 2008. The completion rate thus followed a skewed U curve starting at 72 percent in 2004, dipping to the mid-40s at its lowest point, and then hitting 76 percent in 2010 (figure 2.3).

Except for the National Institute of Business Management (NIBM), no agency records a completion rate lower than 60 percent. The internal efficiency of the MYASD agencies is very similar, with slight variations around the 75 percent

Table 2.4 MYASD Agencies: Training Profile, 2012

Agencies	Total participants	Proportion full-time (%)	Proportion of NVQ (%)
DTET	23,250	79	51
VTA	27,419	88	80
NAITA	36,950	100	20
UNIVOTEC	535	60	100
NIFNE	3,600	72	0
CGTTI	3,324	32	2
NYSC	15,151	72	28
NYC	24,000	100	100
NIBM	11,340	39	0
SLIOP	893	3	3
All	146,462	84	48

Source: MYASD institutional training information.

Building the Skills for Economic Growth and Competitiveness in Sri Lanka
http://dx.doi.org/10.1596/978-1-4648-0158-7

Figure 2.3 MYASD Aggregate Student Intake and Completion Rates, 2004–10

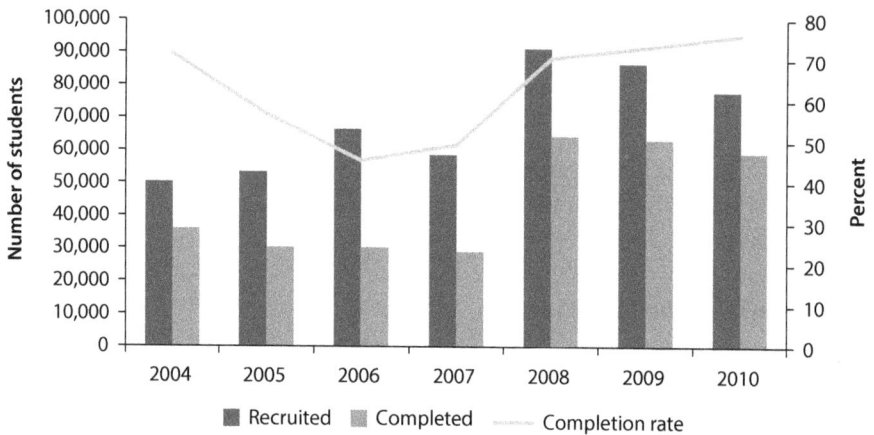

Source: TVEC 2011.
Note: Data are from the following agencies: VTA, CGTTI, DTET, NAITA, NYSC, INGRIN, and NIBM.

average completion rate (table 2.5). A high completion rate does not guarantee that trainees have actually acquired skills by graduation, but it at least indicates their tenacity in completing the course. At 60 percent completion rates in private institutions (chapter 6) are lower than in public institutions. In 2010, the lowest completion rate of 42 percent was recorded by NIBM, which accounts for about 11 percent of total student intake.

External Efficiency

The ultimate measure of the external efficiency of training courses is the income its graduates command. Chapter 4 analyzes the relationship between education, training, and labor market outcomes using the national household skills measurement survey. Although the Skills Toward Employment and Productivity (STEP) survey does not provide data by TVET provider or program, the results show that in terms of wages TVET had an estimated rate of return of 17 percent— twice as much as an additional year of formal education. This suggests that TVET is a profitable investment in Sri Lanka, even though it is not perceived to be as socially rewarding as formal tertiary education.[5]

Several tracer studies provide some information about the external efficiency of TVET providers but they do not yield consistent results. Despite some bright spots, Chandrasiri (2010) found low external efficiency as assessed by employment rates after graduation,[6] which ranged from 25 percent to 63 percent (table 2.6). Even for graduates who find a job within a reasonable time, employment is not always directly linked to the training received.

Chandrasiri (2010) found low employability of TVET graduates in general, though with wide variations among major programs. He also found a number of negative factors affecting the labor market outcomes of TVET graduates: outdated programs, inadequate teaching aids, irrelevant industrial training, insufficient practical work, and inadequate interaction with industry.

Table 2.5 Intake and Completion: MYASD Agencies, 2010

	Recruited	Completed	Dropped	Completion rate (%)	Drop-out rate (%)
DTET	7,221	5,524	1,697	76	24
VTA	23,304	19,640	3,664	84	16
NAITA	24,347	19,342	5,005	79	21
NIBM	8,682	3,613	5,069	42	58
INGRIN	707	660	47	93	7
UNIVOTEC	418	418	0	100	0
CGTTI	344	281	63	82	18
SLIOP	874	660	214	76	24
NYC	11,825	7,375	4,450	62	38
ICTRL	2,187	2,185	2	100	0
All	79,909	59,698	20,211	75	25

Source: MFP 2011.

Table 2.6 Estimated Unemployment Rates of TVET Center Graduates, Various Dates

Survey date	Institution	Unemployment rate (%)
2002	DTET	34
2002	NAITA	28
2002	VTA	63
2005	NYSC	25
2009	VTA	60
2010	DTET	33
2011	Various NGOs	3

Source: Studies quoted in Chandrasiri 2010.

For training institutes, tracer studies identified the following drawbacks: low quality of courses, absence of curricular and resource materials, lack of interest in introducing NVQ courses, delays in starting courses and releasing results, absence of in-plant training or on-the-job training (OJT) for students, inadequate follow-up of graduates and dropouts, and poorly maintained test evaluation records. Adding to performance inefficiencies were inadequate facilities (tools, training equipment, library, sanitary services, and first aid) and lack of curriculum development (Chandrasiri 2010).

Equity Patterns

For the past three decades, equity has been one of the chief concerns of TVET policy makers in Sri Lanka; currently, one of the main objectives of government policy is Skills for All.

Disparities by household income. Not surprisingly, income is a major factor in access to both general and professional education, and dropout rates are higher for trainees who are poorer. Dropping out of a TVET program is often linked to the opportunity cost of foregoing a job to attend a course. Three types of financial aid are available to full-time students: (1) stipends for attendance, based on parental income; (2) bursaries for students from low-income families; and (3) discounted railway and bus season tickets. Most of these schemes are restricted to the neediest trainees attending public technical or vocational centers. Similar strategies support attendance at training for students from other vulnerable groups, such as those with disabilities. The total cost of student welfare is about 1.6 percent of total MYASD recurrent expenditure.

The National Strategy on TVET Policy (Section 14.8; Policy 80) has identified six vulnerable groups that TVET providers should be serving: (1) disadvantaged women, especially those heading households; (2) people with disabilities, both mental and physical; (3) disadvantaged youth, especially school dropouts and former child laborers; (4) poor populations; (5) persons affected by conflict, such as internally displaced persons and ex-combatants; and (6) migrant workers. The government has formulated a variety of strategies to ensure that all vulnerable groups have access to TVET.[7]

Regional disparities. Because of the interplay of supply and demand, although gender discrimination is not pronounced, access to TVET services is unequally distributed between provinces and between economically or otherwise vulnerable segments of the population. TVET services seem to be most intensely used in the richest provinces (table 2.7). The contrast is particularly stark between the Western Province and the Uva and Sabaragamuwa provinces, with the Western Province well ahead in terms of both economic performance and TVET enrollment. However, the pattern is not uniform. For example, in terms of course completion, the Western Province comes in third; the Eastern Province, economically backward after 30 years of violence, ranks ahead of it. There is not enough evidence to identify the respective roles of supply and demand in the skewed distribution, but there may be a leaning toward the supply side. To illustrate, of the 50 public and private centers that received financial assistance from TVEC in 2010/11, 20 are in the Western Province and 10 in the Central Province.

Table 2.7 Economic Performance and TVET Participation by Province, 2009–10
Percent

	Provincial share of GDP	Monthly household income (SL Rs 000)	TVET enrollment per 1,000 residents	TVET completion per 1,000 residents
	2009	2009/10	2010	2010
Western	48.3	47.1	5.8	4.2
Southern	9.7	32.5	4.8	4.3
Eastern	5.0	23.9	5.0	4.4
Central	9.4	31.9	3.0	2.1
Northern	2.4	23.7	4.6	3.4
Sabaragamuwa	6.4	36.1	2.3	1.8
North Western	10.7	35.6	3.5	2.5
Uva	4.6	28.7	2.6	2.2
North Central	3.7	35.6	3.1	2.4
Sri Lanka	100	36.4	4.1	3.1

Source: Chandrasiri 2010.

Uva, North Western, Sabaragamuwa, Northern, and Eastern provinces have both high poverty and low TVET participation rates. The low participation rates of the last two provinces can be attributed primarily to the decades of secessionist conflict. In line with the government's post-conflict development commitments, they therefore merit special attention to TVET activities.

Between 1990 and 2010 poverty fell and TVET participation went up in the Western and Southern provinces. The two account for 58 percent of Sri Lankan gross domestic product (GDP) and 55 percent of TVET enrollments, perhaps because of the rapid expansion of economic activities in Colombo, Gampaha, Kalutara, Galle, Matara, and Hambantota. These six districts together account for 50 percent of Sri Lanka's industrial and 40 percent of its services businesses.

Gender disparities. Like the balance elsewhere in the educational system, gender imbalances in TVET enrollments are not pronounced, but women are limited to a narrow range of skills that disadvantage them in the labor market. Female TVET participation in 2010 was 42 percent (public institutions, 41 percent; private institutions, 52 percent). It also varies enormously by sector. For example, female participation is 90 percent in the medical and health science fields, but only 3 percent in metal and light engineering and 4 percent in automobile repair and maintenance (figure 2.4).

Female participation in DTET, NAITA, VTA, NYSC, and NIBM programs ranges from 32 percent to 50 percent,[8] but women are concentrated in disciplines culturally perceived as "feminine," such as sewing, home science, beauty culture, and secretarial. Although recently more women have been enrolling in computer, accounting, management, and commerce courses, TVET does not seem to be equipped to meet the needs of female school leavers.

The Informal Sector: Skills for the Unskilled

Although the informal sector accounts for close to 66 percent of the workforce, it has no systematic opportunities for skills development. About 51 percent of the nonagricultural workforce and 80 percent of the agricultural workforce operate informally (DCS 2011). Among the other disadvantages for informal workers are not only fewer skills than formal workers (Gunatilaka 2008) but also less general education. Most have had to drop out of school for such reasons as family poverty or a lack of training opportunities after completing primary or O-level education. There is no information about training activities in the informal sector, where NGOs and family-based apprenticeships are common but tend to be unrecorded.

Though the government is planning skills training for informal workers (SSM 2012), many of whom live in rural areas, the current system is not geared to meeting their training needs. Yet creating opportunities for them to acquire skills is intrinsic to increasing their productivity. Some developing countries confronted with the same problem have devised innovative programs that Sri Lanka could look to for possible models (box 2.3).

Figure 2.4 Female Participation in TVET Programs, 2011
Percent

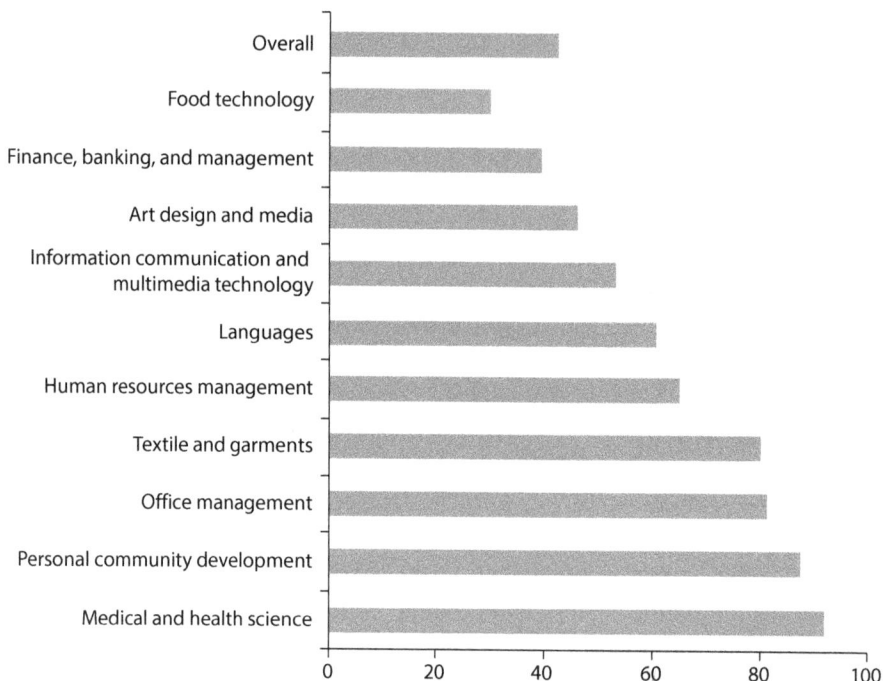

Source: TVEC 2011.

Conclusion

Skills development activities have expanded rapidly over the past 30 years with the active participation of public, private, and NGO providers. Sri Lanka has a well-established structure for delivering TVET services through a wide range of institutions from the certificate to the degree level. But despite reform attempts, organization and management in the sector still need to be built up. The following chapters examine in more detail the cost, financing, and governance of the sector.

Although Sri Lanka has made significant progress in providing access to TVET services to disadvantaged students, considerable disparities exist in access to skills development programs by socioeconomic background, gender, and geographic Since the box has to be continued anyway, please put the rest of this paragraph above the start of the box rather than two pages away location. Female participation in TVET needs to be encouraged and training opportunities extended to poorer districts. Implementing the recommendations of the National Strategy on TVET Provision for Vulnerable People in Sri Lanka would help more members of disadvantaged groups to access training.

Box 2.3 Training for the Informal Sector

Mexico. The Integral Quality and Modernization Program (CIMO), established in 1988, has been effective in reaching small and medium-size enterprises, most of which are informal, to help them upgrade worker skills, improve product quality, and raise productivity. CIMO has now evolved to the point where every year it provides training and industrial services to over 80,000 enterprises and 200,000 employees. By 2000 more than 300 business associations were participating in CIMO, up from 72 in 1988.

CIMO has proved effective in improving the performance of targeted companies. Compared to a control group, CIMO firms increased investments in worker training, had higher rates of capacity utilization, and were more likely to adopt quality control practices. These outcomes were associated with higher productivity.

Kenya. The *Jua kali* (informal sector) project, funded by the International Development Association (IDA), was designed to provide skills and upgrade technology for about 25,000 informal manufacturing workers, increase the access of informal entrepreneurs to services, and improve the policy and institutional environment by removing restrictive laws and policies. A key feature of the project is a voucher program to introduce consumer choice, enabling workers to purchase the training they want wherever they want. Intermediary agencies were selected by competitive tenders to market, allocate, and redeem vouchers throughout Kenya. Impact evaluations showed that employment of graduates was 50 percent higher than before training, and the income of enterprises supported had also increased by 50 percent.

India. The National Alliance of Street Vendors in India (NASVI) offers worker training in information technology, English fluency, and leadership and negotiation, among other skills. For instance, Negotiation Skills Development Training is offered to vendor activists looking to negotiate successfully with institutions and agencies of governance. Participants form groups to role-play scenarios where negotiation is necessary. Leadership Promotion and Negotiation Skills Development is offered to female vendors, who are taught to overcome adversity through better organization and improved negotiation and leadership skills. The training is based on the participative sharing of experiences.

Bangladesh. The Underprivileged Children's Education Program (UCEP), established in the early 1970s, seeks to raise the living standards of poor urban children and their families. It provides the target group of working street children with skills to enhance their employability in the local labor market, often in the informal sector. UCEP is conducted in 30 general schools for non-formal basic education in four major cities. Total enrollment is about 20,000. Skills training is given to a total of 1,400 trainees in three institutions. UCEP has extraordinarily high completion and employment rates, both averaging about 95 percent. Several factors have contributed to its success:

- It provides a solid base of general education.
- It has a clear target group: those who intend to enter the labor force after training as semi-skilled workers.

box continues next page

Box 2.3 Training for the Informal Sector *(continued)*

- It has continuous linkages with industry, which ensure that trainees are acquiring the knowledge, skills, and attitudes sought by employers, and that employers are aware of the competencies of UCEP graduates.
- Students acquire skills and competencies through highly structured and supervised individualized hands-on instruction, rather than being driven by credentials and certificates.
- There is rigorous follow-up of the employment, earnings, and performance on the job of each graduate.

Sources: Johanson and Van Adams 2004; Lopez Acevedo and Tan 2005; Pina *et al.* 2012; World Bank 2001.

Notes

1. For details on general education see World Bank 2005, 2009, and 2011.
2. Preschool in Sri Lanka is almost exclusively private.
3. Specialized programs cover a range of fields, such as construction, farm machinery, gems and jewelry, plantation, health science, printing, telecommunication, and electrical works.
4. An estimated 2,500 or so private and NGO providers were also operating but were not registered with the TVEC. It is not known how many students they have.
5. This perception is almost universal. In a recent nine-country survey (Brazil, Germany, India, Mexico, Morocco, Saudi Arabia, Turkey, the United Kingdom, and the United States), except in Germany a majority of youth stated that society valued academic more highly than vocational paths. It also found that 23 percent of vocational graduates thought that in hindsight they had not chosen the right path and another 42 percent were not sure they had (McKinsey 2012).
6. Studies from a variety of countries do not lead to definitive conclusions about the impact of vocational training. For instance, in OECD countries, TVET graduates are as likely as their peers from either upper secondary or tertiary streams to find a job. However, they earn less (Almeida, Behrman, and Robalino 2012).
7. For more details see TVEC 2010.
8. These institutions jointly account for more than 90 percent of public TVET enrollment.

Bibliography

Almeida, R., J. Behrman, and D. Robalino, eds. 2012. *The Right Skills for the Job?: Rethinking Training Policies for Workers.* Washington, DC: World Bank.

Chandrasiri, S. 2010. "Effect of Training on Labor Market Outcomes." In *The Challenge of Youth Employment in Sri Lanka,* edited by R. Gunatilaka, M. Mayer, and M. Vodopivec, 91–114. Washington, DC: World Bank.

DCS (Department of Census and Statistics). 2011. *Sri Lanka Labour Force Survey Annual Report 2010.* Colombo.

Gunatilaka, R. 2008. "Informal Employment in Sri Lanka: Nature, Probability of Employment, and Determinants of Wages." International Labour Organization, New Delhi.

Johanson, R. K., and A. Van Adams. 2004. *Skills Development in sub-Saharan Africa.* Washington, DC: World Bank.

Lopez Acevedo, G., and H. Tan. 2005. "Evaluating Training Programs for Small and Medium Enterprises: Lessons from Mexico." World Bank Policy Research Paper 3760, World Bank, Washington, DC.

McKinsey Center for Government. 2012. "Education to Employment: Designing a System that Works." McKinsey and Company. http://mckinseyonsociety.com/downloads /reports/Education/Education-to-Employment_FINAL.pdf.

MFP (Ministry of Finance and Planning). "Medium Term Public Investment Outlook for Skills Education Sector (2012–16)." MFP, Colombo, Sri Lanka.

Ministry of Vocational Training and Rural Industries. 1997. "Presidential Task Force on TVET Reforms: Technical Education and Vocational Training Reforms, Policies, Strategies and Action Program." Ministry of Vocational Training and Rural Industries, Colombo, Sri Lanka.

MoE (Ministry of Education). 2005. "School Census. Ministry of Education, Sri Lanka." http://www.statistics.gov.lk/education/censusS%202005.pdf.

———. 2011. "Sri Lanka Education Information 2011." MoE, Sri Lanka. http://www.moe .gov.lk/web/images/stories/statistic/sri_lanka_education_information_2011.pdf.

MoHE (Ministry of Higher Education). 2012. *Sri Lanka Qualifications Framework.* Colombo, Sri Lanka: MoHE.

MVTT (Ministry of Vocational and Technical Training). 2008. *Efficiency of Government and Non-Governmental TVET Provisions.* Unpublished report, Colombo, Sri Lanka.

NAITA (National Apprentice and Industrial Training Authority). 2001. *Report on Tracer Study Survey Results for Monitoring and Evaluation of Vocational Training.* Planning and Information Division, Colombo, Sri Lanka.

———. 2005a. "An Investigation on the Efficiency of the Enterprise-Based Craft Apprenticeship Training Programme Offered by the NAITA." Proceedings of the Research Convention, Ministry of Skills Development and Technical Education, Sri Lanka.

———. 2005b. "Factors Leading to Low Enrolment Rates and High Dropout Rates in Selected Courses Conducted by NAITA." Proceedings of the Research Convention, Ministry of Skills Development and Technical Education, Sri Lanka.

———. 2005c. "A Study to Evaluate the Contribution of Government TVET Institutions for Accomplishing the Training Requirements and Upgrading Occupational Areas in the Industrial Sector." Proceedings of the Research Convention, Ministry of Skills Development and Technical Education, Sri Lanka.

NEC (National Education Commission). 2008. *National Policy Framework on University, Technical and Vocational Education.* Colombo, Sri Lanka: NEC.

NYSC (National Youth Services Council). 2005. "The Diploma in Computer Science Courses Conducted by the National Youth Services Council at the Maharagama Training Centre. Some Proposals for Improvement Based on the Experience of Students Who Have Completed the Course." Proceedings of the Research Convention, Ministry of Skills Development and Technical Education, Sri Lanka.

Pina, P., T. Kotin, V. Hausman, and E. Macharia. 2012. "Skills for Employability: The Informal Economy." Results for Development Institute. http://r4d.org/sites/resultsfordevelopment .org/files/resources/Skills%20for%20Employability%20in%20the%20Informal%20 Economy.pdf.

SSM (Secretariat for Senior Ministers). 2012. *The National Human Resources and Employment Policy for Sri Lanka*. Secretariat for Senior Ministers. Colombo: Government of Sri Lanka.

Tan, H. 2012. "Sri Lanka: Education, Training and Labor Market Outcomes." Background paper for Sri Lanka Skills Development Report, World Bank, Washington, DC.

TVEC (Tertiary and Vocational Education Commission). 2010. *The National Strategy on TVET Provision for Vulnerable People in Sri Lanka*. Colombo: TVEC.

———. 2011. *Labour Market Information Bulletin* (various volumes). Colombo: TVEC.

———. 2012. *Corporate Plan 2012–2016*. Colombo: TVEC.

VTA (Vocational Training Authority). 2001. *Report on Tracer Study Survey Results for Monitoring and Evaluation of Vocational Training*. Colombo.

———. 2005. "Tracer Study on the Participants Who Had Undergone the Career Guidance Awareness Programme Conducted by Vocational Training Authority in Moneragala District." Proceedings of the Research Convention, Ministry of Skills Development and Technical Education, Colombo, Sri Lanka.

World Bank. 2001. *Bangladesh: Education Sector Review*. Washington, DC: World Bank.

———. 2005. "Training and Links to the Labor Market." In *Treasures of the Education System in Sri Lanka: Restoring Performance, Expanding Opportunities and Enhancing Prospects*. Human Development Unit, South Asia Region, 93–118. Washington, DC: World Bank.

———. 2007. *Learning for Working Opportunities: An Assessment of Vocational Education and Training in Bangladesh*. Human Development Unit, South Asia Region. Washington, DC: World Bank.

———. 2009. *The Towers of Learning: Higher Education in Sri Lanka*. Human Development Unit, South Asia Region. Washington, DC: World Bank.

———. 2011. *Transforming School Education in Sri Lanka: From Cut Stones to Polished Jewels*. Human Development Unit, South Asia Region. Washington, DC: World Bank.

CHAPTER 3

Skills Demand in Sri Lanka

Introduction

In recent years Sri Lanka has, like some other developing countries, given high priority to promoting and improving education and training. In particular, its development strategy, based on the 2006 *Mahinda Chintana—Vision for the Future* (MC), has as an integral component the 10-year Education Sector Development Framework and Programme (ESDFP). The ESDFP is designed to (1) increase equitable access to basic education (grades 1–5) and secondary education (grades 6–13); (2) improve the quality of education; (3) enhance economic efficiency and the equity of resource allocation; and (4) strengthen service delivery and monitoring and evaluation (MFP 2010).

The priority given to building skills, especially through technical vocational education and training (TVET), can be seen in the following three MC objectives:

- Improve the quality and relevance of TVET programs by, for example, registration of all vocational training institutions; accreditation and auditing of courses and programs; and reinforcing labor market relevance through collaboration with employers.
- Improve the efficiency of TVET institutions in recruiting and retaining quality staff; providing opportunities for staff development; linking with local and foreign institutions; introducing a quality management system; increasing the number of centers for institutional and apprenticeship-based training; and encouraging the participation of the private sector.
- Improve TVET quality and opportunities for upward career paths by, for example, activating the National Vocational Qualification (NVQ) Framework, competency-based assessments, and recognition of prior learning (RPL); upgrading the nine provincial training institutes into Colleges of Technology; and expanding the University of Vocational Training (UNIVOTEC).

The MC targets specific segments of both the population and the labor market, including youth, small and medium-sized enterprises, and tourism. To create the Five Hub Strategy, key segments of the Sri Lankan economy have been targeted. Every year, about 140,000 young people enter the labor market without job-specific skills (MFP 2010), so there is a substantial need for them to acquire marketable skills, especially those relevant for the targeted segments, to capture their unrealized potential and move Sri Lanka's economy forward. Youth are thus the explicit target for specific skills development programs. Special attention is also directed to small and medium enterprises since skills development would be crucial to enhance their productivity and growth. Tourism has been identified as particularly important, since it is expected to generate 700,000 new job opportunities by 2020, with 20 percent of them in managerial categories (MFP 2010).

To keep the labor market humming at peak efficiency, both academics and policy makers must ascertain which skills employers demand; what barriers there are in the labor market to supplying them and how severe they are; and the possible consequences of any skills shortages. Until recently, answers to these questions have been few because of a lack of data; whatever information exists has been couched in relatively crude terms, and data have mainly been related to hard skills like literacy and numeracy.

This chapter examines recent surveys that collected detailed information from companies on skills demand. It asked specific questions: (1) What is the demand for skills? And what is driving demand? (2) What are the extent, nature, and consequences of skills constraints and mismatches? (3) How effective is the education system—general, TVET, and university—perceived to be in producing skills? Following the framework presented in the introduction, this chapter reviews the skills demand and skills gaps and mismatches identified by employers.

This chapter first analyzes the existence, nature, and consequences of skills constraints in the Sri Lankan economy, including demand drivers, shortages, the types of skills employers are seeking, skills mismatches, and the consequences of skills shortages for firm growth and development. It next describes how firms in Sri Lanka are coping with skills gaps through, e.g., interactions with skills-providing institutions, in-service training, contracting out, and hiring. The chapter then summarizes employer perceptions about the skills provided by the education and training systems. It concludes by discussing policy implications and areas for further research.

Skills Constraints: Existence, Nature, and Consequences

Drivers of Demand for Skills

While many factors might affect skills demand, the ones described next seem particularly relevant to Sri Lanka.[1] Total demand can be seen to contain a mix of such diverse factors as a large contingent of displaced refugees and demographic transition.

Economic growth. While economic growth creates jobs and thus demand for both lower and higher skills, higher-order competencies make it possible to use new technologies and perform complex tasks efficiently. These are becoming particularly important as Sri Lanka moves from a resource-based to a productivity-driven economy.

To help stimulate economic growth and job creation even more, the government has identified five strategic hubs (chapter 1). Within these, strategic segments have been identified, each with its own education and skills needs, since different sectors and industries may not necessarily require the same mix of skills. Tourism, for example, has been identified as of particular strategic importance (MFP 2010); it would seem to need English more than any other skill type. Other industries identified as promising are construction, furniture, transport, and food and beverage, each with unique skills demands.

Technological development and globalization, bringing increased competition. The more Sri Lanka is integrated into global markets, the better educated and trained its labor force must be. Current skills need to be upgraded and workers equipped with skills that enable businesses to compete in global markets.

More foreign competition may heighten innovation (Gorodnichenko, Svejnar, and Terrell 2010). It may also pressure companies not only "to innovate to maintain competitiveness, but also to introduce new ideas, products and business practices, which may spill over to local firms via market interactions" (Dutz and O'Connell 2013, 9–10). This would in turn seem both to require a generally well-educated workforce to generate innovation in the first place and also to spotlight specific skills, such as teamwork and analytical and critical thinking.

In response to globalization, liberalization can help a country stay competitive and perhaps even attract foreign direct investment (FDI). FDI would create jobs and therefore increase demand for skills, with the outcomes depending crucially on how effective institutions and networks at different levels are. In Sri Lanka, for instance, interventions by the Telecommunications Regulatory Commission have only partially succeeded in meeting the full potential for FDI in the sector (Fernando 2006). If full FDI potential is not reached, job creation goals are also not reached, which means less demand for skills than if liberalization had been more complete.

Demographic change. Since the demographic dividend period is expected to end by 2017 (World Bank 2012b), Sri Lanka should also be concerned about ensuring that labor is more productive. Of the 6 percent annual rise in real per capita incomes in East Asia between 1965 and 1990, 20–25 percent is attributable to the demographic dividend. Sri Lanka's dividend seems to have peaked in 2005, when the age-dependency ratio[2] was 46.7 percent; the ratio has since been steadily rising, hitting 49.9 percent in 2011. A more productive labor force will be crucial to sustain MC economic growth rate targets.

As population growth has slowed, fewer people are entering the labor market (World Bank 2012a). Policies to expand the economically active population might include encouraging women and youth to join the labor force, creating conditions to increase domestic demand for labor, and enhancing the quality of the workforce. One way to counter labor force pressures is to equip young and middle-aged Sri Lankans with skills that make them more productive.

Rural-urban migration. Sri Lanka is experiencing a rise in migration from rural to urban areas of workers seeking to earn wages. The evolution began as early as 1977 due to more open economic policies; the export processing zones (EPZs) especially have attracted a huge number of young rural dwellers (Ranathunga 2011). To the extent that these young migrants are unskilled, especially for urban jobs, heavy demand—especially for job-specific technical skills—is being created.

Foreign employment. Many Sri Lankans have emigrated to work, especially in construction. In 2012, for example, of more than a million emigrants, about 250,000 were workers—about 23 percent of new employment. Whereas until recently emigrants were mostly unskilled, increasing migration of skilled labor may heighten domestic skills shortages. While the present impact of emigration is likely to be small, Sri Lanka now has a national policy to ensure "skilled, safe migration" (SSM 2012). Even so, despite the high proportion of migrant workers in total employment—and the associated inflow of remittances (US$4 billion, about 7 percent of gross domestic product [GDP], in 2010)—Sri Lanka does not yet have an effective system to train workers to engage effectively in the labor markets of countries to which they migrate.

Unresolved and new challenges to the education and training systems. Every year about 140,000 new workers leave the Sri Lankan education system unemployable because they lack job-specific skills (SSM 2012). However, the government's Skills for All policy is expected to increase the supply in selected fields (MFP 2013).

Skills Shortages: South Asia and International Evidence

Skills shortages and their possible consequences have received both academic and policy attention, but attention has only recently shifted from viewing skills generically to viewing them as a multidimensional concept covering a variety of types of skills.[3]

In the World Bank Enterprise Surveys, some firms identified lack of an educated labor force as a major or severe constraint throughout South Asia, but Sri Lankan firms are more likely to complain about the lack of an adequate labor force as a major or severe constraint on their operations than those in several other South Asian countries (figure 3.1).

In examining how human capital affects the productivity, innovation, and growth of firms in Sri Lanka, Dutz and O'Connell (2013) found that the share of skills-constrained firms had risen from about 22 percent in 2004 to about 27 percent[4] in 2007. They also found that human capital, measured as worker training, had substantial positive impact on firm productivity and innovation. Thus, eradicating skills shortages in Sri Lanka could have a high return in terms of individual company productivity and innovation.

In Indonesia, di Gropello, Kruse, and Tandon (2011) established that a shortage of skills, though perhaps not yet a major constraint, is certainly emerging as one. This was particularly noticeable in managerial and professional jobs: more than 80 percent of respondents were finding it difficult to fill director

Figure 3.1 Skills Constraints as a Major or Severe Obstacle, South Asia
Percent

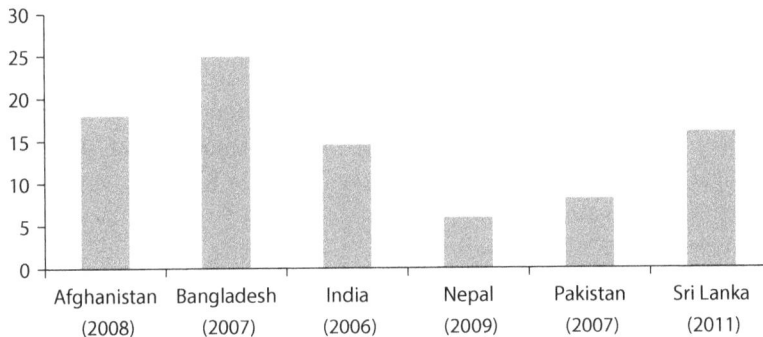

Source: Enterprise Surveys, various years (http://www.enterprisesurveys.org/).

vacancies and more than 60 percent were having trouble recruiting professionals. In the Philippines, di Gropello, Tan, and Tandon (2010) found that skills shortages were emerging as a major problem: the number of weeks to fill professional positions in both services and manufacturing was relatively high for the region, particularly for exporters and those in chemicals, trade, and finance.

Thailand is having similar problems, especially in filling all types of manufacturing vacancies (World Bank 2012a), with large shortages of qualified professional workers (20 percent of firms); skilled production workers (30 percent); and unskilled production workers (48 percent). Notably, a lack of basic and technical skills rather than, say, a shortage of university graduates seems to explain the prevalence of job vacancies, especially in information and communications technology (ICT), English, creative thinking, and behavioral skills (World Bank 2012a).

Recent surveys have gone beyond simply exploring generic skills constraints to consider a range of different but complementary skills. In addition to the Skills Toward Employment and Productivity (STEP) Employer Survey examined here, there is also recent evidence of substantial skills constraints in the Yunnan province in China (Liang and Chen 2014). That study found that the two most important labor factors impeding the operation and growth of Yunnan businesses are finding experienced workers and workers with the appropriate TVET.

Analysis of the Skills Situation from the Employer Side

This section examines three skills demand issues in Sri Lanka: (1) the relevance of the skills of current workers; (2) the types and extent of skills gaps and mismatches, especially in relation to educational institutions; and (3) the education and skill endowments of recent recruits.[5]

Data. The data examined here are mainly from the Sri Lanka Enterprise Survey and the STEP Survey, both carried out by the World Bank (boxes 1.4 and 3.1).

Table 3.1 reports responses to the question about the degree to which an inadequately educated workforce was considered an obstacle in the business environment, using two alternative binary measures (high threshold: severe;

low threshold: major or severe).[6] For the high-threshold measure Sri Lankan firms experience major skills constraints that slightly increased between 2004 and 2011, from about 7 percent to about 9 percent; constraints increased substantially more for the lower-threshold measure, from about 21 percent to about 26 percent.

Among perceived obstacles, an inadequately educated workforce ranks third, after access to finance and the practices of competitors in the informal sector (figure 3.2).[7] Coupled with the findings of recent substantial skills gaps in Sri Lanka, it can be concluded that skills constraints in Sri Lanka are also severe relative to other constraints.

Employers perceive skills constraints as having more impact on firm operations and growth than employment legislation, taxes, and labor costs (figure 3.3). Labor availability—which might be considered a general measure of raw labor supply, adjusted for education and skills—ranks fourth, after finding experienced workers and high employee turnover. Worker technical training ranks third, at about 33 percent—more than double the general education of workers at about 16 percent. This seems to suggest both that the government's recent focus on TVET is well-founded, and that the push for TVET has not yet been successful. This generally agrees with the results of the study for China's Yunnan province (Liang and Chen 2014). Similarly, Rutkowski (2013) found for Vietnam that issues of labor availability in general and TVET in particular ranked high.

Box 3.1 Sri Lanka Enterprise Surveys and the Skills Toward Employment and Productivity (STEP) Survey

In 2004 and 2011, Sri Lanka Enterprise Surveys asking about information for the previous fiscal year were administered to managers. Stratified random sampling was used to select representative firms.[a] To ensure comparability, the sample considered here is restricted to manufacturers (the 2004 survey interviewed only manufacturers; the 2011 survey also interviewed service establishments). In addition, manufacturers represented in the 2011 survey were from industries that overlapped those represented in 2004.[b]

The STEP Employer Survey gathered information from a random sample of employers on company skills needs, hiring (including the skills deficits of prospective employees), training practices, and enterprise productivity, when the respondent is a company executive. The executives were asked, among other things, about requirements for high-skilled (type A) and low-skilled (type B) workers:

(a) *High-skilled/Type A Workers:* managers, professionals, and technicians.
(b) *Low-skilled/Type B Workers:* clerical support workers, service workers, salespeople, skilled agricultural workers, craft and related trades workers, plant and machine operators, and basic occupations. Skills-related questions in the STEP Employer Survey use more detailed groupings of skills than is typical of firm-level surveys, including previous Enterprise Surveys.

a. See Sanchez Puerta *et al.* 2012 and http://www.enterprisesurveys.org/Methodology for more details.
b. Similar to Dutz and O'Connell 2013.

Table 3.1 Skills Constraints in Manufacturing, Sri Lanka, 2004 and 2011 (Share of Firms)

	2004	*2011*
High threshold: Severe	0.069	0.087
Low threshold: Major or severe	0.213	0.266
N	450	301

Source: World Bank Enterprise Survey, Sri Lanka 2004 and 2011 rounds.
Note: The skills demand gap is based on responses to the question "To what degree is an inadequately educated workforce an obstacle to the current operations of this establishment?"

Figure 3.2 Biggest Perceived Obstacle in the Business Environment, Sri Lanka, 2011
Percent

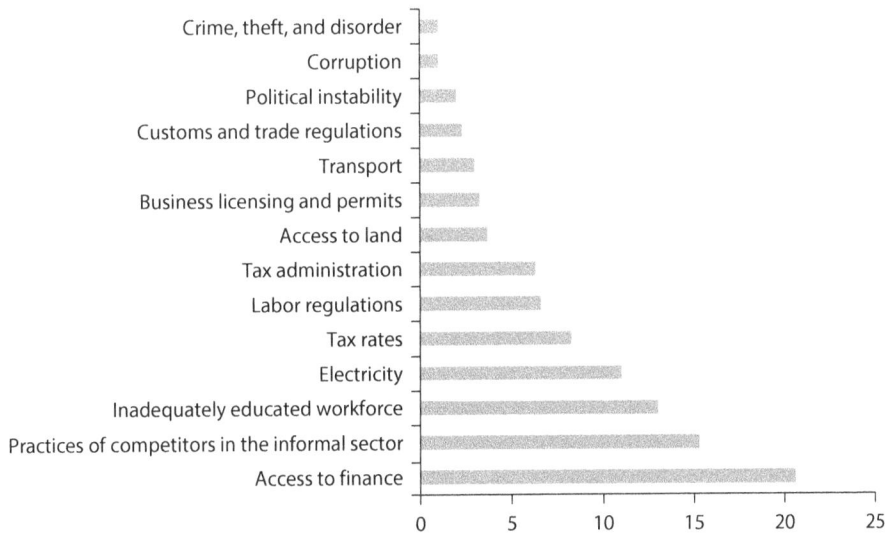

Source: World Bank Enterprise Survey, Sri Lanka 2011 round.

Figure 3.3 Labor Factors That Affect Firm Operations and Growth
Percent

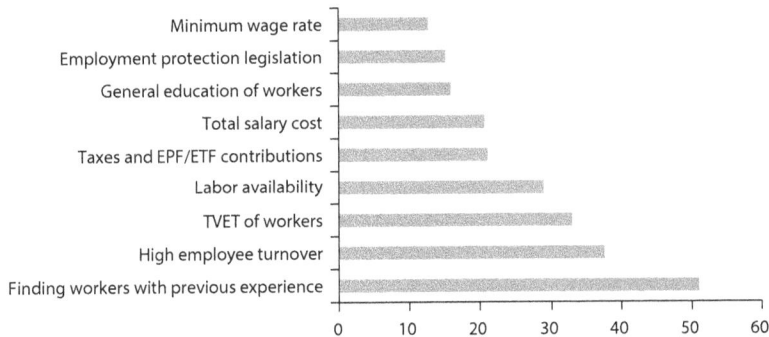

Source: World Bank STEP Survey, Sri Lanka 2012.

Building the Skills for Economic Growth and Competitiveness in Sri Lanka
http://dx.doi.org/10.1596/978-1-4648-0158-7

Figure 3.4 reports on problems encountered when recruiting workers in the past 12 months by hiring category (conditional on encountering problems). Overwhelmingly, the main problem was lack of skills, except for very elementary occupations, where the supply of applicants, skilled or not, was the main challenge. This supports earlier findings, with the added insight that skills are more lacking for white-collar than for blue-collar occupational categories. Similarly, in Yunnan province, more firms were having problems hiring professional and technical workers than less-skilled workers: lack of skills was identified as a serious problem by 73–81 percent of firms hiring professionals and technicians/ associate professionals and over 91 percent of firms hiring plant and machine operators/assemblers/drivers (Liang and Chen 2014). Vietnamese companies also had serious hiring problems, especially those looking for clerks and skilled blue-collar workers, such as craftspeople, machine operators, and assemblers (Rutkowski 2013).

Having established that in recent years Sri Lanka has had considerable skills demand gaps, it is useful to ask what types of skills are in demand—knowledge

Figure 3.4 Skills Shortages, by Job Category
Percent

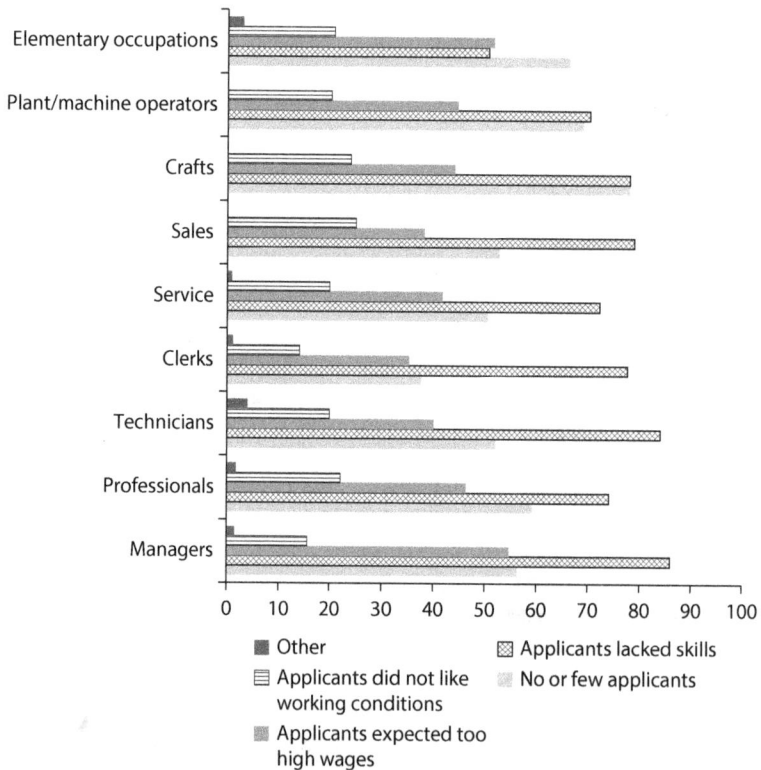

Source: World Bank STEP Survey, Sri Lanka 2012.
Note: The skilled agricultural, forestry, etc. group was excluded because it contained only one observation.

about the source of demand for specific skills can help policymakers address shortages more effectively.

Which Skills Are in Demand?

Job-specific technical skills are important but there is also high employer demand for soft skills, particularly the combined group of leadership, teamwork, and work ethic (77 percent).[7] Asked to assess which group of skills they consider most important for retaining new employees after probation, employers chose job-related skills, but especially so for high-skilled workers (table 3.2). Personality traits (soft skills) were second in general importance, again more so for high-skilled workers.

Figure 3.5 disaggregates the job-related skills underlying the results in table 3.2 to examine the relative importance of each type. Clearly, job-specific technical skills are somewhat more important for retention of low-skilled workers (33.8 percent) than of the more highly-skilled (24 percent). A substantial share of firms ranked literacy in Sinhala or Tamil as most important, again more for low-skilled (21 percent) than for high-skilled workers (18.3 percent). However, about 13.8 percent of firms ranked leadership (soft) skills as most important for high-skilled workers, though only 1 percent did so for low-skilled workers.

Although firms place different values on different skills, across the board the most sought-after skills are job-specific technical skills and language skills, especially English. Job-specific skills are considered particularly important in manufacturing, for both high-skilled (30.2 percent) and low-skilled (47.9 percent) workers.

The demand for English language skills differs most from firm to firm and is high in the strategic sectors identified in the MC. English skills are considered very important in tourism, though more for high-skilled (30.2 percent) than low-skilled workers (25.5 percent), which underscores the importance of building English skills in the system. Job-specific skills are more valued in large firms than in smaller but English literacy is more valued in micro, small, and medium-sized firms—again, a major strategic component of the MC (MFP 2010). For all workers, English skills are much more important for international than domestic firms; for low-skilled workers, for example, about 17 percent of international firms consider English skills most important but only about 7 percent of domestic firms do. English is also valued more for all workers by innovative[8] firms; for

Table 3.2 Job-Related Skills Most Important for Retention Decisions
Percent

	High-skilled		Low-skilled	
	No 1	*No 2*	*No 1*	*No 2*
Personal characteristics (age, appearance, gender, etc.)	22.1	21.2	26.0	22.8
Job-related skills (literacy, numeracy, etc.)	67.6	21.6	59.9	28.2
Personality traits (conscientiousness, emotional stability, etc.)	10.3	57.2	14.1	49.0

Source: World Bank STEP Survey, Sri Lanka 2012.

Building the Skills for Economic Growth and Competitiveness in Sri Lanka
http://dx.doi.org/10.1596/978-1-4648-0158-7

Figure 3.5 Ranking of Job-Related Skills for Retention
Percent

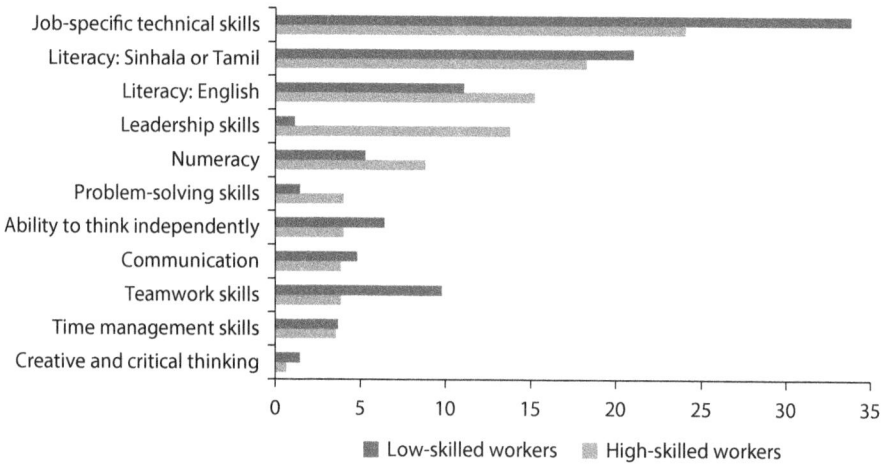

Source: World Bank STEP Survey, Sri Lanka 2012.

high-skilled workers, for example, about 17 percent of innovative firms consider it the most important skill, versus only about 11 percent of non-innovative firms. Perhaps this is merely the flipside of the findings for international firms, reflecting the globalization of innovation. With innovation an MC strategic priority and recognition of globalization as part of the new business model (MFP 2010), English deserves special attention in educational policy. It can help Sri Lanka become part of the globalized and innovative world economy that it envisions, since it is sought after by the types of innovating firms that drive economic growth.

Skills Gaps and Mismatches

Several factors contribute to skills gaps and mismatches in Sri Lanka. First, the economy is evolving rapidly, creating demand for more and better-skilled labor. To stimulate job creation and growth the government has identified priority economic sectors, such as tourism, health, and construction. The MC outlines expected skills needs by occupation that will put additional pressure on the skills supply system, which is not well-prepared and does not have the capacity to meet growing demand. Every year, most of the 140,000 students who enter the labor market without job-specific skills (MFP 2010) are absorbed by the informal economy: their share in the informal sector is 61 percent (agriculture 86 percent; non-agriculture 50 percent) of the total employed there.

Another area where skills gaps are glaring is foreign employment—Sri Lanka's second largest source of foreign exchange after apparel exports. Even though unskilled workers traditionally dominated the group working abroad, more recently demand for skilled labor has gone up, but Sri Lanka does not produce enough workers with the skills foreign employers require. About 77 percent of the job vacancies for skilled labor abroad could not be met (World Bank 2013).

In addition to the gaps resulting from inability to produce skilled labor, there are mismatches between skills demand and supply. The fact that youth unemployment rates are high even as employers complain about the lack of skilled labor suggests that the education and training system is not producing skills that are in high market demand (World Bank 2013). For example, the demand in construction for skilled craftspeople and supervisors is higher than the number who graduate with specializations in these fields. Yet the number of trainees enrolling in computer courses is far above industry demand. The problem can be explained by inadequacies in the country's labor market information system, which does not apprise students of opportunities available. Finally, the quality and relevance of what is taught in education and training institutions often fall short of employer needs, and the skills acquired are often already obsolete.

Household and employer skills measurement surveys make it possible to gather indicative information about skills mismatches in Sri Lanka, although comparisons should be made with caution since the surveys consider different populations on the demand and the supply side. The demand side is analyzed based on the perceptions of formal businesses responding to the employer survey. On the supply side the household survey covered the whole population, including individuals not participating in the labor force, the unemployed, and those working in the informal as well as the formal sector.

To get some indications about education and skills mismatches in the Sri Lankan labor market, responses of individuals in the household survey (separated into high- and low-skilled workers) about their own education and skills were compared with responses to the employer survey related to the education and skills of workers that the respondents think of as representing high- and low-skilled workers. The workers they currently employ can be considered to have the minimal education or skills requirement for jobs in the formal sector. Hence, if the average education or skills stock that employers are looking for exceeds that found in the household survey, there is likely to be a mismatch.[9]

There are substantial mismatches between skills supply and demand in Sri Lanka, especially in terms of higher education and high-skilled workers (figure 3.6).[10] For the population as a whole, for example, 18.2 percent have passed GCE A-levels, 3.2 percent have a bachelor's degree, and 1.1 percent have a master's or Ph.D. However, 56 percent of the employers stated that their average high-skilled workers had passed GCE A-levels, 21.8 percent that they had a bachelor's degree, and 4.4 percent mentioned an advanced degree. The currently employed have more education than the general population. Moreover, there are still substantial mismatches between them and the education employers demand. In other words, the average Sri Lankan adult falls far short of the educational attainment required for formal high-skilled occupations. Since those occupations can contribute most to Sri Lanka's economic development, narrowing the gap needs to be a policy priority. There is also some indication of skills mismatches in low-skilled occupations. Moreover, mismatches are more pronounced for tourism firms, firms that innovate, and firms that have international partners—the very firms that are the main drivers of economic growth.

Building the Skills for Economic Growth and Competitiveness in Sri Lanka
http://dx.doi.org/10.1596/978-1-4648-0158-7

Figure 3.6 Skills Stock of the Labor Force and Employer Requirements
Percent

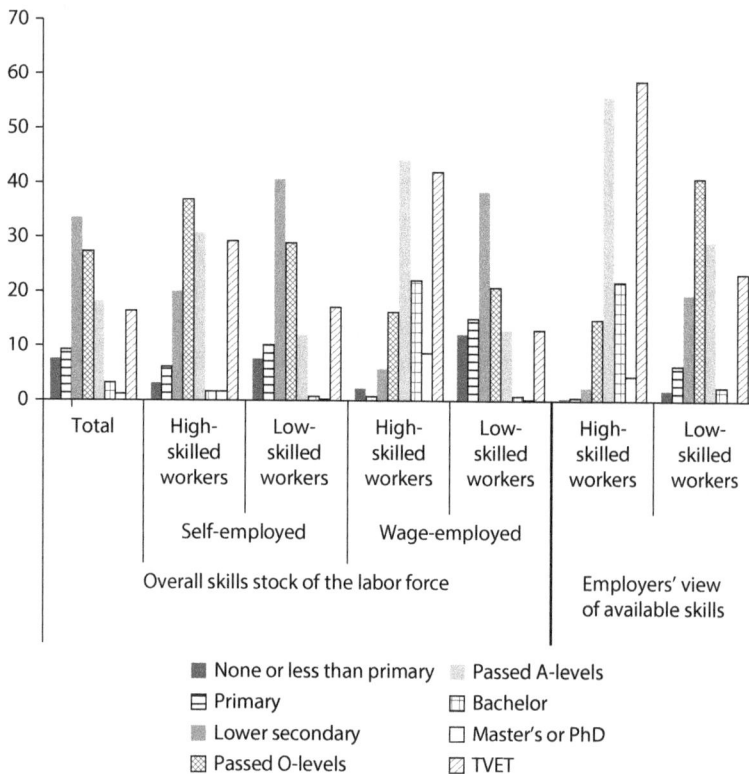

Source: World Bank STEP Survey, Sri Lanka 2012.
Note: Overall skills stock of the labor force is measured from the STEP household survey of the population aged 15–64. The employers' view of available skills is measured from the STEP employer survey and serves as a proxy for the skills demand.

Similar mismatches can be observed between demand for and supply of workers with TVET. While only about 16.4 percent of the population has completed TVET, 59 percent of representative high-skilled workers in formal employment have done so. There is even a substantial TVET mismatch for low-skilled occupations. Here again, mismatches are more pronounced for firms that are international, innovative, and in tourism. While there seem to be substantial gaps in technical skills (English and computer use), the gaps in cognitive skills (reading, writing, and numeracy) and certain soft skills (teamwork and presentation) seem smaller. For example, the general population reports less use of cognitive skills than employers assessing their high-skilled workers. However, there seems to be no mismatch between general population attainments and cognitive requirements for low-skilled occupations. There are also no substantial mismatches between teamwork and presentation skills. However, there is an indication of sizable gaps for English and computer use. For example, only 24 percent of the general population has English language skills but about 41 percent of employers

Figure 3.7 English and Computer Use Skills Available in the Labor Force and Employer Requirements

Percent

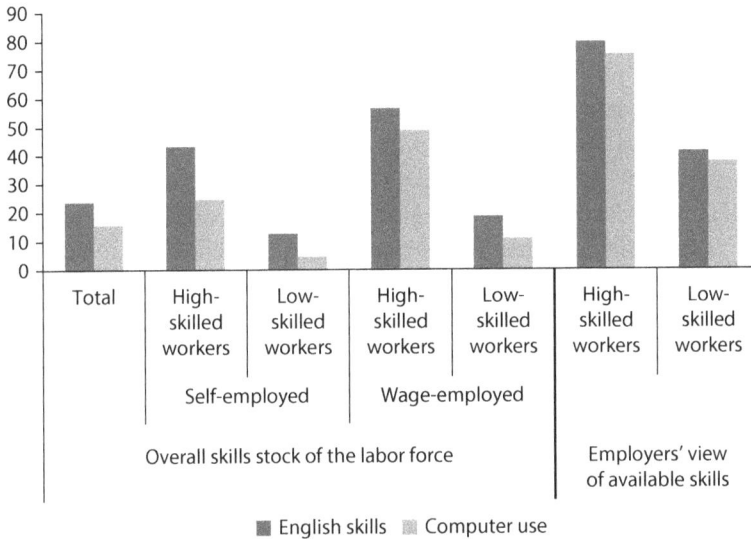

Source: World Bank STEP Survey, Sri Lanka 2012.
Note: Overall skills stock of the labor force is measured from the STEP household survey of the population 15–64 years old. The employers' view of available skills is measured from the STEP employer survey and serves as a proxy for skills demand.

demand English even for low-skilled occupations (figure 3.7). Again, the skills mismatches are more pronounced for firms in tourism, those that innovate, and those that deal with foreign companies.

Consequences of Skills Shortages

Skills shortages can severely harm the production potential of firms.[11] It was found that a substantial skills shortage is associated with production that is about 43 percent lower than it would otherwise be. The STEP Employer Survey also found a negative association between skills shortages and firm productivity for three separate types of skills-related issues—labor availability, general education of workers, and TVET of workers—each of which is negatively associated with total firm production. In the STEP Employer Survey, skills gaps related to TVET are associated with about 76 percent lower production. The magnitudes of the estimated relationship, however, are much less precisely measured than was the case for the Enterprise Survey because fewer firms were available for this analysis.

Skills Constraints: Coping Strategies

This section examines how firms are coping with skills gaps in terms of (1) whether and which types of firms are working with skills-providing institutions; (2) whether and which types are using contractors to address skills shortages; (3) the extent and sources of training; (4) the sources for recruitment and hiring, and how recent hires fare in terms of general education, TVET, and professional certification; (5) what occupations (levels of skill) employers are likely to be looking for in the next 12 months, by sector; and (6) how employers assess the production of skills-providing institutions.

Skills-Providing Institutions

Interactions with skills-providing institutions can be useful for recruitment, training, and work placement. In general there is not much difference in shares of firms interacting with skills-providing institutions by worker type (figure 3.8)— 15.5 percent of firms contacted education and training institutions regarding high-skilled workers (though higher in both manufacturing and services) and 13.9 percent of firms regarding low-skilled workers (higher in tourism). When disaggregating by type of institution, however, it becomes clear that most contact with universities is for high-skilled workers and most contact with TVET institutions is for low-skilled workers.

Training, Firm-based and External

Training is another way to compensate for skills shortages, but it is also important in its own right because it can equip workers with skills that are specific to a certain industry or occupation. In Sri Lanka, firm-based/on-premises training was associated with higher wages but external training was not (Riboud, Savchenko, and Tan 2007). On the firm side, both types of training were found to have substantial impact on performance in Sri Lanka, though especially for internal training (Dutz and O'Connell 2013; Riboud, Savchenko, and Tan 2007; Tan 2012; see chapter 7 for a detailed review of firm-based training).

Figure 3.8 Firm Contacts with Institutions: Across All Firms and by Sector
Percent

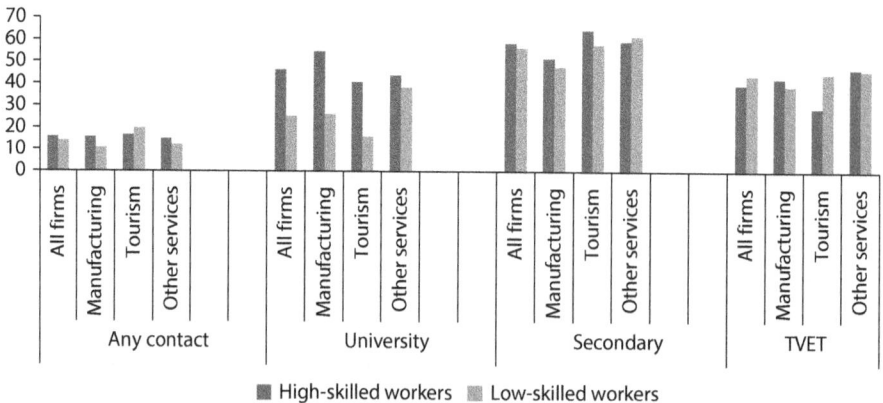

Source: World Bank STEP Survey, Sri Lanka 2012.

Contracting Out

Another way of coping with the skills gaps is to use contractors to compensate for a lack of permanent skilled workers (figure 3.9). At 11.4 percent, contract low-skilled workers are used more than twice as much as contract high-skilled workers (5.3 percent). This is similar to the findings for Yunnan province, where more than 9 percent of firms have used contractors to alleviate shortages of high-skilled workers and more than 17 percent for low-skilled workers (Liang and Chen 2014). When the results for Sri Lanka are disaggregated by sector, the differences become even starker: in manufacturing, 14.4 percent of low-skilled workers are contracted but just 3.3 percent of high-skilled workers. Contractor usage is higher for low-skilled workers across all types of firms except those that are part of a multinational corporation and local nongovernmental organizations (NGOs)—in both of which contractor usage is similar whatever the workers' skill level.

Sources and Qualifications of Recent Hires

Hiring is one of the main ways to address skills gaps. Of the many ways of recruiting employees (figure 3.10), the most common are media advertising and informal channels, such as personal contacts, though informal channels are used more for recruiting low-skilled workers (74 percent) than high-skilled (65.4 percent). This may reflect the scarcity of skills in Sri Lanka: even to recruit relatively low-skilled workers, informal channels must be employed to obtain the number needed. On the other hand, it may indicate that other channels are not functioning well.

An examination of the general education and TVET and professional certification of recent hires underlines the lack of skills available in Sri Lanka. Recent high-skilled hires (table 3.3) are at about the middle in terms of

Figure 3.9 Use of Contractors for Skills Shortages, Full Sample and by Sector and Firm Type
Percent

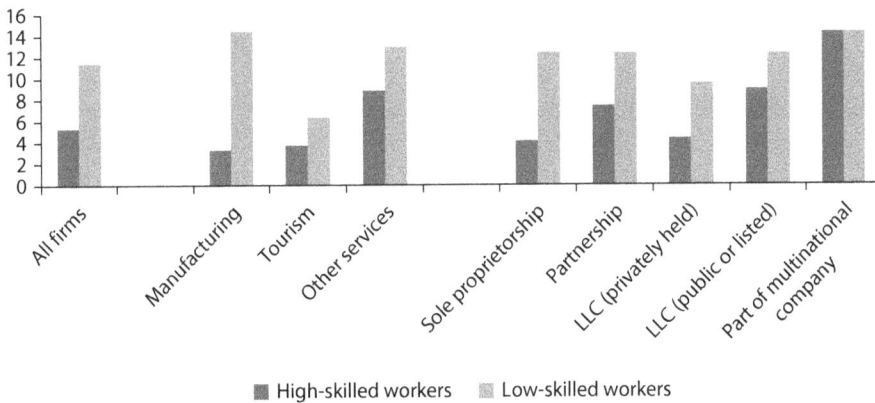

■ High-skilled workers   ▒ Low-skilled workers

Source: World Bank STEP Survey, Sri Lanka 2012.
Note: Only one NGO and one public corporation were part of the sample; they were excluded to simplify the graph.

Figure 3.10 Methods Used to Recruit New Workers
Percent

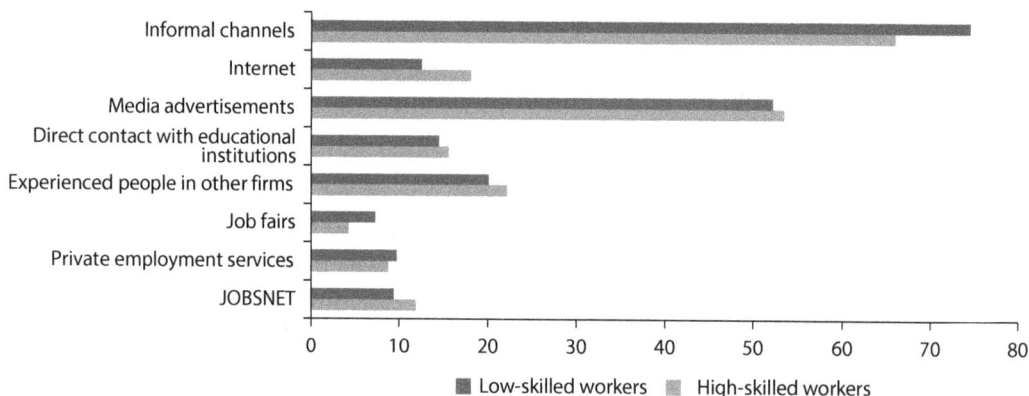

Source: World Bank STEP Employer Survey 2012.

educational attainment, with almost all having completed GCE O- or GCE
A-levels or higher (though only a few are at the very top); of recent low-skilled
hires, about 28 percent have completed no more than grade 8, though about
41 percent completed O-levels and about 27 percent A-levels.

Future Demand: Expected Hiring in the Next 12 Months (2013/14)

Many firms expected to increase their hiring and enlarge their workforce in the
immediate future. The STEP Survey solicited information on numbers of both
current employees and expected employees for 10 different occupations.
Workforce growth for both the skilled and the unskilled is expected in all, ranging from 3.7 percent for service workers to 14.4 percent for crafts and related
trades (figure 3.11). Clearly a widespread strategy for coping with current skills
shortages is substantial future hiring.

Though there are substantial differences between sectors, growth is expected
for all occupations and all sectors except professionals in manufacturing, where
expected growth is virtually zero (figure 3.12). Although demand for more
skilled occupations is quite high—notably professionals in tourism (15.2 percent)
and other services (12.2 percent)—demand for low-skilled workers is mainly in
manufacturing.

How Employers Perceive Skills Production in the Education System

Employers perceive the education system as severely flawed in terms of
producing enough of the right skills. While employers are critical of all
aspects of the system, they are more concerned about general (basic) education than about TVET or university. For example, 68 percent of employers
report that general education "does not meet the skill needs of employers
adequately" while 49 percent say the same about TVET and 52 percent

Table 3.3 Recent Hires: General Education, TVET, and Professional Certification

Percent

	High-skilled workers	Low-skilled workers
General education		
No formal education or incomplete primary	0.0	1.8
Completed primary education (grades 1–5)	0.3	5.8
Completed lower secondary education (grades 6–8)	2.2	19.9
Passed GCE O-level	14.6	41.4
Passed GCE A-level	55.3	26.8
Completed bachelor's degree	20.8	2.1
Completed master's degree	3.4	0.0
Completed PhD or other doctorate	1.0	0.0
Don't know	2.4	2.4
Does this worker have a TVET certificate or degree?		
Yes	51.0	19.2
No	46.3	79.8
Don't know	2.7	1.0
Does this worker have a professional certificate or degree?		
Yes	29.0	6.9
No	68.0	92.3
Don't know	3.0	0.8
N	624	624

Source: World Bank STEP Employer Survey 2012.
Note: Indented rows add up to 100 percent.

Figure 3.11 Expected Hiring in the Next 12 Months, by Occupation

Percent growth

Source: World Bank STEP Employer Survey 2012.

about university (figure 3.13). This is roughly consistent when disaggregating general concerns about the level, kind, and practicality of skills and whether the system produces "enough people with the up-to-date knowledge of methods, materials, and technology" and "enough people with good attitude and self-discipline" (the soft skills)—though in terms of attitude and self-discipline, university education is viewed slightly more unfavorably than general education.

Building the Skills for Economic Growth and Competitiveness in Sri Lanka
http://dx.doi.org/10.1596/978-1-4648-0158-7

Figure 3.12 Expected Hiring in the Next 12 Months, by Occupation and Sector
Percent growth

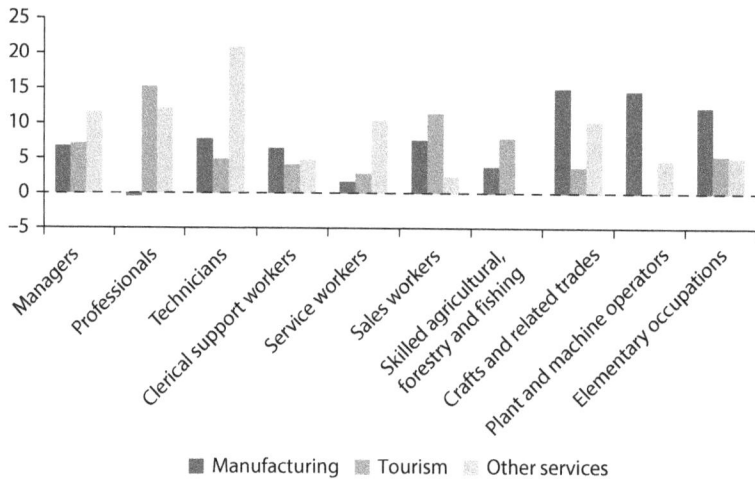

Source: World Bank STEP Employer Survey 2012.

Figure 3.13 Employer Perceptions of TVET, General Education, and University
Percent

The general education, TVET, and university system DO NOT...

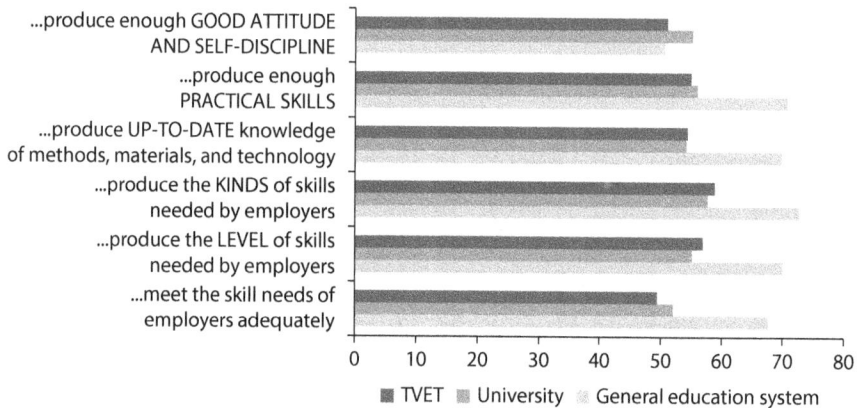

Source: World Bank STEP Employer Survey 2012.

Conclusion and Policy Options

While much is known about generic skills demand and skills constraints in the region, large-scale assessments of more specialized skills, particularly for different types of workers, are relatively recent and still not available for many countries. This chapter has examined demand for skills in Sri Lanka using an employer survey that was designed as part of a World-Bank multicountry skills study as well as other data.

In Sri Lanka, the main drivers of skills demand are economic growth, technological development and globalization, foreign employment, and demographic change. Economic growth and technological development create jobs and therefore increase demand especially for higher-order skills. Increasing integration of the country into global markets requires a better-educated and trained labor force and upgrades of existing skills. While Sri Lanka may reap the demographic dividend to its full extent, it is also likely to soon face a need for a larger economically active population as more people live longer.

While cognitive, soft, and job-specific technical skills are all considered to some degree in deciding whether to retain new employees after probation, soft skills have acquired more prominence than might have been expected. For job-related skills, different economic sectors require different skills. For example, tourism places high value on English skills, especially for high-skilled workers. Subsectors and industries within these hubs will have different needs and will not all require the same mix of skills.

In some cases, the education and skills available in the general population are insufficient to satisfy requirements even for low-skilled workers. Skills gaps prevent labor markets from functioning effectively and make it difficult for individual firms to reach their full production potential. If Sri Lanka is to move to a high-skilled worker economy, this gap must be narrowed.

Employers do not rate the education system favorably in terms of skills production, although they tend to be less critical of the TVET and university components than of general education, which some 64 percent of employers agree "does not meet the skill needs of employers adequately." This perception is persistent in terms of the level, kind, and practicality of skills.

Sri Lanka has launched itself on the right education and skills policy course but more work is needed. Though not yet fully realized, its recent policy initiatives respond to its substantial skills shortages and recognize the detrimental consequences for productivity. To accelerate reform, the findings of this study lead to a number of policy recommendations:

- The high rates of return to firms from closing the skills gaps suggest that higher investment in both general education and formal TVET is warranted. In particular, the government needs to ensure a supportive environment that encourages delivery of high-quality, demand-driven education and training.

- Increasing the direct involvement of industry and employers, especially in TVET, should be a policy priority. For instance, it would be natural and useful to involve industry more directly in the governance and management of TVET institutions to help ensure the quality and relevance of the skills students acquire. The NVQ framework is a move in the right direction through national accreditation of training providers and courses and introduction of competency-based training recognized by employers. It might also be advisable to establish school and industry and sector-specific advisory committees that could also help design training programs and curricula, particularly for TVET.

Building the Skills for Economic Growth and Competitiveness in Sri Lanka
http://dx.doi.org/10.1596/978-1-4648-0158-7

- A better understanding of what comprises skills and the potential consequences of shortages, and continued collection of skills-related data from both
  households and employers, are important to both policy dialogue and research.
  It is to be hoped that researchers will examine these issues for other countries so that detailed and disaggregated comparative skills data are available.
  Follow-up surveys would be useful to enable continuous monitoring and evaluation of changes in demand.

Notes

1. Adapted from Cedefop 2012, 39–40, discussing drivers of change generally; and Shah
   and Burke 2003, 3, discussing skills demand specifically.
2. The dependency ratio is the ratio of dependents—people younger than 15 or older than
   64—to the working-age population—those aged 15–64—multiplied by 100 percent.
3. The same is true for studies of skills on the supply side—see chapter 4 for an analysis
   using a three-dimensional classification (cognitive, soft, and technical skills).
4. Using a stricter (higher-threshold) measure for skills shortages, it can be argued that (1)
   skills shortages in Sri Lanka may not be as severe as these numbers indicate; and (2)
   they may not have risen as severely. Dutz and O'Connell (2013) were interested in a
   set of business environment indicators that went well beyond skills and education.
5. The next section takes the initial univariate analysis of this section a step further by
   exploring multivariate relationships involving skills and skills shortages.
6. Although the 2011 survey covered both manufacturing and service enterprises, the
   2004 survey only covered manufacturers. For comparability purposes, manufacturing
   firm responses were extracted from the 2011 sample for use in this analysis.
7. This information was not collected as part of the 2004 Enterprise Survey.
8. Defined as firms that within the previous three years had introduced any of the
   following: (1) new technologies or (2) new processes within the firm; or (3) new
   products or (4) new services on the market.
9. The standard approach is to compare individuals' education to the educational
   requirements for either specific jobs or occupations, using self-assessment, job analysis,
   and realized matches methods (Leuven and Oosterbeek 2011). With the data available, which are by no means perfect, the best that could be done here for an overall
   assessment of education and skills mismatches was to apply what can be interpreted
   as a variant of the realized matches approach.
10. Skills supply is proxied by education and skills availability data from the STEP house-
    hold survey. Skills demand is proxied by the data coming from the employer survey,
    specifically the percentage of firms that identify that their average high- or low-skilled
    worker has certain education or skills.
11. See Blunch (2013) for details.

Bibliography

Blunch, N-H. 2013. "Skills Demand of Employers in Sri Lanka." Background Paper,
Human Development Division, South Asia Region, World Bank, Washington, DC.

Cedefop. 2012. "Building on Skills Forecasts—Comparing Methods and Applications."
Conference Proceedings, European Centre for the Development of Vocational

Training, Research Paper 18, Publications Office of the European Union, Luxembourg.

di Gropello, E., with A. Kruse and P. Tandon. 2010. *Skills for the Labor Market in Indonesia: Trends in Demand, Gaps, and Supply*. Washington, DC: World Bank.

di Gropello, E., with H. Tan and P. Tandon. 2010. *Skills for the Labor Market in the Philippines*. Washington, DC: World Bank.

Dutz, M. A., and S. D. O'Connell. 2013. "Productivity, Innovation and Growth in Sri Lanka: An Empirical Investigation." World Bank Policy Research Working Paper 6354, World Bank, Washington, DC.

Fernando, A. 2006. "Regulation and FDI: Sri Lankan Telecommunications Industry." Photocopy, Department of Management, Monash University, Melbourne, Australia.

Gorodnichenko, Y., J. Svejnar, and K. Terrell. 2010. "Globalization and Innovation in Emerging Markets." *American Economic Journal: Macroeconomics* 2 (2): 194–226.

Leuven, E., and H. Oosterbeek. 2011. "Overeducation and Mismatch in the Labor Market." In *Handbook of the Economics of Education*, edited by E. A. Hanushek, S. J. Machin, and L. Wößmann. Amsterdam: North-Holland, Elsevier.

Liang, X., and S. Chen. 2014. *Developing Skills for Economic Transformation and Social Harmony in China*: A Study of Yunnan Province. Washington, DC: World Bank.

MFP (Ministry of Finance and Planning). 2010. *Mahinda Chintana—Vision for the Future*. Department of National Planning, Ministry of Finance and Planning, Government of Sri Lanka, Colombo. http://www.treasury.gov.lk/publications/mahindaChintanaVision -2010full-eng.pdf.

———. 2013. "Chapter 2: Investing in Human Capital towards Knowledge Economy." In *Sri Lanka Skills Report*, Ministry of Finance and Planning, Government of Sri Lanka, Colombo.

Ranathunga, S. P. B. 2011. "Impact of Rural to Urban Labour Migration and Remittances on Sending Household Welfare: A Sri Lankan Case Study." Munich Personal RePEc Archive, MPRA Paper 35943. http://mpra.ub.uni-muenchen.de/35943/.

Riboud, M., Y. Savchenko, and H. Tan. 2007. *The Knowledge Economy and Education and Training in South Asia*. Washington, DC: World Bank.

Rutkowski, J. 2013. "Beyond 'Hard Skills': Workforce Skills in the Eyes of Employers." Draft, Europe and Central Asia Region, World Bank, Washington, DC.

Sanchez Puerta, M. L., A. Valerio, G. Pierre, and S. Urzúa. 2012. "STEP Skills Survey Data Analysis Methodology Note." Draft. Social Protection and Labor Department, World Bank, Washington, DC.

Shah, C., and G. Burke. 2003. "Skills Shortages: Concepts, Measurement and Implications." ACER, Centre for the Economics of Education and Training Working Paper 52, Monash University, Melbourne, Australia.

SSM (Secretariat for Senior Ministers). 2012. *The National Human Resources and Employment Policy for Sri Lanka*. Secretariat for Senior Ministers. Colombo: Government of Sri Lanka.

Tan, H. 2012. "Sri Lanka: Education, Training and Labor Market Outcomes." Background paper for the Sri Lanka Skills Development Report, World Bank, Washington, DC.

World Bank. 2008. *Skill Development in India—The Vocational Education and Training System*. Report 22, Human Development Sector, South Asia Region, Washington, DC.

———. 2012a. *Leading with Ideas: Skills for Growth and Equity in Thailand*. Bangkok: World Bank.

———. 2012b. *Sri Lanka—Demographic Transition: Facing the Challenges of an Aging Population with Few Resources*. Report 73162-LK, Human Development Unit South Asia Region, World Bank, Washington, DC.

———. 2013. *System Approach for Better Education Results—Workforce Development: Sri Lanka, Country Report*. World Bank, Washington, DC.

CHAPTER 4

Skills Supply, Education, and Labor Market Outcomes

Introduction

Sri Lanka has the most educated population in South Asia (see chapter 2), having reduced the illiterate share of its population from 30 percent in the 1960s to 15 percent by 2010. The proportion of Sri Lankans with secondary education is comparable to Malaysians, though much lower than South Koreans. However, as in the rest of South Asia, in 2010 only about 2 percent of Sri Lankans had completed more than secondary education—substantially less than in Malaysia and the Republic of Korea.

Despite the impressive expansion of access to primary and secondary education, quality is emerging as a problem. For example, a mere one-third of primary school children master language and mathematics skills. In tertiary education, both the relevance of current programs and the employability of graduates are questionable. Relatively few students are enrolled in programs that the nation has defined as priorities, and for many it takes a considerable time after graduation to find their first job (Gunatilaka, Mayer, and Vodopivec 2010).

Because Sri Lanka's economy is changing rapidly (see chapter 3), the skill levels and composition of the general population and high youth unemployment are of critical policy concern. It is imperative that the education and training systems build skills that are relevant for export-oriented and expanding sectors and occupations in high demand. Systems need to be flexible to react promptly to changes in demand by upgrading worker skills and to equip youth for the labor market. There is great policy interest in understanding how the education system in general, and post-school technical and vocational education and training (TVET) in particular, can help to address these problems.

In 2012 a detailed household skills measurement survey was carried out to assess the current stock of skills, how they are formed, and the relationship between education, training, and labor market outcomes (box 1.4). This chapter addresses the skills supply part of the conceptual framework presented in figure 1.6, asking: (1) What is the skills composition of the Sri Lankan labor force?

(2) Are the skills that students acquire in general education and TVET relevant to the growing and globalizing Sri Lanka economy? (3) What types of skills improve labor market outcomes, such as employment and earnings?

This chapter first describes the education and skills profile of the Sri Lankan population in terms of general education, TVET, and apprenticeship. It also studies how skills are formed by the general education and TVET systems. Then it analyzes the link between skills and labor market outcomes; returns to education and skills; and the relationship between skills and employment, underemployment, and self-employment. Finally, the chapter summarizes the findings and offers policy recommendations.

Education and Skills Profile of the Workforce

General Education Profiles

Sri Lankans in general have considerable schooling; 83 percent of those aged 15–65 have completed at least lower secondary education. Only 1.4 percent of the Skills Toward Employment and Productivity (STEP) sample had no education at all, 6.2 percent had not completed primary education, 9.2 percent had completed only primary education, 33.5 percent had progressed into lower secondary, 14 percent had passed GCE O-levels, 18.2 percent had passed GCE A-levels, and 4.3 percent had completed a bachelor's or a master's degree.

People living in urban areas tend to be more educated than those in rural areas, and youth have more education than adults. For example, 24.2 percent of the urban population but only 14.2 of the rural reported the highest level of education as GCE A-levels (figure 4.1). Youth were more likely than adults to report the highest level of education as lower secondary, GCE O-levels, upper secondary, or GCE A-levels. Considerably more adults than youth had no education at all or had at best finished primary school. However, fewer youth than adults reported tertiary education, most likely because they are still in school.

There is gender parity in education completion, but despite the policy of free education, people from poorer backgrounds had fewer years of education than those from higher-income families. A larger share of women than men reported GCE O-levels, upper secondary, and GCE A-levels as the highest level completed (figure 4.1), and a larger share of men reported completing no more than grade 9. Figure 4.2 details years of education by asset quintile,[1] a proxy for household wealth. People in the lowest quintile have on average 7.6 years of education and those in the highest 11.6 years.

TVET and Apprenticeship

Technical and vocational skills are typically formed in the TVET and apprenticeship systems. In Sri Lanka, 16 percent of those aged 15–64 had completed vocational education or training and 15 percent had completed an apprenticeship (table 4.1). The proportion of both was higher in urban areas than in rural and for men rather than women, but fewer youth than adults completed either, perhaps because some youth have not yet ended their education. Based on

Figure 4.1 Highest Level of Education Completed, by Region, Gender, and Age
Percent

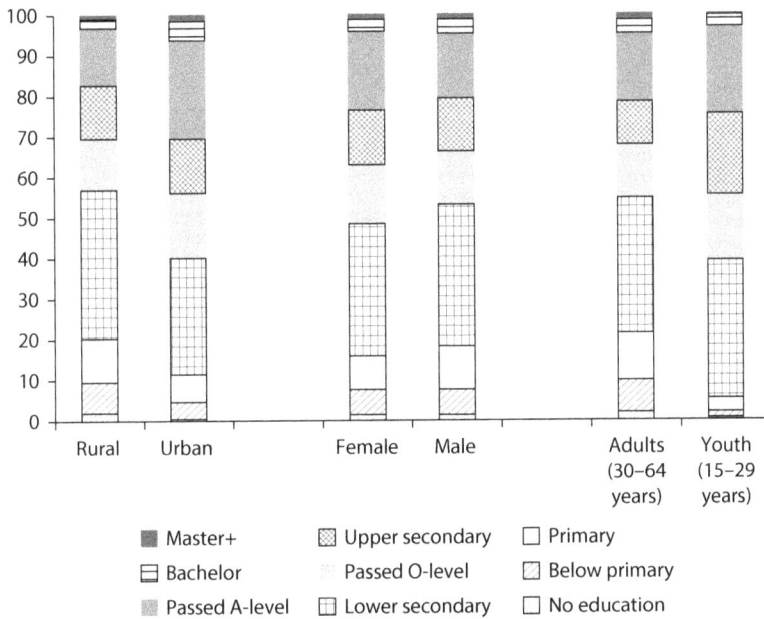

Legend:
- Master+
- Bachelor
- Passed A-level
- Upper secondary
- Passed O-level
- Lower secondary
- Primary
- Below primary
- No education

Source: STEP household survey.

Figure 4.2 Education and Training, by Wealth Quintile

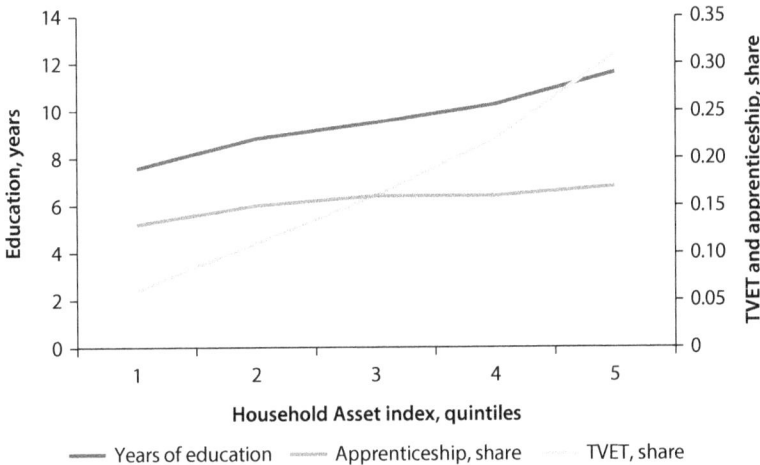

— Years of education   Apprenticeship, share   TVET, share

Source: STEP household survey.

regression analysis, after controlling for other characteristics gender, urban/rural, and youth/adult differences are statistically significant (Savchenko 2013).

In the absence of a direct comparison of population shares with TVET in other countries, enrollment in TVET as a percentage of total secondary education enrollment can serve as a proxy. With 5.3 percent, Sri Lanka is lagging behind

Table 4.1 Percent of the Sample with TVET or Apprenticeship Experience

	Region			Gender		Youth	
	Mean	Rural	Urban	Female	Male	Adults (ages 30–64)	Youth (ages 15–29)
TVET	16	14	20	16	18	17	15
Apprenticeship	15	14	18	13	19	17	12

Source: STEP household survey.

Korea (11.8 percent) and Malaysia (6.2 percent) but is ahead of other countries in South Asia, such as India (0.8 percent), Bangladesh (3.3 percent), and Pakistan (3.9 percent) (EdStats 2011).

The TVET system in Sri Lanka consists of certificate, diploma, and degree programs (figure 4.3a; see also chapter 2 for details). Most TVET students complete vocational training at the certificate level; few get more advanced training. Most students graduate from certificate programs (73 percent), 14 percent receive professional diplomas, 12 percent technical diplomas, and only 1 percent a vocational technology degree (figure 4.3b).

Most apprenticeships are informal. The formal apprenticeships managed by the NAITA represent workplace training based on a structured curriculum; however, only 37 percent of the STEP respondents surveyed had had certified formal apprenticeships. The average duration of formal apprenticeships was about eight months and of informal apprenticeships six months.

While there is a clear vertical path through the TVET system, there is no horizontal mobility between general education and TVET. The minimum required to enroll in the TVET system is completion of grade 9, but some programs may require GCE O-levels. The TVET system requires that all students go through all National Vocational Qualification (NVQ) levels no matter how much general education they have, so that students with more education are often in the same classrooms as those with less. The fact that more of those with GCE A-levels or higher than those educated through grade 11 or less have TVET education (figure 4.4) suggests that students who do not qualify for university on the first try may opt for TVET and try to get into university the following year.

Though the public sector provides most TVET, it tends not to coordinate with business. Despite a fairly active private sector, most students still obtain TVET from public institutions. According to Tertiary and Vocational Education Commission (TVEC) estimates, in 2011 98,948 students were in public TVET programs and 52,859 in private (see chapter 6). Similarly, in the STEP survey, it was found that 68 percent of respondents undertook TVET in public or public statutory institutions (VTA, NAITA), 29 percent in private institutions, and 3 percent in NGOs.

There is wide variation in the types of skills and the quality of what is taught in TVET institutions. The most popular field is information and communication technology (ICT), the choice of 22.5 percent of respondents. Other popular fields are education (8.7 percent), manufacturing (8.1 percent), sewing (7.3 percent), and auto and home appliance repairing, engineering, and business

Figure 4.3 The National Vocational Qualification (NVQ) System and Distribution of Student Population by NVQ Level

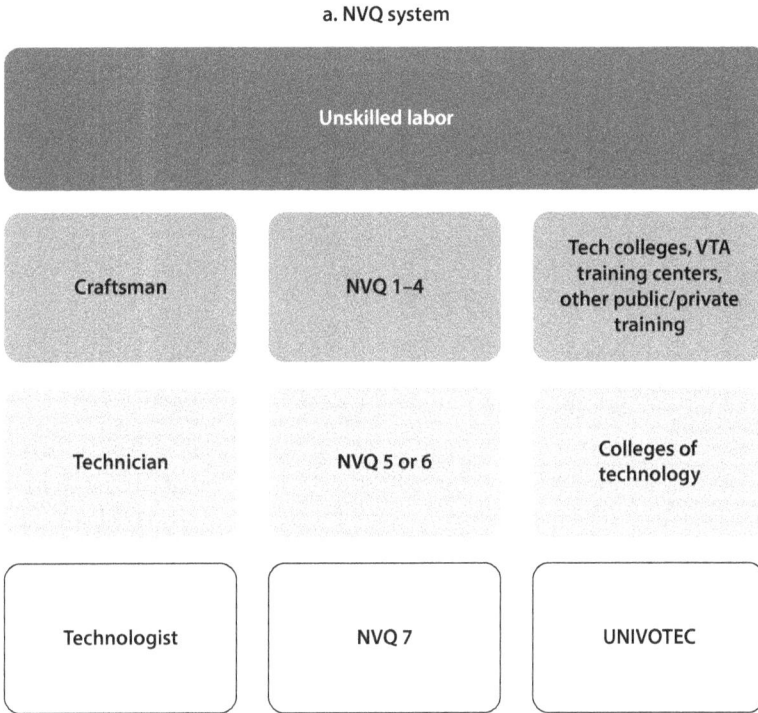

a. NVQ system

Unskilled labor		
Craftsman	NVQ 1–4	Tech colleges, VTA training centers, other public/private training
Technician	NVQ 5 or 6	Colleges of technology
Technologist	NVQ 7	UNIVOTEC

Source: Mahinda Chintana 2010.

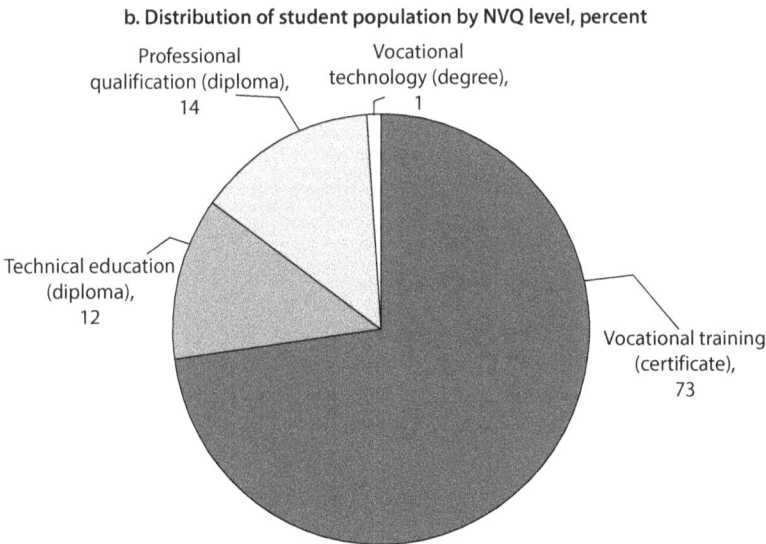

b. Distribution of student population by NVQ level, percent

Professional qualification (diploma), 14

Vocational technology (degree), 1

Technical education (diploma), 12

Vocational training (certificate), 73

Source: STEP survey.

Building the Skills for Economic Growth and Competitiveness in Sri Lanka
http://dx.doi.org/10.1596/978-1-4648-0158-7

Figure 4.4 Population with TVET, by Level of Education
Percent

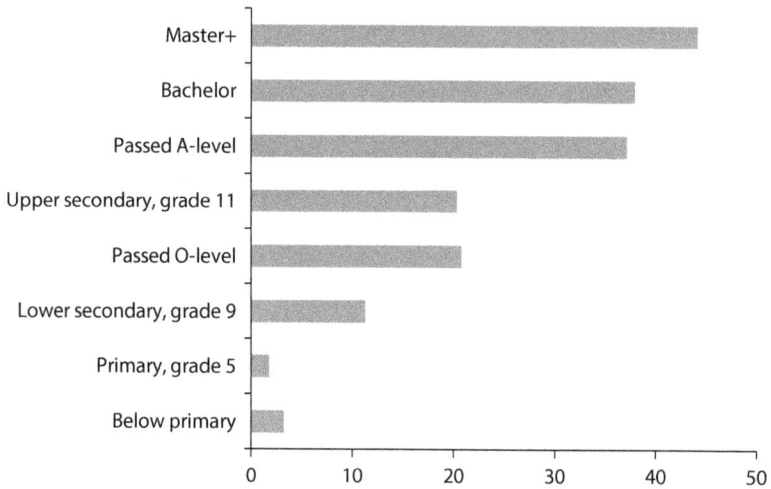

Source: STEP household survey.

(about 6 percent each). While some public institutions are well-managed and generate the needed skills, many have no connection with labor markets and the skills they teach are obsolete. Private providers often teach subjects of high social demand that are not necessarily demanded by labor markets (see chapter 6).

Despite the low social demand for TVET, 56 percent of those who had chosen it believe that a technical qualification gives better job and salary opportunities; another 27 percent thought it would help them get a job faster; and 11 percent had chosen TVET because either they could not get into university or there was no university accessible. The natural question is whether these expectations were met, and indeed 61 percent of respondents felt that TVET opened more job opportunities in Sri Lanka or abroad, and helped them to be more confident at work. Unfortunately, 24 percent of those with TVET qualifications were either not employed or not in the labor force. Another 15 percent felt that TVET did not open up employment opportunities.

Skills Profiles

The STEP survey is one of the first to investigate skills composition in developing countries. Research from economics, psychology, sociology, and medical science, among other fields, has demonstrated that cognitive, soft, and technical skills determine not only labor market outcomes but also social behavior in general (Sanchez Puerta *et al.* 2012). There is also evidence that the environment (family, school, social networks, policy interventions, and so on) can modify these skills. But most studies of the economics of skills (their production and impact) have dealt with developed rather than developing and emerging economies.

As described in chapter 1, the STEP survey characterizes a worker's skills in terms of three categories: cognitive, soft, and technical. Subdomains identified are the result of detailed analysis of instruments that measure prototypical compo-nents of the three types of skills.[2] The cognitive skills that STEP assessed were reading, writing, and numeracy, with an objective test in reading. Soft skills were assessed in terms of the Big Five personality traits (extraversion, conscientiousness, openness, emotional stability, and agreeableness), long-term perseverance, hostility bias, decision making, risk and time preferences, teamwork, and presentation and interpersonal skills. The technical skills assessed were job-specific: technology use, computer use, mechanical skills, machinery and equipment use, autonomous working skills, English skills, and incidence of physical tasks.

In developed countries cognitive skills have been found to affect a variety of outcomes ranging from academic achievement and labor market outcomes to health and social behavior (Cawley, Heckman, and Vytlacil 2001; Gottfredson 1997; Hanushek and Wößmann 2008, 2009; Hartigan and Wigdor 1989; Heckman, Stixrud, and Urzúa 2006; Herrnstein and Murray 1994; Mulligan 1999; Murnane and Willett 2000; Neal and Johnson 1996; Tyler, Murnane, and Willett 2000; Urzúa 2008). Glewwe, Huang, and Park (2011) found that in China's developing Gansu Province, cognitive skills affect decisions about whether children stay in school or enter the labor force. Many studies have found that cognitive skills have a positive impact on earnings and that introducing cog-nitive skills into the earnings equation decreases the coefficients on education variables or makes education insignificant (Alderman *et al.* 1996 for Pakistan; Blunch 2009 for Ghana; Boissiere, Knight, and Sabot 1985 for Kenya and Tanzania; Moll 1998 for South Africa). Reviewing the evidence for links between cognitive ability and educational systems and labor market outcomes in develop-ing countries, Glewwe (2002) concluded that (1) more research is needed on how education policies shape learning and skills; and (2) cognitive ability directly affects wages and may be the most important predictor of worker productivity.

More educated individuals report using basic cognitive skills more often and more intensely (figure 4.5). The likelihood of reading at work or at home is lower in Sri Lanka than in Bolivia, the Lao People's Democratic Republic, Vietnam, or Yunnan province of China at all education levels. Use of writing skills in Sri Lanka is similar to Yunnan but lower than in Bolivia, Lao PDR, or Vietnam. Sri Lanka's use of numeracy skills is on a par with other countries, for example Vietnam. It is noteworthy that the intensity of the use of cognitive skills increases dramati-cally with secondary and postsecondary education. Regression analysis confirms that cognitive skills are closely correlated with educational levels, with the high-est marginal increase occurring at the primary level, which is where cognitive skills are mainly formed. Later, cognitive skills tend to grow more sophisticated. Since mastery of cognitive skills (literacy and numeracy) is a prerequisite to entering higher levels of education, any government intent on improving the cognitive skills of the population should allocate resources to primary and secondary schools.

People living in urban areas are more likely to read, write, and use numeracy skills (figure 4.6), and use them more intensely, than rural residents. For exam-ple, while only 64 percent of the rural population read at home or at work,

Figure 4.5 Cognitive Skills, by Level of Education
Percent

a. Reading intensity, by level of education completed

b. Writing intensity, by level of education completed

■ Low ■ Medium ■ High

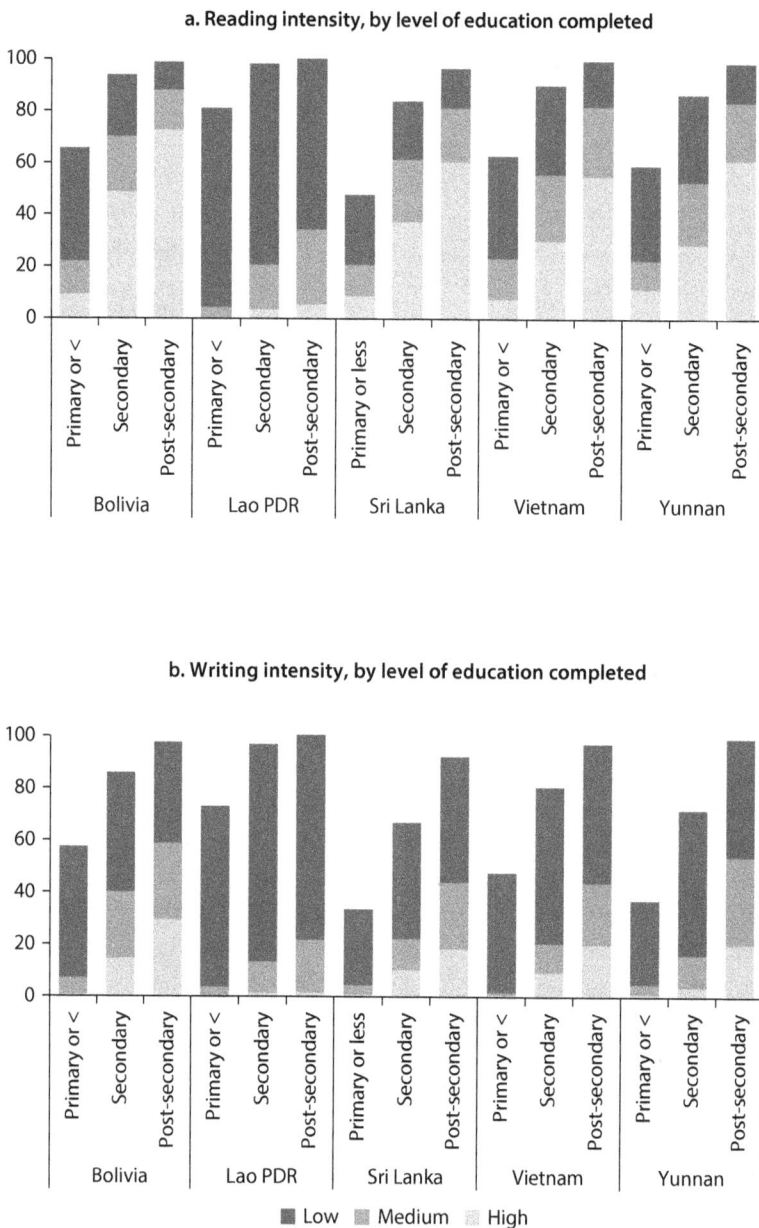

figure continues next page

Figure 4.5 Cognitive Skills, by Level of Education *(continued)*
Percent

c. Numeracy intensity, by level of education completed

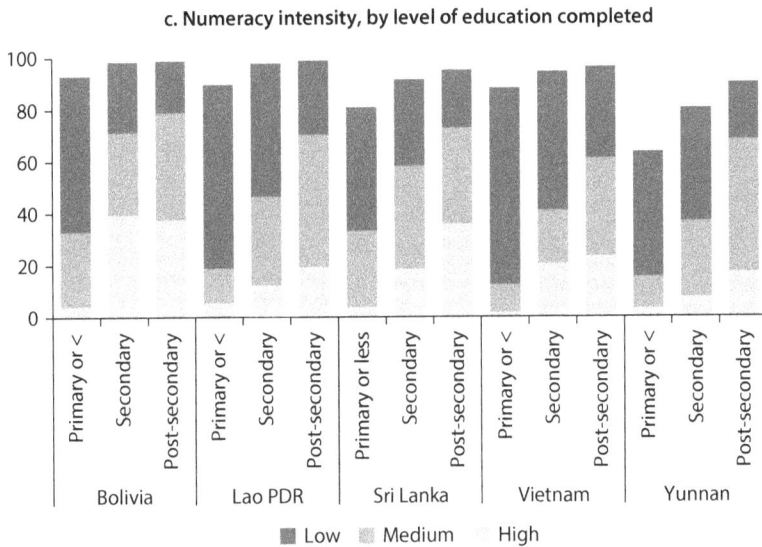

Source: Sanchez and Valerio 2013.

Figure 4.6 Distribution of Cognitive Skills, by Area and Type of Employment
Percent

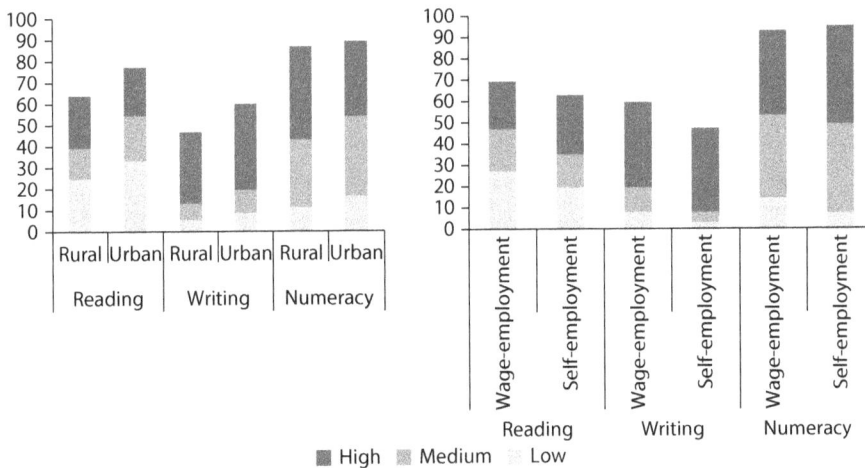

Source: STEP household survey.

77 percent of urban dwellers do so regularly. Moreover, 9 percent of urban residents normally write documents longer than 25 pages versus 5 percent of rural residents.

There are also substantial differences in the use of cognitive skills by type of employment: 59 percent of wage-earners write at work or at home, but only

47 percent of the self-employed do so; also, wage-earners on average read and write longer documents and do more sophisticated calculations.

Despite the high literacy rates, one in 10 Sri Lankans, especially those with no more than primary education, say that lack of literacy skills slows career progression. While 42 percent of people with no education, 23 percent who did not complete primary education, and 19 percent who completed only primary education reported that lack of reading and writing skills prevented them from getting a job, a promotion, or a pay raise or prevented them from developing their own business, only 5–7 percent of people with O-levels or more did so (figure 4.7). Rural residents and men complained more often about lack of literacy skills than urbanites and women.

Globalization and the growth and development of economies and firms have brought a technological transformation that requires different types of skills for good job performance, such as ability to operate computers and the latest machinery or to communicate with clients in a foreign language. Around the world, a lack of workers with technical and soft skills often constrains production (di Gropello, Kruse, and Tandon 2011; di Gropello, Tan, and Tandon 2010; World Bank 2010, 2012a). Sri Lanka is not an exception (see chapter 3): 46 percent of employers there considered job-specific skills the most important factor in deciding whether to retain a low-skilled worker and 38 percent said the same about retaining a high-skilled worker. Moreover, firms subject to skills constraints are less productive (chapter 3). Increasing adoption of active labor market policies around the world, usually specifying certain types of training, suggests a general recognition of the need to improve technical skills (Card, Kluve, and Weber 2010).

Only 16 percent of Sri Lankans use computers, 24 percent have English skills, and 23 percent have mechanical skills (table 4.2). There are substantial differences

Figure 4.7 Lack of Literacy Skills as a Barrier to Career Development
Percent

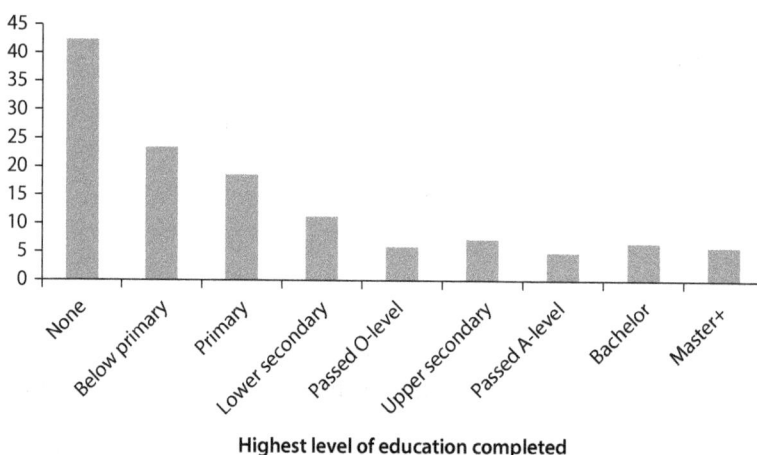

Highest level of education completed

Source: STEP household survey.

in skills use by area and type of employment. Demand for technical skills is clear: 75 percent of employers require computer skills of high-skilled workers and 38 percent require them of low-skilled workers. Moreover, the government envisages expansion in tourism, ICT, and high-value-added export-oriented sectors, all of which require these skills. There are substantial geographic differences in computer skills: only 8 percent in rural areas have them versus 28 percent in urban areas. And while 44 percent of high-skilled workers use computers and 54 percent speak English, only 8 percent of low-skilled workers use computers and 16 percent speak English.[3] Finally, use of computer skills at work in Sri Lanka seems to be much lower than in other developing countries (figure 4.8): About 55 percent of workers in Yunnan and 35 percent of workers in Bolivia and Vietnam use computers at work, compared to less than 30 percent in Sri Lanka.

Technical skills are shaped both by general education (upper secondary and above) and TVET. Formation of computer and English skills begins at GCE O-levels (figure 4.9), with substantial relative increases at GCE A-levels, master's and above, and TVET.

While foundational cognitive skills and job-specific skills are both important, the demand for soft skills is rising, especially for teamwork, presentation skills, and conscientiousness (see chapter 3). Recent studies have found that noncognitive skills affect earnings (Glewwe, Huang, and Park 2011; Heckman, Stixrud, and Urzúa 2006; Mobius and Rosenblat 2006; Mueller and Plug 2006; Nyhus and Pons 2005; Salgado 1997; Urzúa 2008) and employment and occupation status (Borghans, ter Wel, and Weinberg 2008; Heckman, Stixrud, and Urzúa 2006; Urzúa 2008; Waddell 2006). It thus appears that soft skills may be more important to some labor market outcomes than cognitive ability (Bowles, Gintis, and Osborne 2001; Glewwe, Huang, and Park 2011; Heckman, Stixrud, and Urzúa 2006; Segal 2008; Urzúa 2008). In the long run, Goff and Ackerman (1992) suggest, soft skills are more important to economic success than cognitive.

Table 4.2 Skills Used by Area and Type of Employment

Percent

	Technology	Computer	English	Mechanical	Manual
Total	51.8	15.6	23.9	22.6	41.3
Area					
Rural	43.4	8.0	15.2	13.6	46.1
Urban	58.2	28.4	36.9	15.7	31.6
Worker type					
Low-skilled	45.3	8.1	16.0	21.6	48.4
High-skilled	76.6	44.1	54.0	26.3	14.1
Employment type					
Wage-earners	56.7	21.0	28.7	21.6	40.3
Self-employed	43.9	6.6	15.8	25.3	42.5

Source: STEP household survey.

Figure 4.8 Computer Use at Work
Percent

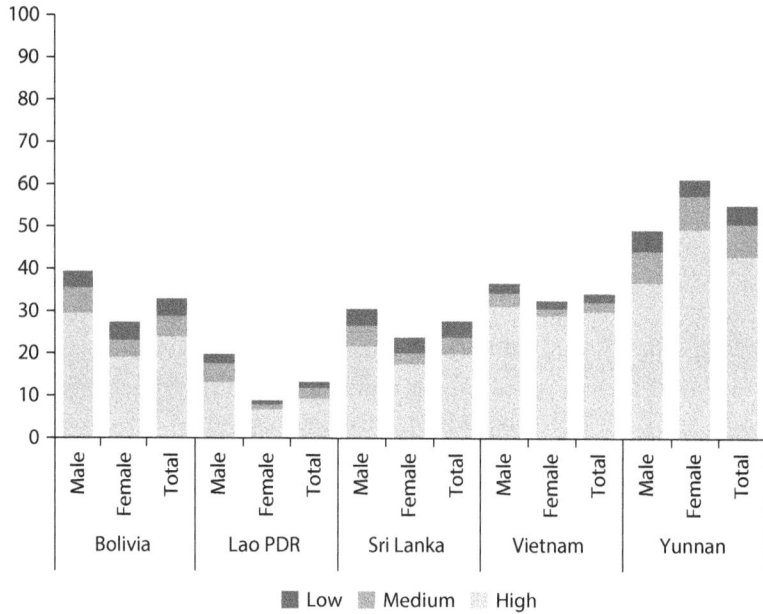

Source: Sanchez and Valerio 2013.

Except for openness, personality traits seem not to be acquired in the educa-tion system, although presentation and teamwork skills are shaped by both general education and TVET (figure 4.10). Openness, presentation, and team-work skills increase substantially with both general education and TVET. But since employers highly value some of the soft skills, such as conscientiousness, that education and training systems do not seem to produce, there could be room for better course content.

Skills and Labor Market Outcomes

The labor market in Sri Lanka is characterized by low unemployment, high underemployment, and a large informal economy. According to the Labor Force Survey (LFS), Sri Lanka made incredible progress in bringing down unemploy-ment from 9 percent in 2000 to 5 percent in 2010 (World Bank 2012b). Of the STEP respondents, 59 percent were in the labor force,[4] and only 6 percent of those were unemployed. Of the employed, 18 percent were underemployed[5] and 37 percent self-employed.[6] The average weekly earnings of an employed worker are approximately SL Rs 5,100 (table 4.3).

Urban residents, women, and youth participate in the labor force much less than rural residents, men, and adults (table 4.3). Moreover, women and rural residents are more likely to be underemployed than other groups. Given the Sri Lankan demographic transition, sustained high growth will depend on

Figure 4.9 Technical Skills by Level of Education

Percent

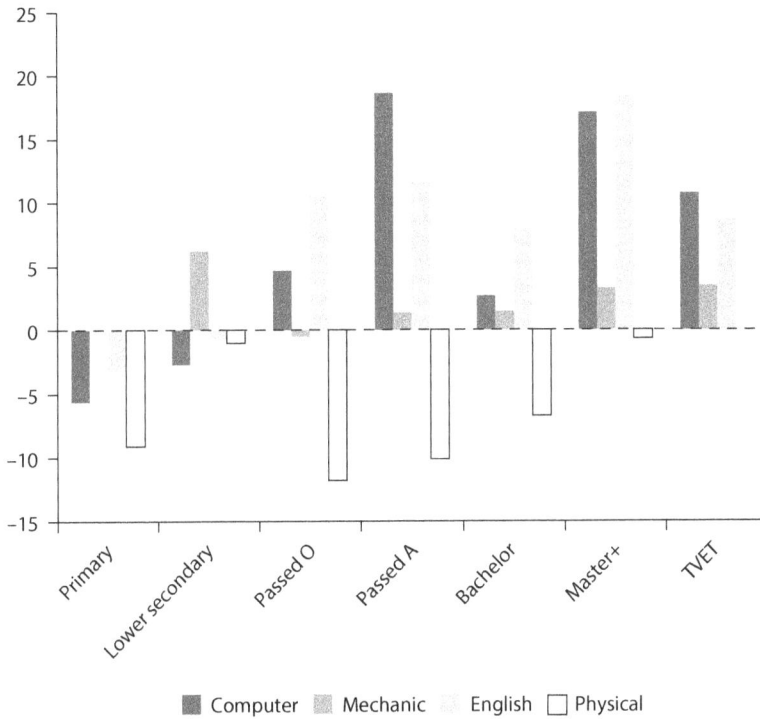

Computer   Mechanic   English   Physical

Source: STEP household survey.
Note: Change in skills in primary education is compared to the below-primary level; from secondary on, the change represents an increase in skills compared to the level of previous education. Other controls are gender, province, rural/urban, parental education, age, household wealth, and marital status.

raising labor productivity and attracting more entrants into the labor force. Only 47 percent of youth is in the labor force, and those who do participate are three times more likely to be unemployed (13 percent) than adults (4 percent). Only 56 percent of the urban population is in the labor force compared to 61 percent of the rural, but one of every five rural residents is underemployed. Women are only half as likely to be in the labor force as men and are more likely to be underemployed.

Informality is a big issue in the Sri Lankan economy; 62 percent of workers are employed in the informal labor market. In the STEP survey (as in this report), informality was proxied by self-employment. Women were found more likely (42 percent) to be self-employed than men (33 percent). Only 24 percent of youth were self-employed compared to 40 percent of adults. Combined with low youth labor force participation and high unemployment, this suggests that young people are waiting to get formal jobs, though as time goes by they may accept informal jobs.

While earnings increase with general education and TVET, the relationship between education and training and other labor market outcomes is less obvious

Figure 4.10 Change in Soft Skills by Level of Education
Percent

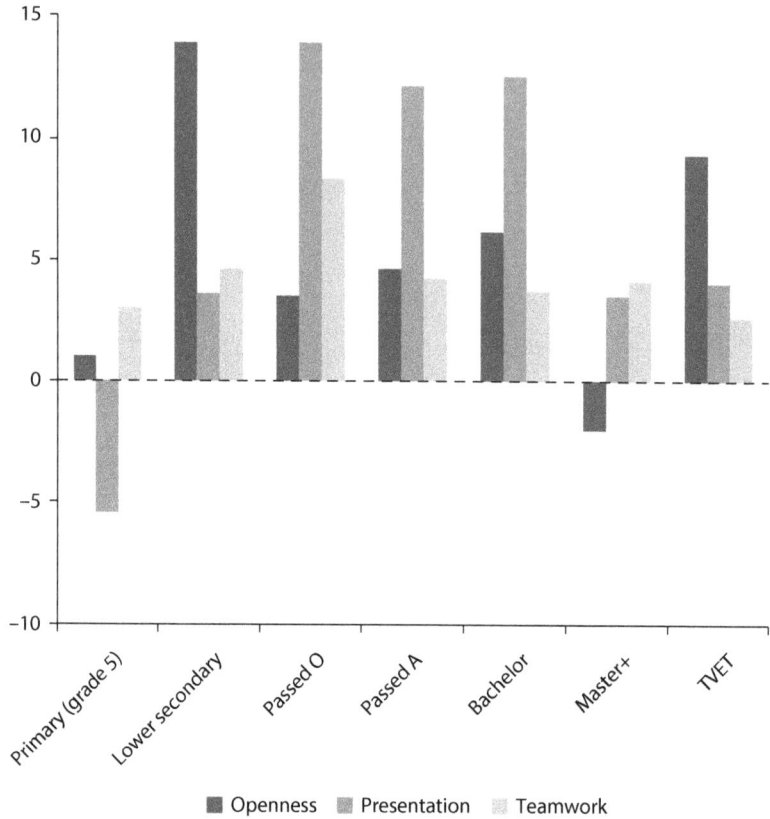

Source: STEP household survey.
Note: Change in skills in primary education is compared to the below-primary level; from secondary on, the change represents the increase in skills compared to previous education. Other controls are gender, province, rural/urban area, parental education, age, household wealth, and marital status.

Table 4.3 Labor Market Outcomes by Demographic Characteristics

	Labor force participation (%)	Unemployment (%)	Underemployment (%)	Self-employment (%)	Weekly earnings of employed, SL Rs
Total	59	6	18	37	5,098
Rural	61	6	21	37	4,622
Urban	56	6	14	37	5,818
Female	43	10	22	42	3,729
Male	85	3	15	33	5,990
Adults (aged 30–65)	64	4	18	40	4,928
Youth (aged 15–29)	47	13	17	24	5,749

Source: STEP household survey.

Table 4.4 Labor Market Outcomes by Education and Training

	Labor force participation (%)	Unemployment (%)	Underemployment (%)	Self-employment (%)	Weekly earnings of employed, SL Rs
Education					
No education	61	8	26	13	2,891
Below primary	66	4	14	35	2,936
Primary (grade 5)	65	3	18	34	3,431
Lower secondary (grade 9)	58	5	19	43	4,520
Passed GCE O-level	52	8	19	47	4,844
Passed GCE A-level	61	7	17	28	7,049
Bachelor's	84	8	18	7	7,322
Master's+	82	0	29	7	11,269
Training					
No TVET	56	6	18	38	4,698
TVET	73	8	17	34	6,573
No apprenticeship	56	6	19	38	5,018
Apprenticeship	75	4	16	35	5,425

Source: STEP household survey.

(table 4.4). Individuals with TVET and apprenticeship training are more likely to participate in the labor force than those without. More than 80 percent of those with bachelor's degrees and above are in the labor force. Unemployment is higher for the uneducated and people with O-levels, A-levels, and bachelor's degrees than for other education levels. It is also higher for those who completed TVET than for those who did not.[7] Self-employment peaks at 47 percent for those with no more than GCE O-level education, while 93 percent of those with bachelor's degrees and above work in the formal economy.

Returns on higher education (GCE A-levels and above) and on TVET have been rising,[8] but neither formal nor informal apprenticeship improves wages. Meanwhile, returns on primary, lower secondary, and GCE O-level education have been dropping for more than 10 years (figure 4.11); and between 2000 and 2012 the premium for passing A-levels relative to GCE O-levels went up from 17 percent to 31 percent and the premium for earning a bachelor's degree or more relative to GCE A-levels went from 35 percent to 54 percent. Tan (2012) found that an additional year of schooling pushed up monthly wages by 5–10 percent.

Once education is controlled for, self-reported reading, writing, and numeracy do not yield additional returns.[9] Even though some studies found that cognitive skills have a significant impact on earnings, the impact of self-reported cognitive skills was positive but not statistically significant. It may be that the basic self-reported measure of cognitive skills is not robust enough; adding a reading test would be very useful. Or it may be that cognitive skills by themselves are not significant (Glewwe, Huang, and Park 2011) and the education variables capture the effect completely.

Figure 4.11 Wage Premiums, by Level of Education
Percent

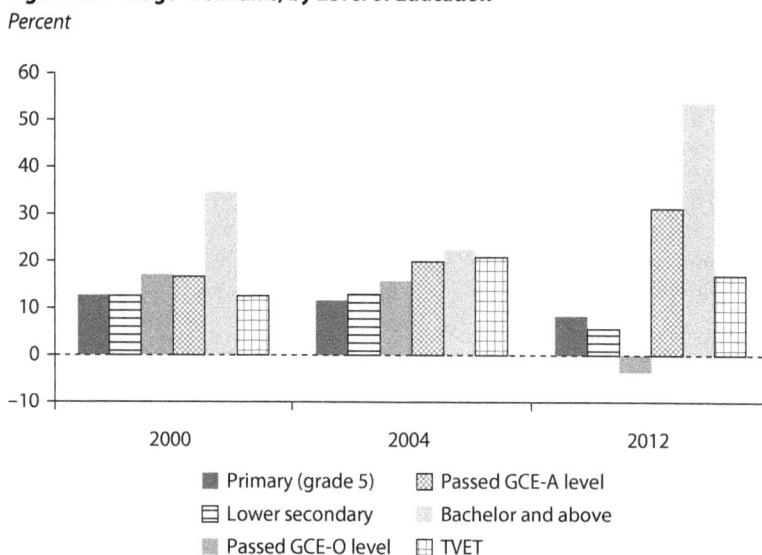

Sources: LFS 2000 and 2004; STEP household survey 2012.
Note: The first bar for each year reflects the wage premium for completed primary education relative to no education or incomplete primary; the second last bar reflects the wage premium for completing bachelor's and above relative to passing GCE A-levels. The last bar is TVET relative to non-TVET. The wage premiums are the differences in the coefficients of a regression of log hourly wage on basic controls (education, TVET, gender, urban, province, age, and age squared). With additional controls the qualitative results are robust to other specifications.

Not only are technical skills associated with higher wages but incorporating them into the regression decreases the magnitude of the education coefficients.[8] For example, those who apply the following skills earn more: technology 38 percent more an hour, mechanical 25 percent, computer skills 21 percent, and English 16 percent. Even after controlling for education the returns are statistically significant, which suggests that there is a premium for technical skills that the education variable does not capture. In addition (figure 4.12), taking skills into account in the analysis somewhat decreases the premiums associated with any given level of education. It appears that employers value specific technical skills in addition to education.

Though socio-emotional skills are valued in the labor force, their returns do not exactly correspond to what employers identify as the most important traits. One standard deviation increase in extraversion, openness, emotional stability, or agreeableness is associated with 5–7 percent higher hourly wages. However, the return on conscientiousness is close to zero and not significant even though (see chapter 3) most employers identify it as the most important socio-emotional trait (64 percent for high-skilled workers, 70 percent for low-skilled). Unlike technical skills, bringing socio-emotional skills into the analysis does not decrease the magnitude of returns to education. Surprisingly, though presentation and teamwork skills were positively related to earnings, the finding was not statistically significant.[9]

Figure 4.12 Returns on Education after Controlling for Technical Skills
Percent

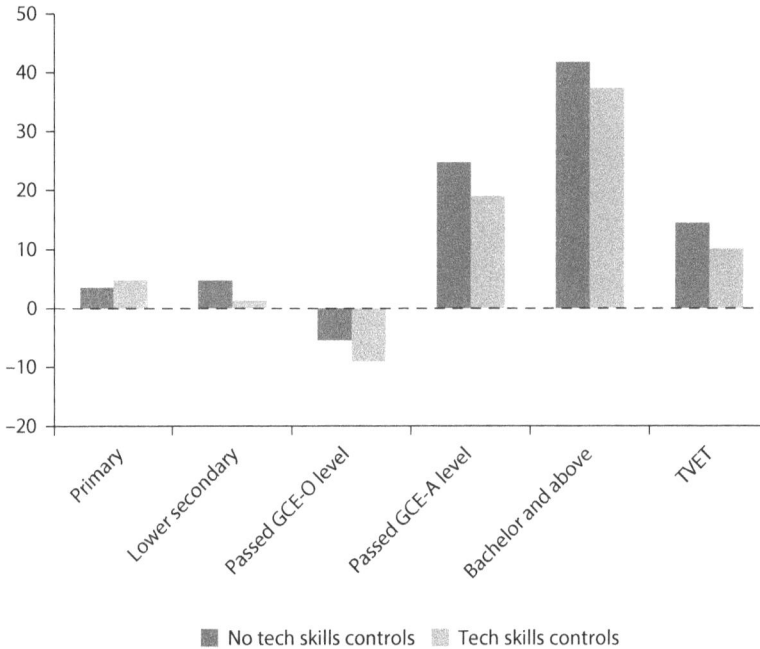

■ No tech skills controls   ░ Tech skills controls

Source: STEP household survey.
Note: Other controls were technical skills, gender, province, rural/urban area, age, age squared, occupation, and sector.

Only writing, numeracy, teamwork, and long-term perseverance have a statistically significant relationship with the probability of being employed, and there is no relationship between employment and technical skills. According to the regression analysis, there are no statistically significant differences in employment probability between different levels of education or receipt of TVET, which suggests that unemployment is idiosyncratic rather than education-specific.[10]

Workers with technology, computer, and presentation skills are less likely to be underemployed. Technology skills decrease the likelihood of underemployment by 7 percent, computer skills by 10 percent, and presentation skills by 2 percent. Combined with the wage premiums associated with technology and computer skills, these results underscore the importance of these technical skills for the labor market. As with employment probability, education level and TVET do not have a statistically significant relationship with underemployment; the fact that urban residents are less likely to be underemployed suggests that working hours in urban jobs may be more highly regulated, which in its turn could be because the formal economy is more prevalent in urban areas.

Some technical and soft skills (computer, technology, English, perseverance, and decision making) are associated with a lower probability of being in the informal economy (figure 4.13), as is completion of a bachelor's degree or

Figure 4.13 Probabilities of Being Self-Employed, by Skill
Percent

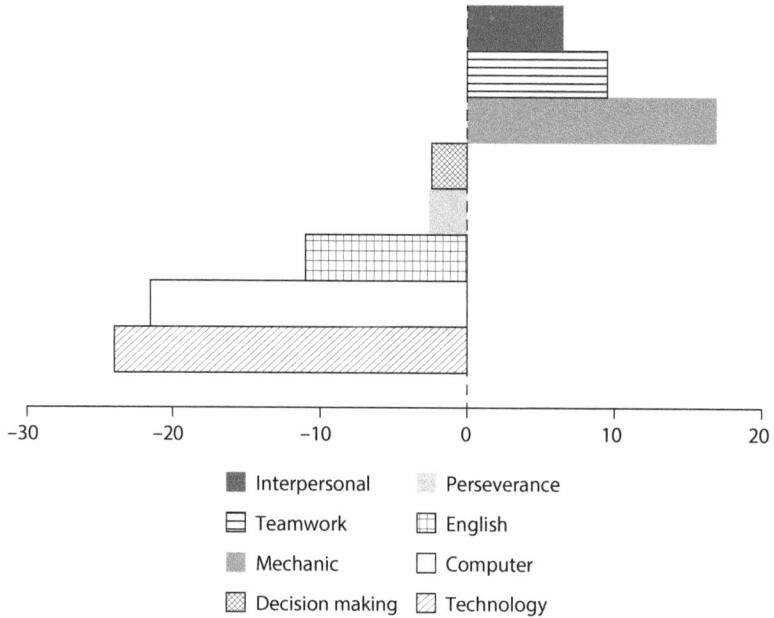

Source: STEP household survey.
Note: Other controls were education, gender, province, rural/urban, age, marital status, and number of children.

beyond. For example, those with technology skills are 24 percent less likely to be self-employed than those without, those with computer skills 22 percent less likely, and those competent in English 11 percent less likely. However, mechanical skills are associated with a higher probability of being self-employed. As for soft skills, long-term perseverance and decision making are associated with less probability of being self-employed, but interpersonal and teamwork skills increase the likelihood of participating in the informal economy. People who have completed only lower secondary or passed only GCE O-levels are more likely to be self-employed; those with a bachelor's and above are less likely to be self-employed than those with less than complete primary education.

Conclusion and Policy Options

This is the first effort to assess the skill levels of the Sri Lankan labor force that goes beyond standard measures of education. This chapter drew upon findings from the STEP household survey and other sources. The main findings are these:

• *The Sri Lankan labor force is the most educated in South Asia in terms of education attainment.* The STEP survey found that more than eight out of 10 adults in Sri Lanka have completed at least lower secondary (grade 9). More than one adult out of six has completed vocational education or training and the same proportion has completed an apprenticeship program. More than two-thirds of TVET students graduate from certificate programs, but only a few of these move on to more advanced technical studies. Most apprenticeships are informal.

- *Despite the high degree of education in Sri Lanka, the overall skills stock of the workforce is much lower at advanced levels (for example, tertiary education) than in middle- and high-income countries like Malaysia and South Korea.* Moreover, the self-reported likelihood of using reading and writing skills is lower than in other countries that STEP surveyed, though the use of numeracy skills is on par with them. Urban and formal jobs require more cognitive skills than rural and informal. Although apparently well-educated, 10 percent of the population say that the lack of cognitive skills prevents them from getting better jobs. Self-reported reading, writing, and numeracy skills are closely correlated with the amount of schooling, with the highest marginal increases below GCE O-levels. This indicates that cognitive skills are formed early in education. More educated individuals report using basic cognitive skills more often and more intensely.

- *The supply of technical skills for which there is high demand, such as English and computer skills, is quite low.* Moreover, there are substantial differences in the supply between urban and rural populations and higher- and lower-skilled workers. These skills are formed in upper secondary and above and in TVET.

- *Most noncognitive skills, except for openness, presentation, and teamwork, are not acquired in the general education or TVET systems.*

- *The labor market in Sri Lanka is characterized by low unemployment, a large informal economy, and relatively high underemployment.* In particular, and of special concern, unemployment of youth is high, labor force participation of women is low, underemployment is high (especially for women and rural residents), and so is participation in the informal economy.[11]

- *The returns on more education (GCE A-levels and above) and TVET have been rising.* However, neither general education nor TVET affects the probability of employment. There are no returns to apprenticeship in terms of either earnings or employment.

- *Technical skills, such as English, technology, and computer capability, improve the quality of employment.* These skills are associated with a lower probability of being self- or underemployed.

- *While self-reported writing and numeracy are associated with a higher likelihood of being employed, they do not significantly affect earnings after education is accounted for.*

- *There is a significant positive relationship between several socio-emotional skills, technical skills, and earnings.* The fact that soft and technical skills have returns beyond education mirrors labor market demand (chapter 3) and the government strategy for skills development. Incorporating technical skills into earnings regressions reduces the magnitude of the education coefficients. This suggests that in addition to certain schooling requirements, employers also value specific technical skills.

It appears that TVET is a good investment for Sri Lanka: it improves worker earnings and equips them with skills relevant to the labor market. However, to implement the *Mahinda Chintana* vision, TVET needs to be reformed to better respond to emerging skills demands. The following policy considerations are suggested:

- *Build up the quality of primary and secondary education to better transfer cognitive skills.* Basic cognitive skills lay the foundation for acquisition of technical and more complex cognitive skills. Because basic skills are learned in primary and secondary school, improving the quality of early learning is crucial for building solid cognitive skills.

- *Expand the supply of technical skills by improving TVET and upper secondary education.* Technical skills enhance individual success in the labor market. Employers increasingly demand them from workers, and the government considers technical skills to be drivers of economic growth. Since technical skills are formed in upper secondary, postsecondary, and TVET, that is where interventions are needed.

- *Simplify horizontal links between TVET and general education.* There is a clear vertical path through the TVET system for a worker who completes lower secondary education to progress from craftsperson to high-skilled technician. However, there is no horizontal mobility between general education and TVET. To progress through the TVET system, students must complete all NVQ levels no matter how complete their general education, which makes the learning process inefficient and creates additional costs. Design and approval of the Sri Lanka Qualifications Framework was a step toward great mobility, but it has not yet been operationalized.

- *Introduce soft skills into general education.* Though there are returns to soft skills in terms of earnings and probability of wage employment, the general education and vocational systems do not make much effort to produce them. Mainstreaming soft skills into both general education and TVET curricula is therefore essential (box 4.1).

- *Expand the awareness of students and the general population about the TVET path.* Though there is low social demand for it, the returns on TVET are relatively high. A campaign to increase social demand might begin by introducing technical and vocational classes into secondary education curricula.

Box 4.1 Soft Skills in Youth Training Programs in Latin American Countries

Youth in many countries in the Latin America and Caribbean region face issues similar to those of youth in Sri Lanka: high unemployment, poor quality of jobs for those who are employed, and higher participation in the informal sector than adults. In response to these problems, countries in the region have implemented a variety of policies and programs, such as job training, career counseling, providing better information about vacancies, support for self-employment, provision of incentives to private firms to hire young people, temporary public sector jobs, and subsidies to unemployed youth.

The overarching goal of job training is to increase the probability of trainees finding formal jobs and improve the quality of employment. Though programs are financed with public funds, at US$400–750 the per capita training costs are relatively low. The programs provide the market-relevant skills that employers demand. Some of the programs provide participants not only with technical training and internships or on-the-job training in firms but also with supplementary classroom soft skills training. For example, participants in *Juventud y Empleo* in the Dominican Republic receive 75 hours of soft skills training, those in *Jovenes en Accion* in Colombia clock up to 360 hours of combined technical and soft skills training, and *Procajoven* in Panama provides 150 hours in training. The courses are designed to enhance such soft skills as social abilities (for example, conflict resolution and teamwork); personal growth (for example, self-esteem and persistence); and communication skills.

While most impact evaluations look at how these programs affect labor market outcomes overall, the preliminary impact evaluation of a randomized experiment in the Dominican Republic youth training program suggests that the soft skills taught in the program combined with work experience improved the labor market outcomes of participants.

Sources: Gonzalez-Velosa, Ripani, and Rosas-Shady 2012; Martinez 2012.

- *Review the apprenticeship system.* Apprenticeship as currently organized does not earn returns in terms of either employment opportunities or earnings. It should be reviewed to ensure that it provides market-relevant skills.

- *Improve collection of information about TVET.* As TVET becomes crucial for producing the skills needed to achieve MC goals, it is necessary to regularly collect information on who has obtained it. Unfortunately, the Labor Force Surveys discontinued asking all working-age respondents about TVET in 2004. To monitor TVET graduates and its labor market outcomes, the Department of Census and Statistics (DCS) should revert to the practice of asking all working-age individuals TVET questions when the personal characteristics of household members are enumerated.

- *Periodically evaluate the impact of the major TVET programs.* TVET quality and relevance are important to ensure that the skills provided are those which the labor market requires. Thus, periodic evaluations of the impact of major TVET programs within a quasi-experimental framework would help to inform policy decisions aimed at making the system more responsive to the labor market.

Notes

1. The asset index was constructed to proxy for the wealth of the household by using principal component analysis of the assets reported. The principal component analysis covered (1) household ownership of consumer durables such as a radio, television, bicycle, or car; and (2) characteristics of the dwelling in which the household lives, such as the walls, roof, floor, number of rooms per capita, main source of drinking water, main source of energy for cooking and for lighting, main type of toilet facilities, whether the household has a small garden plot, and agricultural land. This methodology, developed by Sanchez and Valerio (2013) is based on Filmer and Scott (2008).

2. See Savchenko (2013) for a description of how the variables were constructed.

3. To make the measurements comparable to the employer surveys, high-skilled workers are defined as those who are managers, professionals, or technical and associate professionals. The rest are considered low-skilled.

4. A person is defined as being out of the labor force if he or she was not working and was not trying to find a salaried or waged job or had not tried to start a business in the past four weeks.

5. Underemployment is defined as in the Sri Lanka LFS: people who work less than 35 hours a week and would like to work more for the same pay rate.

6. Workers are defined as wage-employed if they identified their main occupation as wage worker or employee and as self-employed if it was their own economic activity with or without hired labor, or employer, or farmer.

7. Regression analysis shows that these relationships are not statistically significant.

8. In checking if self-reported intensity of reading, writing, or numeracy has implications for wages, the regression results suggest that intensity of cognitive skills has a statistically significant relationship with earnings only if education is not accounted for. Once education variables are included in the regresssion, the intensity of cognitive skills is no longer significant. This could imply that the education variable captures the relationship between cognitive skills and earnings.

9. For detailed analysis, see Savchenko (2013)

10. For a detailed analysis of employment, underemployment, and self-employment, see Savchenko (2013).

11. According to the Sri Lanka LFS, 63 percent of the labor force was in the informal economy in 2011, but the STEP survey does not use exactly the same measure of informality. Thus, it was approximated by the self-employment rate, which is 37 percent. Also, official underemployment reported in the LFS is 2.8 percent; the study used a similar definition of underemployment.

Bibliography

Alderman, H., J. Behrman, D. Ross, and R. Sabot. 1996. "Decomposing the Gender Gap in Cognitive Skills in a Poor Rural Economy." *Journal of Human Resources* 31 (1): 229–54.

Blunch, N. H. 2009. "Multidimensional Human Capital, Wages and Endogenous Employment Status in Ghana." In *Labor Markets and Economic Development*, edited by R. Kanbur and J. Svejnar, 367–85, London and New York: Routledge.

Boissiere, M., J. Knight, and R. Sabot. 1985. "Earnings, Schooling, Ability and Cognitive Skills." *American Economic Review* 73 (5): 926–46.

Borghans, L., B. ter Wel, and B. A. Weinberg. 2008. "Interpersonal Styles and Labor Market Outcomes." *Journal of Human Resources* 43 (4): 815–58.

Bowles, S., H. Gintis, and M. Osborne. 2001. "Incentive-Enhancing Preferences: Personality, Behavior, and Earnings." *American Economic Review* 91 (2): 155–58.

Card, D., J. Kluve, and A. Weber. 2010. "Active Labour Market Policy Evaluations: A Meta-Analysis." *Economic Journal* 120 (548): F 452–77.

Cawley, J., J. Heckman, and E. Vytlacil. 2001. "Three Observations on Wages and Measured Cognitive Ability." *Labour Economics* 8 (4): 419–42.

di Gropello, E., H. Tan, and P. Tandon. 2010. *Skills for the Labor Market in the Philippines.* Washington, DC: World Bank.

di Gropello, E., A. Kruse, and P. Tandon. 2011. *Skills for the Labor Market in Indonesia: Trends in Demand, Gaps, and Supply.* Washington, DC: World Bank.

DTET (Department of Technical Education and Training). 2002. "Tracer Study of Technical College Graduates 1995–1996." Conducted in collaboration with DCS and National Education Research and Evaluation Centre, University of Colombo, Sri Lanka.

EdStats. 2011. Education Statistics Database. World Bank, Washington DC.

Filmer, D., and K. Scott. 2008. "Assessing Asset Indices." World Bank Policy Research Working Paper 4605, Washington, DC.

Glewwe, P. 2002. "Schools and Skills in Developing Countries: Education Policies and Socioeconomic Outcomes." *Journal of Economic Literature* 40 (2): 436–82.

Glewwe, P., Q. Huang, and A. Park. 2011. "Cognitive Skills, Non-Cognitive Skills, and the Employment and Wages of Young Adults in Rural China." Paper presented at the annual meeting of the Agricultural and Applied Economics Association, Pittsburgh, PA, July 24–26.

Goff, M., and P. L. Ackerman. 1992. "Personality-Intelligence Relations: Assessment of Typical Intellectual Engagement." *Journal of Educational Psychology* 84 (4): 537–53.

Gonzalez-Velosa, C., L. Ripani, and D. Rosas-Shady. 2012. "How Can Job Opportunities for Young People in Latin America be Improved?" Technical Note IDB-TN-345, Inter-American Development Bank, Washington, DC.

Gottfredson, L. S. 1997. "Why g Matters: The Complexity of Everyday Life." *Intelligence* 24 (1): 79–132.

Gunatilaka, R., M. Mayer, and M. Vodopivec. 2010. *The Challenge of Youth Employment in Sri Lanka.* Washington, DC: World Bank.

Hanushek, E., and L. Wößmann. 2008. "The Role of Cognitive Skills in Economic Development." *Journal of Economic Literature* 46 (3): 607–68.

———. 2009. "Do Better Schools Lead to More Growth? Cognitive Skills, Economic Outcomes, and Causation." NBER Working Paper 14633, National Bureau of Economic Research, Cambridge, MA.

Hartigan, J. A., and A. K. Wigdor. 1989. *Fairness in Employment Testing: Validity Generalization, Minority Issues and the General Aptitude Test Battery.* Washington, DC: National Academy Press.

Heckman, J., J. Stixrud, and S. Urzúa. 2006. "The Effects of Cognitive and Noncognitive Abilities on Labor Market Outcomes and Social Behavior." *Journal of Labor Economics* 24 (3): 411–82.

Herrnstein, R., and C. Murray. 1994. *The Bell Curve: Intelligence and Class Structure in American Life.* New York: Free Press.

Mahinda Chintana. 2010. http://www.treasury.gov.lk/publications/mahindaChintana Vision-2010full-eng.pdf.

Martinez, S. 2012. http://www.iza.org/conference_files/ALMP2012/martinez_s_dr.pdf.

Ministry of Skills Development and Technical Education. 2005. "Proceedings of the Research Convention 2005." Colombo, Sri Lanka.

Mobius, M., and T. Rosenblat. 2006. "Why Beauty Matters." *American Economic Review* 96 (1): 222–35.

MoE (Ministry of Education, Sri Lanka). 2011. Sri Lanka Education Information, MoE. http://www.moe.gov.lk/web/images/stories/statistic/sri_lanka_education _information_2011.pdf.

Moll, P. G. 1998. "Primary Schooling, Cognitive Skills and Wages in South Africa." *Economica* 65 (258): 263–84.

Mueller, G., and E. S. Plug. 2006. "Estimating the Effect of Personality on Male-Female Earnings." *Industrial and Labor Relations Review* 60 (1): 3–22.

Mulligan, C. B. 1999. "Galton vs. The Human Capital Approach to Inheritance." *Journal of Political Economy* 107 (S6): 184–224.

Murnane, R. J., and J. B. Willett. 2000. "How Important Are the Cognitive Skills of Teenagers in Predicting Subsequent Earnings?" *Journal of Policy Analysis and Management* 19 (4): 547–68.

NAITA (National Apprentice and Industrial Training Authority). 2001. *Report on Tracer Study Survey Results for Monitoring and Evaluation of Vocational Training.* Planning and Information Division, Colombo, Sri Lanka.

Neal, D. A., and W. R. Johnson. 1996. "The Role of Premarket Factors in Black-White Wage Differences." *Journal of Political Economy* 104 (5): 869–95.

Nyhus, E. K., and E. Pons. 2005. "The Effects of Personality on Earnings." *Journal of Economic Psychology* 26 (3): 363–84.

Riboud, M., Y. Savchenko, and H. Tan. 2007. *The Knowledge Economy, Education and Training in South Asia.* Washington, DC: World Bank.

Salgado, J. F. 1997. "The Five Factor Model of Personality and Job Performance in the European Community." *Journal of Applied Psychology* 82 (1): 30–43.

Sanchez Puerta, M. L., A. Valerio, G. Pierre, and S. Urzúa. 2012. "STEP Skills Survey Data Analysis Methodology Note." Draft, Social Protection and Labor Department, World Bank, Washington, DC.

Sanchez Puerta, M. L., and A. Valerio. 2013. "STEP Surveys Results." Background paper, Social Protection and Labor Department, World Bank, Washington, DC.

Savchenko, Y. 2013. "Skills Development in Sri Lanka: Skills Supply, Education and Labor Market Outcomes." Background paper, World Bank, Washington, DC.

Segal, C. 2008. "Motivation, Test Scores, and Economic Success." Working Paper 1124, Department of Economics and Business, Universitat Pompeu Fabra (UPF), Barcelona, Spain.

Tan, H. 2012. "Sri Lanka: Education, Training and Labor Market Outcomes." Background paper for Sri Lanka Skills Development Report, World Bank, Washington, DC.

TVEC (Tertiary and Vocational Education Commission). 2012a. Corporate Plan 2012–2016 (in TVEC docs folder). http://www.tvec.gov.lk/pr/images/Corporate_Plan%20 2012-2016-edited.pdf.

———. 2012b. National Vocational Qualifications Framework. http://www.tvec.gov.lk /pdf/NVQ_Framework.pdf.

Tyler, J. H., R. J. Murnane, and J. B. Willett. 2000. "Do the Cognitive Skills of School Dropouts Matter in the Labor Market?" *Journal of Human Resources* 35 (4): 748–54.

Urzúa, S. 2008. "Racial Labor Market Gaps: The Role of Abilities and Schooling Choices." *Journal of Human Resources* 43 (4): 919–71.

VTA (Vocational Training Authority). 2001. *Report on Tracer Study Survey Results for Monitoring and Evaluation of Vocational Training.* Colombo, Sri Lanka.

Waddell, G. 2006. "Labor-Market Consequences of Poor Attitude and Low Self-Esteem in Youth." *Economic Inquiry* 44 (1): 69–97.

World Bank. 2005. *Treasures of the Education System in Sri Lanka: Restoring Performance, Expanding Opportunities and Enhancing Prospects.* Human Development Department, South Asia Region. Washington, DC: World Bank.

———. 2010. *Providing Skills for Equity and Growth: Preparing Cambodia's Youth for the Labor Market.* Human Development Department, East Asia and Pacific Region. Washington, DC: World Bank.

———. 2012a. *Leading with Ideas: Skills for Growth and Equity in Thailand.* Washington, DC: World Bank.

———. 2012b. *World Development Indicators.* Washington, DC: World Bank.

CHAPTER 5

Cost and Financing of Technical and Vocational Education and Training

Introduction

The Sri Lanka technical and vocational education and training (TVET) sector has been the subject of innumerable studies, reports, plans, and strategies. Few, however, have tackled its financing.[1] One reason for this is that estimating how much funding is channeled to TVET activities is not easy. TVET institutions serve a variety of clients, from school leavers to mid-career employees, and course formats are organized to suit different needs. A number of government entities are responsible for TVET activities; assignment of the responsibilities changes whenever government portfolios are reshuffled; and expenditures on technical training activities are often not recorded as a separate line item. Most private TVET is conducted outside the formal sector, and when nongovernmental organizations (NGOs) offer TVET, their reporting methods are not always uniform.

While many countries have to deal with these issues to varying degrees, they are particularly challenging in Sri Lanka. TVET financing is not well-documented, and assessing the efficiency of spending is daunting because the relationship between spending and outputs—let alone outcomes—is elusive. Financial data are scarce, and those available are often inconsistent. This chapter therefore makes no attempt at comprehensive coverage of all types of providers.

A great deal can be learned from between-country comparisons, but selecting comparison countries is a delicate enterprise. Sri Lanka's comparators for the purposes of this chapter are (1) the other countries in the South Asia region; (2) countries at a similar economic level to Sri Lanka as defined by gross national income (GNI) per capita; and (3) countries whose economic or education trajectory can serve as an example or a source of inspiration. Most countries in the last group are in East Asia.

In this chapter the first section analyzes spending on TVET countrywide; the second discusses efficiency and funding issues down to the production unit (training centers); the third concentrates on TVET management and governance; and the closing section highlights lessons learned and identifies options for Sri Lanka.

Expenditures in the Aggregate

Aggregating all TVET expenditures and every funding source involves scanning the entire spectrum of agents providing TVET, from official public authorities to private training centers (often informal and undeclared, and sometimes transient) and adding up both what they spend and what they bring in. Although private providers cater to almost a third of TVET clients, little is known about their financing. The bulk of this section, therefore, unpacks information on the public sector, adding only guesstimates about private TVET financing.

The Public Sector

Public funds allocated to TVET are primarily from the central government. Most spending in the provinces is channeled through funds levied at the center.

Central Government Spending

A number of ministries manage and finance TVET institutions. Data on sources, composition, and destinations of monies are also widely dispersed. But although more than a dozen ministries sponsor training institutions, most TVET activities and resources are concentrated in five: Youth Affairs and Skills Development (MYASD); Health (MoH); Construction, Engineering Services, Housing and Common Amenities (MoCESHCA); Economic Development (MoED); and Agriculture (MoAg). Spending by other ministries is minimal.

Ministry of Youth Affairs and Skills Development (MYASD). Between 2000 and 2010 primary responsibility for TVET shifted from one ministry to another (box 2.1), but the MYASD is now the main public provider of funding, since TVET-related activities constitute its focal mission.

MYASD spending on TVET has been increasing steadily for a decade. In current terms, total spending went up on average by 22 percent a year, with exceptions only in 2004, 2007, and 2009 (table 5.1). However, in real terms, the growth, though vigorous, was less spectacular, quadrupling between 2000 and 2011 (figure 5.1). This also translated into a rather tentative increase in the share in gross domestic product (GDP) of public spending on TVET (figure 5.2).

Although total public spending comprises both recurrent and development expenditures, their patterns are quite different. About two-thirds of total MYASD spending is recurrent; for the past decade, development spending has

Table 5.1 Ministry of Youth Affairs and Skills Development—Total Expenditures, 2001–11
Current Rs million

	2001	2002	2003	2004	2005	2006	2007	2008	2009	2010	2011
Total expenditures	1,134	1,329	1,813	1,846	2,288	3,529	3,657	5,966	5,283	5,840	8,585
Δ (%)		17	17	36	2	24	54	4	63	−11	11	47

Source: Ministry of Finance and Planning (MFP) 2003–12, Budget Estimates.
Note: Not included is spending in 2000–09 by the Ceylon German Technical Training Institute, Ocean University, National Youth Service Council, and National Youth Corps.

Figure 5.1 Total MYASD Expenditure in Current and Constant Prices, 2000–11

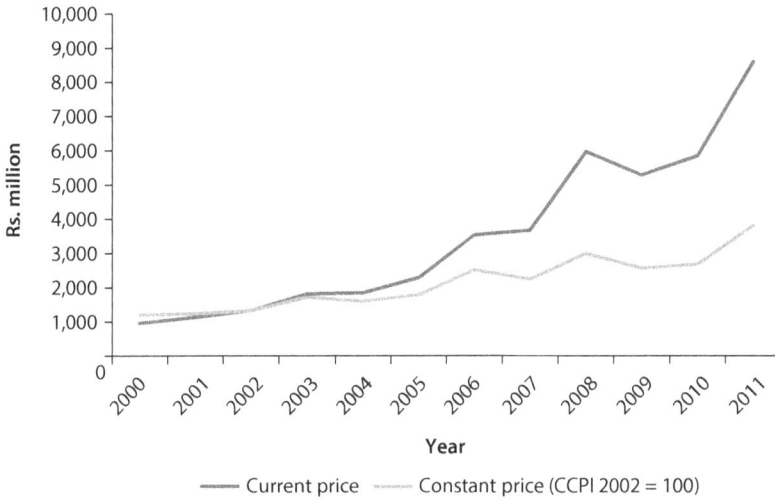

Sources: MFP 2003–12, Budget Estimates (current prices); Central Bank Annual Report 2011; Colombo Consumer Price Index (CCPI).
Note: Constant prices for 2000 and 2001 are based on the 1952 CCPI series.

Figure 5.2 MYASD Expenditure as a Share of GDP, 2000–11
Percent

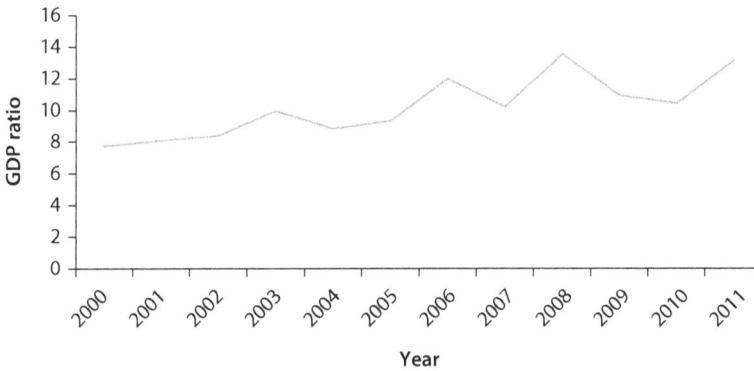

Source: MFP, Central Bank.

been relatively stable at 31–58 percent of total expenditure, though it has increased slightly over time. The share of donor funding varies from 7 percent to 46 percent but is heading downward. The divergence of the two ratios suggests that as development expenditures increase, they become less dependent on donor funding.

Foreign funding to the MYASD, currently about 10 percent of total TVET spending, is unpredictable. It has been volatile, although it is clearly trending down (figure 5.3). Initial forecasts of donor contributions for 2010, 2011, and

Figure 5.3 Share of Donor Financing in MYASD Budget, 2001–11
Percent

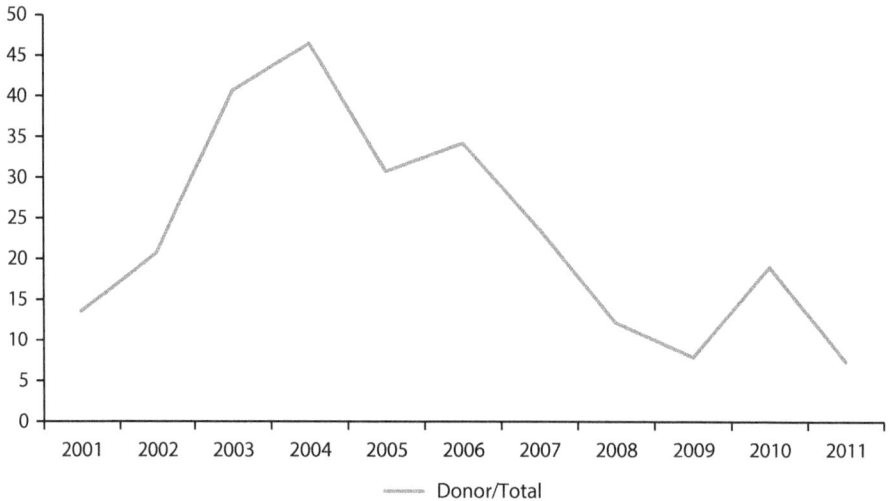

Donor/Total

2012 proved pessimistic; the forecast for 2013–14 is for more than 20 percent of the total ministry budget. Swings and uncertainty in foreign investment make long-term planning difficult.

In addition to the MYASD, four other ministries fund about 12 percent of the government-sponsored training centers. Each ministry manages its TVET activities differently.

Ministry of Health. The MoH allocates significant amounts to staff training. Its Education, Training and Research Unit (ET&R) coordinates, monitors, and evaluates skills training for nursing officers, paramedical staff, and technical service providers. On request, in the same schools it also trains at its expense support staff (for example, attendants and dispensers) for other public institutions, such as the Ministry of Indigenous Medicine, army hospitals, and police hospitals. The budget share of ET&R human resources development activities, which are considered equivalent to TVET activities, averaged 6.2 percent for 2000–11 (range: 4.3 percent in 2000 to 7.2 percent in 2011). In constant price terms, the unit's budget doubled.

Ministry of Construction, Engineering Services, Housing and Common Amenities. Expenditures linked to TVET represent a significant share of the total MoCESHCA budget, but recent allocations to the ministry have been sized down. All MoCESHCA vocational training is conducted by the Institute for Construction Training and Development (ICTAD). Most ICTAD programs are operated by either the Construction Equipment Training Centre (CETRAC), for long-term training, or the Operator Training Centre (OTC) for short-term training. The two units received about 5 percent of the total ministry budget in

Figure 5.4 Ministry of Construction, Engineering Services, Housing and Common Amenities Expenditures on Training, 2007–11

Current SL Rs 000

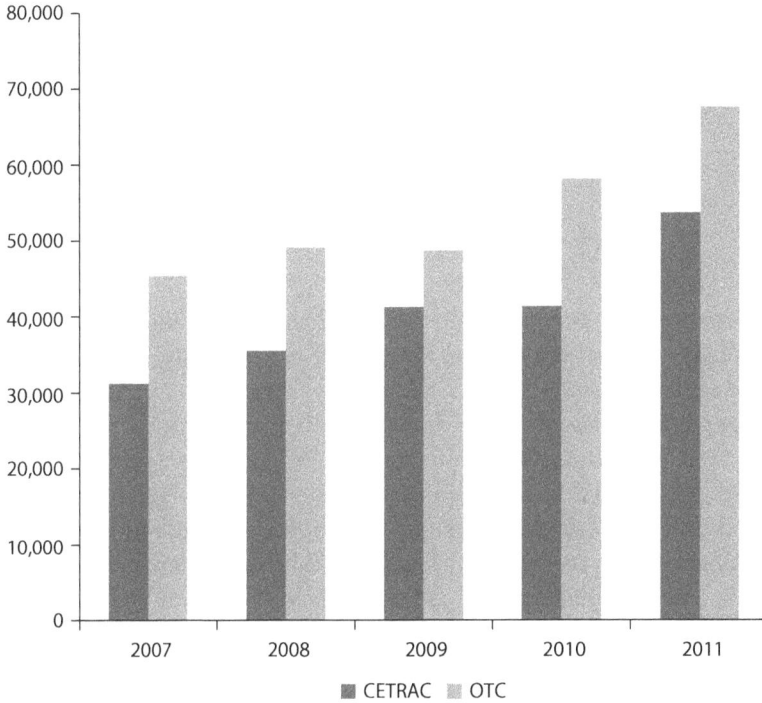

■ CETRAC ▥ OTC

Source: ICTAD Finance Division (unpublished document).

2011—half their allocation in the two previous years. For 2007–11 average annual growth of MoCESHCA's TVET budget in current prices was 6 percent; inflation was 6.7 percent (figure 5.4).

Ministry of Economic Development. The MoED manages a large, self-financing tourism training institute. Since 2010 the ministry has also hosted the Sri Lanka Institute of Tourism and Hotel Management (SLITHM), which had been the responsibility of the Ministry of Tourism. The SLITHM, a major provider of training for the booming tourism industry, is financially self-sufficient.

Ministry of Agriculture. The MoAg receives the second-highest TVET allocation. It runs six training centers that received about 1 percent of its total budget in 2010. Although MoAg budgets as a whole have since seen only moderate increases, allocations for training have jumped to 5–6 percent of the total (table 5.2). MoAg also spends more than twice its allocation for extension and training activities.

Table 5.2 Ministry of Agriculture Expenditure on TVET, 2010–14
SL Rs thousands

	2010	2011	2012[a]	2013[b]	2014[b]
Recurrent	178,738	218,000	235,000	251,000	274,000
Capital	65,649	127,465	120,000	143,000	166,000
Total	244,387	345,465	355,000	394,000	440,000
Training activities/Total ministry budget (%)	1	6	6	5	6

Source: MFP, Budget estimates.
a. Estimates.
b. Projections.

Other Ministries with Training Responsibilities. Nine other ministries have government training centers,[2] but because together they serve only about 3 percent of all public center trainees, they are dealt with as a single cluster. Estimates of their TVET spending are based on the number of their students, on the assumption that their cost per trainee is the same as that of the ministries that provide most TVET. Because sessions are of different lengths—some trainees are part-time and others full-time—and the fields of study differ, it seems more prudent to estimate a range than a single average cost. The study therefore estimated that the total they spent (recurrent and capital) is 4–10 percent of what MYASD spends.

Training and Capacity Building. Most ministries have a small training and capacity-building budget that averages about 1.1 percent of capital expenditure, but there are considerable variations. Training and capacity building, also called human resource development, is budgeted as capital expenditures. Ministries in charge of infrastructure typically spend less than 1 percent of their capital budget on training and capacity building while the human resources group devotes almost 7 percent. Even among the main TVET providers, inter-ministry dispersion is great, from less than 0.1 percent for the MoED to 25 percent for the MYASD. Finally, because a number of activities financed by this budget line are not strictly speaking TVET, only half the envelope has been taken into account in the estimate of aggregate TVET spending.

Provincial Government Spending. The Thirteenth Amendment to the Sri Lankan Constitution distinguishes three types of expenditures based on where the responsibilities lie: (1) the Provincial Council List, over which the councils have full power; (2) the Concurrent List, in which provincial and central authorities are equally responsible for expenditures; and (3) the Reserved List, which is at the sole discretion of the central government. Activities directly or indirectly linked to TVET are found in all three: education on the Provincial Council List; higher education on the Concurrent List; and professional occupations and training—where most TVET items would fall—on the Reserved List. For planning purposes, the government has set five major categories, which cover 23 areas. However, TVET is not one of them. It seems to have been incorporated into education, which is in the social infrastructure development category. Provinces have two sources of revenue: a block grant for recurrent expenditures and the Provincial Specific Development Grant for capital outlays. It was not possible to ascertain their specific spending on TVET.

It is estimated that the provinces are responsible for about 1 percent of total TVET spending. A straightforward estimate of the direct contribution of provinces to TVET activities is not possible.[3] According to the 2009 Annual Report of the Finance Commission (FC), the body mandated to identify provincial finances, provincial revenues represented about 3.4 percent of total government revenues in 2009. For this study the analysis then looked at partial data for three subsectors that absorb most of the provincial budget related to TVET in the Western Province, namely agriculture, education, and small industries, and at data for industrial development in the Sabaragamuwa Province, where most vocational training is held. In both cases, outlays for TVET represent about 1.2 percent of the province's spending. This percentage was then applied to all provinces, resulting in a total close to SL Rs 1 billion.

The Private Sector

Private providers of TVET in Sri Lanka are many and diverse (see chapter 6).[4] Of about 1,250 private centers, 77 percent are for-profit, 16 percent are NGOs, and the rest are either companies training their own staff (4 percent) or professional associations offering training to members or chambers of commerce. Training centers may be run or financed by national operators only, foreign agencies only, or a mix of the two. What each spends can vary tremendously, depending, for instance, on (1) whether they are for-profit; (2) the training provided (from bakery to mechatronics); (3) demand for courses; (4) course length (from a few days to two years); and (5) the quality of training inputs (and hence outputs). Many providers are unwilling to give out financial information, often because they are not registered.

Private sector spending on TVET is estimated to be about half of the MYASD TVET budget. The estimate was reached by applying information from a limited number of institutions to the entire private sector, on the assumption that in the aggregate the differences would offset each other. This method provides reasonable orders of magnitude. To make the approach more reliable, the results of three lines of enquiry were compared: (1) cost per trainee and total number of trainees who completed sessions; (2) expenditures per center and total number of centers in the country; and (3) total fees paid by all centers as a proxy for their expenses. This produced a spread of 1–4 between the two extreme values. Selecting the median value for the purpose of aggregation put private TVET spending at half that of MYASD and twice that of the MoH.

Finally, trainees also contribute significantly to TVET financing through fees and related expenses. One way to estimate these expenses is to observe specific institutions, such as Don Bosco Technical College, but a more reliable route is to compare the results of the most recent Skills Toward Employment and Productivity (STEP) Household Skills Measurement Survey with information obtained using the previous method. A critical advantage of the household survey is that it provides information not only on fees paid but also on related out-of-pocket expenses. Apparently, fees actually represent on average only 25–50 percent of trainee cash outlays.

National Aggregates and International Comparisons
Total TVET Spending
After having identified all possible actors, it is necessary to sum up TVET spending and estimate orders of magnitude for aggregate spending. Rather than relying on a single figure, a low and a high case were designed to test the sensitivity of results for several sources of funds—the total for the high case is about 50 percent more than for the low (table 5.3).

Recognizing how sensitive the results are to the method of calculation, it appears that TVET spending is less than 0.5 percent of GDP. Taking into account all sources, Sri Lanka allocates 0.23–0.34 percent of its GDP to TVET (table 5.4), of which the public sector accounts for two-thirds.

An International Perspective
There is no indisputable yardstick by which to establish that Sri Lanka's spending on TVET is too low, too high, or about right. However, assessing whether investment is or is not sufficient may not be the most relevant task. As international comparisons have demonstrated for primary and secondary general education (Vegas and Coffin 2012), and more recently for tertiary (World Bank 2012), the amount spent is not a foolproof predictor of performance; how funds are spent and for what is more relevant.

For a start, how does Sri Lanka's allocation compare with other countries? As there are no international time series that allow for direct comparison with

Table 5.3 Aggregate Spending on TVET-Related Activities, 2010 or Nearest Year

	High case		Low case	
	(SL Rs million)	Distribution (%)	(SL Rs million)	Distribution (%)
MYASD	5,840	31	5,840	45
MoH	1,525	8	1,525	12
MoCESHC	99	1	99	1
MoED (SLITHM)	176	1	176	1
MoAg	244	1	244	2
Other ministry training centers	565	3	261	2
Internal ministry training and capacity building	2,015	11	1,344	10
Provinces	937	5	937	7
Private sector	4,099	22	1,100	8
Households	3,406	18	1,554	12
Total	18,907	100	13,080	100
Of which: Public sector	11,402	60	10,426	80

Sources: Based on MFP, FC, and STEP Household Skills Measurement Survey data and interviews.

Table 5.4 Spending on TVET as a Percentage of GDP, All Sources, 2010 or Nearest Year
Percent

Ministry/Agency	High case	Low case	Medium case
MYASD	0.10	0.10	0.10
MoH	0.03	0.03	0.03
MoCESHC	0.002	0.002	0.002
MoED (SLITHM)	0.003	0.003	0.003
MoAg	0.004	0.004	0.004
Other ministry training centers	0.01	0.00	0.01
Training and capacity building	0.04	0.02	0.03
Provinces	0.02	0.02	0.02
Private sector	0.07	0.02	0.05
Household expenditure	0.06	0.03	0.04
Total	0.34	0.23	0.29
Of which: Public sector	0.20	0.19	0.19

Sources: Based on MFP, FC, and STEP Household Skills Measurement Survey data and interviews.

Table 5.5 Public Spending on Education, Selected Countries, Percentage of GDP, 2008–10

	2008	2009	2010
Bangladesh	2.4	2.2	—
Nepal	3.8	4.7	4.7
Pakistan	2.9	2.7	2.4
Sri Lanka	—	2.1	—
South Asia average	4.2	4.2	3.7
Indonesia	2.8	3.5	3.0
Malaysia	4.1	5.8	—
Philippines	2.7	2.7	—
Thailand	3.8	4.1	3.8
World average	4.8	5	3.8
Number of countries	123	95	55

Source: UNESCO Institute of Statistics.
Note: — = not available.

Sri Lanka, the assessment begins with an analysis of spending on general education by region.

Spending on General Education. Sri Lanka devotes a smaller slice of its national wealth to general education as a whole than its neighbors in South Asia or countries further east. Using UNESCO Institute of Statistics (UIS) figures for 2008–10 (data for Sri Lanka are available only for 2009), it is apparent that Sri Lanka is investing less in general education than other countries in South Asia, most of which are low-income countries (LICs), or its comparators, most of which are middle-income countries MICs (table 5.5).[5] Yet despite its low level of public investment, Sri Lanka's indicators for primary and secondary education are ahead of those in most other South Asian countries.

Building the Skills for Economic Growth and Competitiveness in Sri Lanka
http://dx.doi.org/10.1596/978-1-4648-0158-7

An examination of the proportion of public spending allocated to education compared to the country's total budget shows that Sri Lanka has a lower allocation than its mostly LIC neighbors or the other comparators (table 5.6)—another possible indication that general education is not a priority for Sri Lanka.[6] Nevertheless, with a few exceptions, the countries that allocate the highest shares of GDP to public spending on education do not necessarily allocate a higher share of total governmental spending. In fact, the correlation between the two indicators is feeble.[7]

Investing in TVET: Sri Lanka and Elsewhere. Although under-resourced, Sri Lanka's public sector TVET seems to benefit from relatively favorable intrasectoral prioritizing. There is no universally accepted definition of what constitutes TVET, which complicates comparisons. UIS provides international data on the share of technical and vocational education in total education spending, but the indicator is available only for 20 countries, of which only one is a comparator country and two are in South Asia. Sri Lanka is not one of them.

At about 11 percent, Sri Lanka's share of public spending on TVET in the entire education sector budget is about twice as high as the average computed for the UIS countries (table 5.7). Very few countries have a higher percentage: Poland and Ethiopia do, but they are not renowned for their TVET systems; yet in Switzerland, which spent 13 percent in 2006, higher than the OECD average (OECD 2009a), TVET is considered successful.

Sri Lanka's public spending on TVET appears to be more generous than its spending on general education, perhaps because policy makers may be giving more attention to the former than the latter. More research is necessary before this can be confirmed.

Table 5.6 Public Spending on Education as a Percentage of Total Public Spending, Selected Countries, 2008–10

	2008	2009	2010
Bangladesh	14.0	14.1	—
Nepal	19.1	19.5	20.2
Pakistan	—	11.2	9.9
Sri Lanka	—	8.1	—
Average South Asia	15.0	13.3	13.2
Brazil	17.4	16.8	—
Indonesia	17.9	21.1	17.1
Malaysia	17.2	18.9	—
Philippines	16.9	15.0	—
Korea, Rep.	15.8	—	—
Thailand	20.5	20.3	22.3
Average	16.9	17.3	19.7
World average	15.7	14.9	15.5

Source: UIS.

Note: — = not available.

Table 5.7 TVET-Related Public Expenditure as a Share of the Total Education Budget, Selected Countries, 2000–09

Percent

	2000	2001	2002	2003	2004	2005	2006	2007	2008	2009	2000/09 Average
Albania	..	..	4.9	8.4	6.8	7.1	..	..	—	—	6.8
Algeria	6.7	7.4	7.4	7.9	6.2	7.8	7.5	..	—	—	7.3
Bangladesh	..	2	..	..	..	..	..	..	—	—	2.0
Costa Rica	6.2	6.6	7.3	6.5	5.2	5.6	..	..	—	—	6.2
Liberia	..	..	..	..	..	7.6	5.9	7.1	4.9	—	6.4
Moldova	5.4	..	..	..	4	..	..	..	—	—	4.7
Pakistan	4.9	5.2	5.7	..	..	..	..	..	—	—	5.3
Senegal	1.6	2.3	3.3	3.1	..	..	..	..	—	—	2.6
Turkey	..	..	8	..	..	..	..	..	—	—	8.0
Sri Lanka	—	—	—	—	—	—	—	—	—	10.5	—

Source: UIS.

Note: .. = negligible; — = not available.

Table 5.8 MYASD TVET Spending, by Sector, 2013

Percent

Hotel and tourism	35
Automobile technology	33
ICT	19
Construction	7
Fisheries, marine, and navigation	3
Medical and health sciences	2

Source: MYASD 2013 budget estimates.

Expenditures, Efficiency, and Funding

The next, more difficult, question is how efficiently the money is spent. A first step toward an answer is to document the composition of aggregate expenditure and follow the flow of funds down to the agency and service delivery levels. The next steps are to estimate unit costs and attempt to identify factors that affect them. Finally, after an analysis of revenue sources and a snapshot of the situation from the trainee perspective, it becomes possible to tease out the equity situation.

Composition and Destination of Expenditure Allocations
How the MYASD Spends Its Resources

MYASD investments target priority sectors (table 5.8). The allocation of recurrent and development funds by economic sector suggests that MYASD targets the sectors with the most growth potential and those most in need of skilled workers.

MYASD is development-oriented, and a high proportion of its budget is for capital investments. For the last three years, the shares of recurrent and capital expenditure have taken opposite paths, with the latter increasing to the point that at 55 percent it is now where the former was three years ago (figure 5.5).

Figure 5.5 Share of Recurrent and Capital Expenditure in the MYASD Budget, 2009–12

Percent

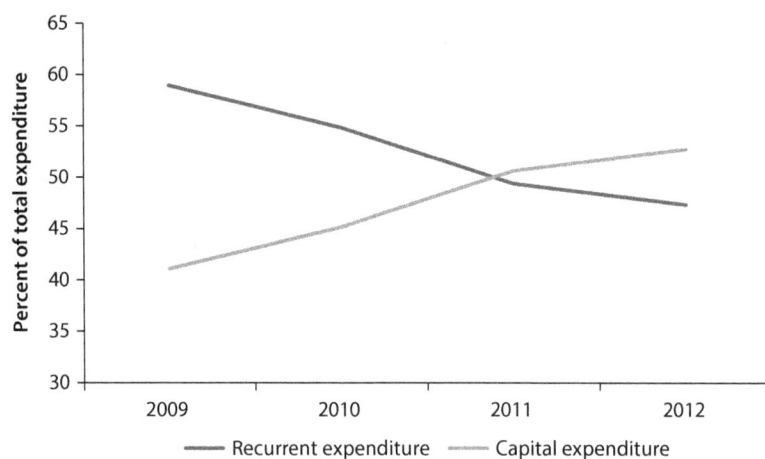

Source: Based on MFP, Budget Estimates.

Table 5.9 Spending, by Category, MYASD and All Ministries, 2012

Percent

	MYASD	All ministries
Total operational	3	68
Total development	97	32
All	100	100
Total recurrent	42	50
Total capital	58	50
All	100	100

Source: MFP, Budget Estimates.

The MYASD is spending only a tiny share of its resources on operations (table 5.9). To understand why, a detailed examination of the budget is necessary.

Recurrent Expenditure. Two-thirds of the MYASD recurrent budget is transferred to specialized ministry agencies; less than 30 percent goes to the cluster "personnel emoluments + welfare programs + retirement benefits" (table 5.10).[8] For the government as a whole, personnel emoluments and associated spending account for 58 percent of recurrent expenditure, and for the Ministry of Education (MoE), it is 70 percent. The difference is that the MYASD does not itself conduct training but instead devolves such activities to specialized agencies, which pay salaries from their budgets.

Capital Expenditure. The composition of the MYASD capital budget has changed radically in the past three years. Transfers to institutions form the largest slice

Table 5.10 Distribution of the Recurrent Budget—MYASD, MoE, and All Ministries, Various Years
Percent

	All ministries			Ministry of Youth Affairs & Skills Development			Ministry of Education
	2010–13	2010	2012	2010–13	2010	2012	2010
	Change	Composition		Change	Composition		Composition
Personnel Emoluments							
Of which:	10	38	38	19	29.00	27.0	55.0
Salaries and wages	13	21	22	17	21.00	19.0	—
Other allowances	6	15	15	26	8.00	8.0	—
Traveling expenses	6	2	2	73	0.40	0.5	0.2
Supplies	12	9	9	82	2.00	2.0	1.0
Maintenance expenditures	11	1	1	123	1.00	1.0	0.1
Services	13	5	4	67	4.00	4.0	5.0
Transfers							
Of which:	16	46	47	30	65.00	65.0	38.0
Welfare programs	18	5	5	292	0.40	1.0	25.0
Retirement benefits	28	15	17	640	0.03	0.2	—
Public institutions	17	6	6	28	63.00	62.0	1.0
Contributions to Provincial Councils	—	14	15	—	—	—	—
Total	12	100	100	30	100.00	100.0	100.0

Source: MFP, Budget Estimates.
Note: — = not applicable.

Table 5.11 Distribution of the Capital Budget—MYASD, MoE, and All Ministries, Various Years
Percent

	MYASD			MoE	All ministries
	2010	2011	2012	2011	2011
Rehabilitation and improvement of capital assets	1	2	15	19	9
Acquisition of capital assets	5	4	12	41	32
Capital transfers	37	44	51	1	15
Of which: Public institutions	37	44	50	1	10
Acquisition of financial assets	0	1	1	0	18
Human resource development	41	15	1	37	1
Other capital expenditure	16	33	21	3	24
Total	100	100	100	100	100

Source: MFP, Budget Estimates.

(and the share is increasing), exceeding by a very wide margin transfers made on average by all ministries and the MoE in particular (table 5.11).

It is possible to infer the level of budget execution by comparing actual spending with forecasts. The latter go through two steps: an estimate and then a revised estimate. The difference between the two is minimal, but the difference between estimates and actual budgets is significant. In 2010 the forecast underestimated actual spending by 10 percent; in 2011 the forecast overestimated it by almost 30 percent.[9]

Building the Skills for Economic Growth and Competitiveness in Sri Lanka
http://dx.doi.org/10.1596/978-1-4648-0158-7

Table 5.12 MYASD Transfers to Public Institutions, 2010–12

	2010	2011	2012	2012
	Value (SL Rs million)			(%)
Vocational Training Authority of Sri Lanka (VTA)	883	1,410	1,450	
National Youth Services Council (NYSC)	549	760	797	
National Apprenticeship & Industrial Training Authority (NAITA)	647	941	988	80
Ceylon German Technical Training Institute	202	277	282	
University of Vocational Technology (UNIVOTEC)	111	129	159	
National Institute of Fisheries & Nautical Engineering (Ocean University)	86	230	255	17
Tertiary and Vocational Education Commission (TVEC)	50	76	82	
National Human Resource Development Councils	19	33	39	3
Total government contribution to these institutions	*2,547*	*3,856*	*4,052*	100
Total MYASD expenditure (recurrent and capital)	5,840	8,585	8,617	

Source: MFP, Budget Estimates.

Public Agencies Supported by the MYASD. Among the eight public agencies receiving TVET funding from the MYASD, three account for one-third of the total ministry budget. Two-thirds of the recurrent MYASD budget and half of its capital budget are channeled to these eight agencies. The weight of their financing differs widely (table 5.12), as do their missions, roles, and sizes. The Vocational Training Authority of Sri Lanka (VTA), the National Youth Services Council (NYSC), and the National Apprenticeship and Industrial Training Authority (NAITA) share 80 percent of the total budget dedicated to agencies. Another three—service providers that are mostly post-secondary—receive about 17 percent (table 5.12). Finally, two councils, one of them the Tertiary and Vocational Education Commission (TVEC), share the remaining 3 percent. While the budget does not show subsidies to private providers, they do get some support from TVEC. In 2010/11, for instance, they received assistance for "contribution to the cost of machinery."[10]

Information about what public training centers operated by MYASD agencies spend is not exhaustive. Most of what is presented here comes from the Department of Technical Education and Training (DTET) institutional survey, which had four modules: training performance, staff skills, facilities, and finance. Although the survey targeted centers run by 10 MYASD agencies, financial information was provided only for NYSC and NAITA. Because survey quality is mediocre in terms of both representation and type of information reported, it needs to be interpreted with caution.

The main features emerging from the data collected from the NAITA and NYSC training centers are these (table 5.13):

- Total recurrent expenditures differ widely, with NAITA centers spending about three times more than NYSC centers.
- The disparities in capital spending are even larger.
- In both sets of centers, recurrent expenditures tend to be stable over time.

- In both, the centers spend more on capital than on recurrent items.
- The major chunk of recurrent expenditure in NYSC centers goes to remuneration of nonpermanent staff, whether teaching or not and regardless of the trade and the location.

Unit Costs

Estimating unit costs in a sector as heterogeneous as TVET is problematic. Unlike in primary education, averages say little. One factor that makes comparisons difficult is the huge variation in the duration of training programs (table 5.14). The course variations testify to the variety of TVET available and to the diversity of trainees (youth, adults, first-time job seekers, mid-career employees, school leavers, the unemployed). Ideally, the best measure of unit costs is the per-graduate cost. However, because of this diversity, costs per participant are sometimes more meaningful. In most cases, as is normal practice, unit costs are estimated on the basis of recurrent items only. However, since TVET courses are supposed to be at least partially based on equipment and machinery, estimates that include capital costs are also relevant here. The following section presents the results of two approaches, the first based on estimates completed by MYASD itself and the second on direct observations during this study.

MYASD Estimates

On average, unit costs in MYASD institutions are relatively moderate. Per-participant costs are computed for the agency as a whole, not by training center.

Table 5.13 Average Annual Expenditure, NAITA and NYSC Centers, 2009
Current SL Rs

	NAITA	NYSC
Average recurrent expenditure	467,278	180,316
Average capital expenditure	1,486,253	229,438
Average total expenditure	1,953,532	409,755
Capital expenditure as a percent of total expenditure (%)	76	56

Source: Data from the DTET survey.
Note: Data based on fewer centers.

Table 5.14 Examples of Course Duration

MoCESHC—CETRAC long-term program	3–36 months
MoCESHC—CETRAC short-term program	5–10 days
MoCESHC—OTC	5–15 days
MYASD—SDFL	1–5 days
MoH—Various programs	3–36 months
MoED—SLITHM long-term program	3 years
MoED—SLITHM short-term program	3–6 months
Western Province (Small Industries)	6–12 months
Sabaragamuwa (Industrial Development)	3–12 months
Don Bosco	6–24 months

Except for UNIVOTEC, unit costs range from SL Rs 12,000 to SL Rs 80,000 (table 5.15). The average is SL Rs 33,000 for recurrent and SL Rs 16,000 for capital elements. The share of capital expenditure varies widely, depending on the type of training.

These values take on more significance in relation to per capita GDP. With per-student recurrent spending averaging 12 percent of per capita GDP, unit costs for TVET fall between those for primary and for higher education and are slightly above the figure for all types of education (table 5.16). UNIVOTEC's figures are triple Sri Lanka's higher education average. This may be because UNIVOTEC has fewer than 500 students, significantly less than any other Sri Lankan university.

Size effect on the pattern of unit costs was tested on the eight MYASD agencies. Economies of scale are apparent in the unit cost and enrollment data for the agencies, even if UNIVOTEC is excluded (figure 5.6).

Alternative Estimates

SLITHM data made it possible to differentiate between per-participant and per-graduate costs. The former are clearly higher than was estimated for MYASD centers and closer to those for UNIVOTEC. When enrollments shot up in 2009, unit costs began to shrink (table 5.17), but the number of graduates increased much more slowly, so costs per graduate rose.

Table 5.15 Agencywide Annual Unit Costs in Public Training Centers, 2011
SL Rs 000

	Recurrent	Capital	Total
DTET	44	12	56
VTA	32	22	55
NAITA	16	12	28
NYSC	53	15	68
CGTTI	39	41	80
UNIVOTEC	262	116	377

Source: MYASD 2012.

Table 5.16 Per Student Recurrent Costs as a Percentage of Per Capita GDP, 2011
Percent

TVET, minimum[a]	6
TVET, maximum[a]	92
TVET, average[a]	12
Higher education[b]	33
Primary education[c]	7
All levels	9

Sources: a. MYASD 2012 data.
b. World Bank 2009.
c. World Bank 2011b.

Figure 5.6 Unit Costs in MYASD Agencies and Number of Participants, 2011

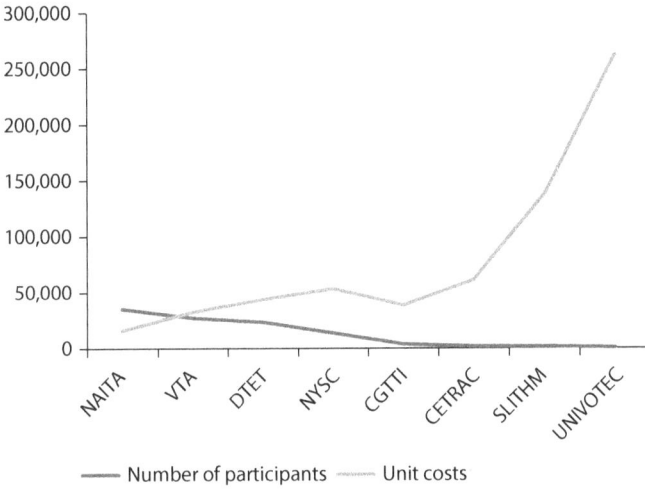

Source: MYASD data.

Table 5.17 SLITHM Annual Unit Costs, 2008–11

	2008	2009	2010	2011	Change 2008–11 (%)
Enrollees	899	1,385	1,274	1,361	51
Unit cost per enrollee (SL Rs thousand)	172	113	138	154	−11
Graduates	651	859	745	761	17
Unit cost per graduate (SL Rs thousand)	238	183	236	275	16

Source: SLITHM.

Sri Lanka's TVET unit costs appear to be midway between those for primary and for secondary education in South Asia. The 10–25 percent of per capita GDP spent on each TVET trainee falls well within the region's general education average and is about average for comparators and upper-middle-income countries (UMICs) (figure 5.7).

A final test was conducted with OECD data, which do not show per-student expenditures for TVET but do show them for postsecondary/non-tertiary education, a reasonable proxy. In general OECD per-student TVET spending is (1) significantly higher than spending on primary students; (2) similar to what is spent on upper secondary students; and (3) usually less than spending at the tertiary-type GCE A-level[11] (table 5.18). Sri Lanka seems to follow the OECD pattern.

Factors Affecting Costs and Efficiency

Though there is not enough information to decide whether a low unit cost reflects highly efficient use of resources or delivery of low-quality products, more

Figure 5.7 Per Student Expenditure as a Percentage of Per Capita GDP, Comparator Countries, 2007 and 2009

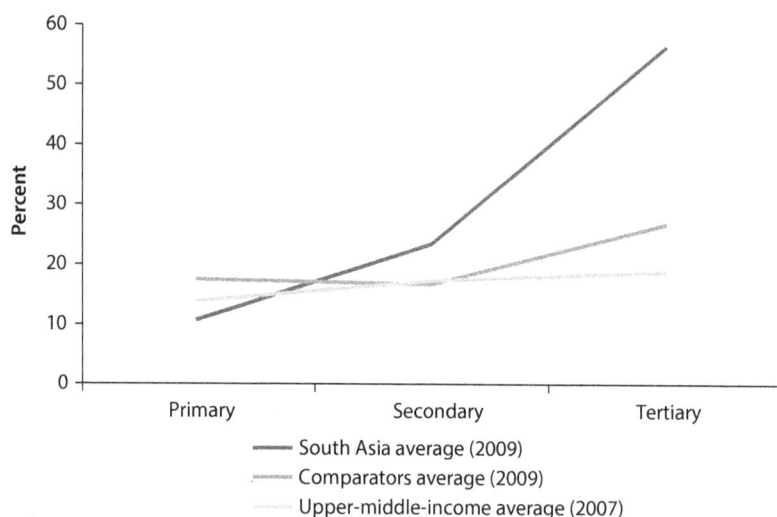

Legend:
— South Asia average (2009)
⋯ Comparators average (2009)
⋯ Upper-middle-income average (2007)

Source: UIS.

Table 5.18 Ratio of Per Student Expenditure in Postsecondary/Nontertiary Education to Per Student Expenditure in Various Levels of Education, Selected Countries, 2009

	Primary	Upper secondary	Tertiary
Czech Republic	0.5	0.3	0.2
Estonia	1.4	1.1	1.1
Germany	1.3	0.8	0.5
Hungary	1.1	1.1	0.5
Netherlands	1.5	1.0	0.7
New Zealand	1.4	1.1	0.8
Poland	1.5	1.5	1.0
South Africa	2.7	—	1.2

Source: OECD 2012, Table B1.1a.
Note: — = not available.

comprehensive investigation can illuminate the reasons for cost variations. Three aspects are reviewed here: course content, staffing, and teacher qualification. Finally, the relationship between spending and center performance is examined.

Why Costs Vary: Course Content

The obvious factor to be taken into account is the wide variety of courses that training centers offer. Skills development spans the entire spectrum of activities in agriculture, industry, and services. Unit costs in industrial disciplines are within a narrow range and there is little variation in types of courses. There is enough information from the Don Bosco Technical College and the Advanced

Technological Institutes (ATIs) to demonstrate how course type relates to the costs of industrial training. Don Bosco per trainee costs, standardized on a monthly basis, vary from about SL Rs 16,200 for welding to about SL Rs 2,300 for motorcycle mechanics—a ratio of 7 to 1. However, if the unusually high cost of welding classes is excluded, the ratio between the second-most expensive course, motor winding, and the cheapest drops to 4 to 1. Computer and bakery courses are both close to the average of about SL Rs 6,000.

Although average unit costs are higher in ATIs, they are of the same order of magnitude, though within a much narrower range. Of the four courses common to both types of institutions, three at ATIs have higher unit costs. The results suggest that the field is not a major source of cost differentiation, at least within the relatively homogeneous industrial sector, where the capital intensity of courses is fairly standard. It also appears that status and level of qualification do not affect unit costs much, even though not-for-profit centers have lower unit costs for courses leading to higher qualifications than centers run by the public sector.

Why Costs Vary: Input Mix

The share of salaries in TVET center spending is notably lower than in general education. In both Don Bosco Technical College and the ATIs (figure 5.8) salaries for academic staff represent a relatively small share of recurrent expenditure (58 percent for Don Bosco; 48 percent for ATIs). This is characteristic of TVET institutions. How their non-salary recurrent expenditures are structured differs strikingly, however, because for ATIs overhead costs exceed a third of the total as against the more usual 10 percent for the Don Bosco Technical College.

Data from provincial training centers and from the DTET survey show a more nuanced picture. While confirming that the salary bill of provincial centers can be low, it also appears that the bill can sometimes reach levels comparable to those in general education. NAITA and NYSC training centers break new ground: total remuneration (salaries for all categories of staff plus allowances) often consumes almost all the recurrent budget. However, spending linked to inputs needed for practical training is generally categorized not as recurrent but as capital expenses. NAITA and NYSC centers also tend to spend more on capital than on recurrent spending. NYSC centers devote about 57 percent of total capital expenditure to machinery and equipment and NAITA devotes anywhere from 18 percent to 100 percent for the same purpose.

Why Costs Vary: Staffing

The opportunity to practice with competent teachers on real equipment and materials (computers, engines, electrical circuits, or bakery ovens) is of utmost importance. In looking at staffing in the MYASD centers three conclusions emerge (table 5.19): (1) there are wide disparities in total staff per center; (2) trainee-to-teacher ratios average almost 40 to 1 and vary substantially but are high in many agencies[12]; and (3) the ratio of nonacademic to academic staff is more concentrated; in agencies not chiefly devoted to training, such as DTET, there is usually more than one nonteaching staff member for each teacher.

Building the Skills for Economic Growth and Competitiveness in Sri Lanka
http://dx.doi.org/10.1596/978-1-4648-0158-7

Figure 5.8 Expenditure Distribution, Don Bosco Technical College and ATIs, 2011–12

Percent

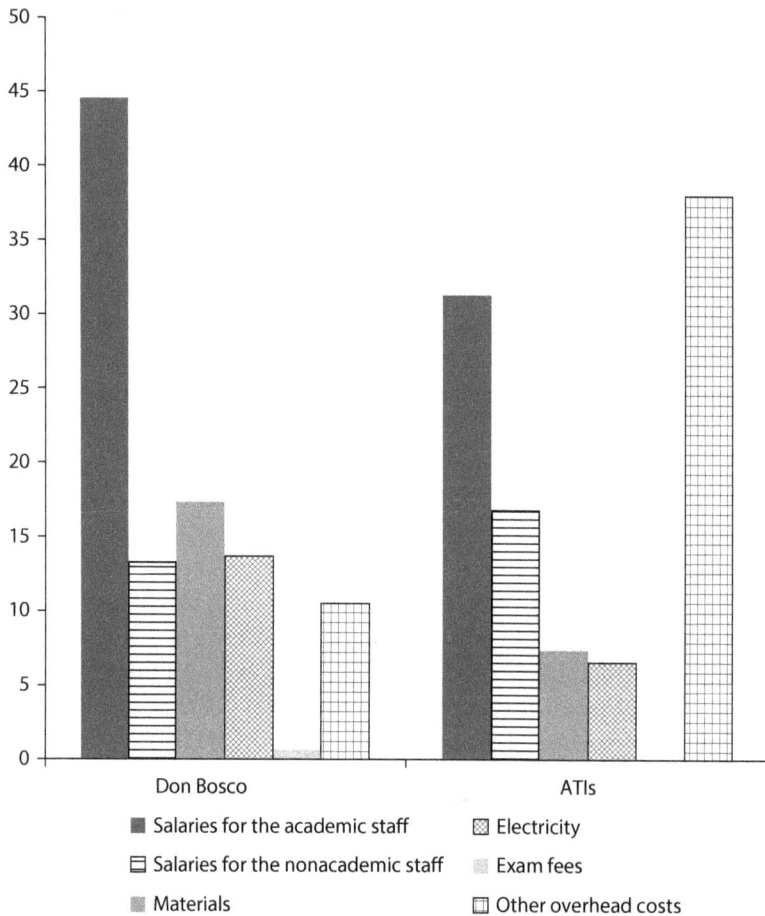

Sources: Don Bosco Technical College and ATI finance divisions.

Intensive reliance on contractual rather than permanent instructors suggests that centers attempt to maximize flexibility and responsiveness. The DTET survey of training centers found that their staffing situation varies significantly (table 5.20):

• Of the 11 NYSC centers whose responses to the survey can be considered reliable, only 5 have more than 10 staff.
• The number of nonacademic staff per instructor ranges from 0.6 to 2.5.
• The proportion of visiting or contractual academic staff varies from none to 100 percent, with a slight propensity to increase with the number of instructors.

Building the Skills for Economic Growth and Competitiveness in Sri Lanka
http://dx.doi.org/10.1596/978-1-4648-0158-7

Table 5.19 MYASD Agency Staffing Profile, 2010

	Number of centers	Total staff	Academic staff	Nonacademic staff	Total staff per center	Nonacademic staff per instructor	Trainee-to-teacher ratio
DTET	38	1,977	135	1,842	52	13.6	53
VTA	264	1,618	1,100	518	6	0.5	21
NAITA	125	626	277	349	5	1.3	88
NIBM	4	156	34	122	39	3.6	255
INGRIN	1	26	15	11	26	0.7	47
UNIVOTEC	1	166	44	122	166	2.8	10
CGTTI	2	223	152	71	112	0.5	2
SLIOP	1	32	28	4	32	0.1	31
NYSC	36	538	369	169	15	0.5	32
ICTRL	1	73	14	59	73	4.2	156
All	473	5,435	2,168	3,267	11	1.5	37

Source: MFP Medium-Term Public Investment Outlook for Skills Education Sector (2012–16).

Table 5.20 NYSC Centers: Staffing Composition and Status, 2011

Center #	Total staff	Total academic staff	Total non-academic staff	Non-academic staff per instructor	Visiting/contractual academic staff	Permanent academic staff	Ratio of permanent to visiting/contractual staff
1	12	5	7	1.4	2	3	1.5
2	7	2	5	2.5	1	1	1.0
3	14	6	8	1.3	3	3	1.0
4	7	3	4	1.3	0	3	—
5	5	2	3	1.5	1	1	1.0
6	6	4	2	0.5	0	4	—
7	9	7	2	0.3	7	0	0.0
8	9	5	4	0.8	0	5	—
9	12	3	9	3.0	0	3	—
10	11	7	4	0.6	7	0	0.0
11	20	8	12	1.5	0	8	—
	112	52	60	1.2	21	31	1.5

Source: DTET survey data.
Note: — = not available.

Staffing held steady for 2006–11 in terms of both total volume and composition (academic, nonacademic, permanent, contractual).

Although they are generally seasoned teachers, most center instructors lack solid experience in industry. NAITA centers rely more heavily on contractual teachers, who comprise on average 88 percent of all their instructors.[13] Even though in general education such high dependence on nonpermanent staff could be considered a weakness, for vocational training it may reflect the agility of

Building the Skills for Economic Growth and Competitiveness in Sri Lanka
http://dx.doi.org/10.1596/978-1-4648-0158-7

centers in reacting to ever-changing demands. The many small centers cannot afford to keep a sizable number of permanent staff; instead, they call upon external instructors, who are also more likely to have industrial experience.

Drawing on external instructors can serve institutions well if the teachers have the required qualifications and expertise. This seems generally to be the case (DTET survey). In both NYSC and NAITA centers, the overwhelming majority of instructors have at least completed a vocational degree[14] and also have solid teaching experience (table 5.21).[15] However, their industrial experience is not broad. Not even half the NAITA instructors have more than one year of practical experience. This is a source of concern; practical experience should be a condition for teaching in vocational training centers.

Financial incentives are not sufficient to attract and retain qualified instructors, especially in the public sector. The third ingredient from a costing perspective is remuneration. On average, permanent TVET instructional staff in public training centers are better off than their MoE counterparts. For instance, monthly entry-level salaries for DTET civil servants start at SL Rs 22, 935, significantly higher than the SL Rs 16,100 for starting teachers in school. In the SLITHM, assistant lecturers begin at a monthly salary of SL Rs 24,725, and senior lecturers start at SL Rs 32,550. The difference is accentuated by the number of years in service (figure 5.9). Salary is only part of the total remuneration,[16] which includes various allowances, but those are similar in the two ministries. By and large, salaries of civil servants are lower than for workers in the private sector with the same qualifications.[17]

The scenario is different for nonpermanent staff, who are often the real pool of instructors because they give centers the flexibility to adjust numbers and types of trainers to market demand. They are usually paid by the hour. Informal sources suggest that the hourly rate ranges from SL Rs 175 in the public sector to SL Rs 500 in the private. In comparison, the hourly minimum wage on plantations is SL Rs 515.[18] Assuming that contract trainers work three hours a day three days a week, they would earn about SL Rs 6,800 a month in the public sector and nearly SL Rs 19,400 in the private sector. In the public sector, then, they earn the equivalent of the minimum wage for unskilled or semiskilled permanent workers. (However, the comparison cannot be carried too far: nonpermanent instructors most likely hold several jobs, either in different training centers or away from TVET, since they can scarcely make a living working part-time in a single center.)

Table 5.21 Qualification and Experience of NYSC and NAITA Academic Staff, 2011

	Number of academic staff	Percent with at least a GCE A/L	Percent with at least one year of industrial experience	Percent with at least one year of teaching experience
NYSC	140	88	61	90
NAITA	76	74	46	71

Source: DTET survey.
Note: Figures are only indicative because of possible errors in interpreting questionnaires.

Training Center Revenues

Public TVET centers rarely seek alternative sources of income, such as what they could generate from their own productive activities. They recover some of their costs through fees. Private for-profit and NGO centers have more diversified revenues. Most revenues for public centers are allocations from ministry budgets. Opportunities to tap other sources of funds are limited by constraining regulations; they are more common in centers that do not receive public support.

Still, there are some special cases, such as the MoCESHCA centers. The OTC and the CETRAC get less than half their revenues from the government (table 5.22), and fees are charged for several of their offerings.

The two centers operating as part of the ICTAD Institute, especially the CETRAC, bring in revenues from renting out facilities and equipment, testing, workshop repairs, seminars and customized courses for targeted audiences, and

Figure 5.9 Earning Profiles of School Teachers, Principals, and SLITHM Assistant Lecturers

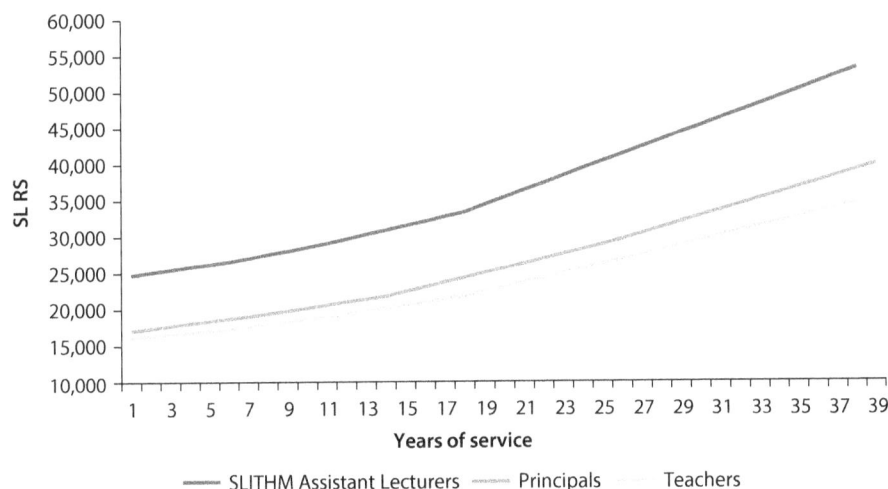

Source: Teachers and principals: Public Administration Circular No: 06/2006(VIII); SLITHM assistant lecturers: SLITHM.
Note: The SLITHM earning curve is based on the assumption that promotion rules for SLITHM lecturers are the same as those for teachers.

Table 5.22 CETRAC and OTC: Government Grants and Other Incomes, 2007–11
Current SL Rs million

| | CETRAC | | | | OTC | | | |
	Government grants	Other income	Total income	Government grants/ total income (%)	Government grants	Other income	Total income	Government grants/ total income (%)
2007	8	15	23	35	11	15	26	42
2008	12	14	26	46	13	20	33	39
2009	12	13	25	48	13	20	32	41
2010	12	11	23	52	14	20	34	41
2011	12	17	29	41	15	22	37	41

Source: Ministry of Construction, Engineering Services, Housing and Common Amenities.

Building the Skills for Economic Growth and Competitiveness in Sri Lanka
http://dx.doi.org/10.1596/978-1-4648-0158-7

consultancy services. This suggests that public institutions can diversify their revenues despite the regulatory straightjacket. Realistically, however, such possibilities are open only to centers in urban areas.

The ICTAD centers are not the only examples of state-controlled training centers managing to diversify their resources. The six SLITHM hotel schools draw revenues from training activities, renting facilities, and charges for meals. Except in 2008 and 2009, these accounted for one-third to two-thirds of their total income. Four of the six hotel schools did run deficits over the last five years, but management issues seem to have been the main problem.[19] The VTA's Hotel School in Ahangama charges outsiders a minimal fee for use of its facilities.

SLITHM has a variety of income sources, including the proceeds of two levies: The Tourism Development Tax, levied on airline and ship voyage tickets, goes entirely to the Ceylon Tourist Board to be used to promote Sri Lanka tourism, with part of it earmarked for SLITHM.[20] The Embarkation Tax, paid by every traveler leaving Sri Lanka by air or sea, fuels two special funds, portions of which are also channeled to SLITHM.[21] Together, since 2008 these have accounted for 75–81 percent of total SLITHM revenues; fees represent about 15 percent (table 5.23). Unlike its hotel schools, SLITHM manages to make a profit from its activities.

Although quite common in many countries, channeling monies through a national competitive fund is not a mainstream approach for TVET in Sri Lanka. The only significant example is the Skills Development Fund Ltd.(SDFL), which has been dormant for several years. This fund, which is available for MYASD agencies and also for industry-based training, is thus only a marginal source of TVET financing.

The education offices in the Western Province are an example of public training centers that have income-generating programs. About 40 such programs are managed by the Department of Examinations centers in Colombo, Kalutara, and Gampaha districts. They cover fields as diverse as hand sewing, beauty culture, computers, woodwork, and electrical work, all of which are offered to unemployed school leavers.

Table 5.23 SLITHM Sources of Revenue, 2008–11

Percent

Year	Tourism development levy (TDL)[a]	Embarkation levy	Government grants	Student fees and other income[b]	Other income[c]	Income/profit from Hotel Samudrad	Loan income	Total income
2008	78.9	—	—	17.7	2.7	0.7	0.1	100
2009	24.1	50.4	1.2	14.5	2.6	7.0	0.1	100
2010	53.9	25.7	—	13.4	0.9	6.1	0.1	100
2011	26.9	53.7	—	14.0	0.8	4.5	0.1	100

Sources: Annual Accounts Data Base, SLITH Management, MoED 2008, 2009, 2010 & 2011.

Note: — = not available.

a. For 2008, the figure shows the sum of the two taxes.

b. Student fees and other income includes fees for the full-time courses and tailor-made or part-time courses of the hotel schools, payment of special assignments, income from travel and tourism, and hotel schools income.

c. Other income includes leasing facilities, auctions, and sales income for restaurant meals.

Table 5.24 Sources of TVET Funding, Bangladesh, 2007
Percent

	Public institutions		Private institutions	
	Vocational education	*Vocational training*	*Vocational education*	*Vocational training*
Government grants	75.2	69.0	54.6	0.0
Tuition and other fees	4.9	20.1	14.5	76.8
Sale of products	3.2	6.0	7.3	0.8
Income from training	4.9	0.0	9.2	6.5
Others	11.8	4.9	14.4	15.9
Total	100	100	100	100

Source: World Bank 2007.

The general pattern seen in Sri Lanka, especially the heavy reliance on public funds, is not unique. The model is characteristic of countries that have not yet relaxed rules against alternative sources of financing. Bangladesh demonstrates that revenues generated by public centers for vocational training or education are minimal and those generated by private centers are small compared to the fees they charge (table 5.24).

The Trainee Perspective: Fees and Allowances

Although generally low or zero fees combined with small allowances to attend courses are meant to lure trainees, they are not a sufficient incentive to either attract or retain them. In some cases, such as adult trainees currently employed or looking for a job, however, trainees both contribute to the cost of courses and are also compensated for the opportunity cost linked to attending them.

Four categories of courses are offered free to trainees: (1) some courses provided by centers (for instance, in the Western Province short-term agriculture department courses and all programs run by the Department of Small Industries); (2) courses in specified disciplines; (3) courses for specific audiences (for instance, government employees in agriculture taking courses at the agriculture department's Bomuwala Institute in the Western Province); and (4) a combination of the last two (for instance, school-leavers attending the 3-year CETRAC program on construction equipment and mechanical maintenance).

For other courses, fees are charged by the day for short-term courses and by the month for medium- and long-term courses. Fees vary widely depending on trade and discipline, type of organization, and clientele. They tend to be higher for courses in hydraulic system maintenance, motor mechanics, hospitality, and computer studies. Looking at the short-term courses offered by SLITHM, CETRAC, OTC, and Don Bosco centers, the ratios of highest to lowest fees vary from 1.3 to 13.4 (table 5.25). Based on the SLITHM, CETRAC, and OTC centers, the relationship between fees and unit costs seems rather loose in the public sector (0–28 percent of per-trainee costs). At the Don Bosco centers, fees make up 23–73 percent of unit costs.

Table 5.25 Fee Ranges, Selected Training Centers, 2011 or Nearest Year
Current SL Rs

	Daily		Monthly		Total	
	Minimum	*Maximum*	*Minimum*	*Maximum*	*Minimum*	*Maximum*
CETRAC	1,800	4,700	—	—	3,500	18,000
Don Bosco	1,000	1,500	—	—	9,000	30,000
OTC	600	3,800	—	—	3,000	40,250
SLITHM	—	—	3,000	3,500	9,000	21,000
SDFL	4,000	4,500	—	—	—	—

Source: Information provided by the centers.
Note: Total fees include admission and monthly fees. — = not applicable.

Allowances paid to trainees are meant to incentivize attendance, attract target groups, and compensate for foregone gainful activities. In some cases (for example, unemployed school leavers), trainees do not have to pay fees. In 2000, a Public Administration Circular established that trainees attending practical training in public institutions should be paid a daily allowance. However, it adds that with few exceptions (NAITA and ATIs), practical training should be limited to six months and the allowance should be paid "only if necessary provision is available" and no other allowance or remuneration is made. In 2012, the daily allowance was SL Rs 500. In all cases, allowances are small, and always lower than the fees charged.

Allocation Mechanisms

Finance Act No. 38 of 1971 and related regulations spell out the mechanism for allocating funds to public institutions. Ministries and departments, state corporations, boards, and other corporate bodies, non-profit-oriented public corporations, and public institutions can obtain budgetary support from line ministries. Even if support is not sought, project plans are to be sent to the Department of National Planning (DNP), which appraises all projects submitted for parliamentary approval and prepares related plans as part of its Public Investment Program (PIP). The National Budget Department prepares budget estimates for the following fiscal year based on estimates finalized by the DNP.

The 2012–14 PIP projects a significant increase in TVET investments. About 74 percent are expected to be funded from foreign sources—a testimony to how much the sector depends on sources not fully under the control of sector authorities. In 2012, after extensive negotiations, the MYASD was finally allocated 76 percent of its initial request.

The budgeting process is arbitrary, relates neither to performance nor to national priorities, and seems to be opaque and inefficient. Budget estimates are based on the traditional "negotiated" approach. Even allocation of recurrent expenditures is not strictly based on inputs, such as number of students. Budget estimates do not take into account such outcome indicators as student and employer satisfaction with the quality and relevance of training. How Sri Lanka allocates funding to TVET is thus suboptimal. A major problem is that the largest increases go to the institutions that spent the most in the past, no matter whether they did so efficiently or whether they made efforts to improve access and course quality and relevance.

Public TVET providers may charge fees for part-time courses, and public enterprises may revise their charges and prices to yield an operational surplus so that they can meet current expenses from the funds generated. However, this policy does not incentivize public TVET providers to be innovative, since any income they raise is deducted from their budget allocations. Earned income is not treated as income that can be used for institutional development.

Audit

Public TVET institutions are audited at two levels. First, the Internal Audit Unit (IAU) ascertains whether financial reporting standards are being followed and whether the use of resources is appropriate. It also verifies the reliability of accounting, appraises how well staff carry out their tasks, and assists in monitoring progress made on development work undertaken by the institutions. However, the IAU is mostly a reporting agency.

The Auditor General also reviews the accounts and submits a report to the Committee on Public Enterprises of the Parliament, which reviews public institution performance on the basis of the Auditor General's report. While this can be considered a useful policy measure to make public TVET providers aware of their ultimate responsibility to Parliament, it does not ensure that they will be financially accountable in terms of fulfilling expected development targets.

Governance and Management

The preceding sections suggest both underinvestment in TVET and inefficient use of resources. However, financing practices and performance are heavily contingent upon the governance environment within which stakeholders operate. In Sri Lanka, the situation is complicated by the heterogeneity of the sector and the gap between official procedures and actual practices. This section reviews allocation mechanisms, accountability, autonomy, and planning and oversight.

Accountability and Autonomy

The central authorities tightly control the expenses of public TVET providers, yet providers are not held accountable for performance and have no real incentives to respond to, much less anticipate, demand. Officially, public TVET providers have considerable autonomy, but in fact, they are all strictly supervised by the government, which is their main revenue source. Although the SDFL should be a special case because of its public/private nature, in fact the Treasury appoints all the members and the chair of its governing board.[22]

The Tertiary and Vocational Education Act sets out TVET governance arrangements and related financial regulations. Most MYASD institutions were instituted post-1978. Dependence on public funds often translates into central administrative control and ministry micromanagement (for example, staffing). Central control makes it hard for institutions to plan strategically.

Planning, Information, and Oversight

Public TVET is both supply-driven and poorly coordinated. The TVEC prepares a corporate strategic plan with sector-specific goals and targets. Each public provider prepares plans according to MFP guidelines. The development framework of the government gives directives for equal access to education, quality jobs, secured living, maintaining quality standards, and offering productive educational opportunities for young people. Although it also states that "the technical education and vocational training of the country will change into a demand-driven and cost-effective system," it gives no guidelines or instruments to achieve this reasonable objective.

The main obstacle in planning to reach this objective is the lack of information from employers about demand, both current and expected. TVEC's Labor Market Information Unit publishes useful data on employment and unemployment and also on job advertisements. However, informal discussions suggest that providers do not systematically use the information available; and as is common around the world, employers have difficulties forecasting their medium-term needs, which depend heavily on the economic situation, global and local. For these reasons, TVET strategic planning is simply an administrative requirement, not an attempt to forecast client and stakeholder needs.

The governing boards of TVET institutions are dominated by public servants and tend to be more regulative than market-driven. Except for the broad policy directives of the MC, there is nothing to ensure managerial efficiency and accountability. Executives of public TVET institutions tend to lack management flexibility. Confronted with acute financial problems and quality crises, they are not in a position to adopt innovative financing strategies. Most are even less prepared to plan for the long term.

Secretaries in supervising ministries are accountable for the funds released to public TVET providers. Similarly, TVET agency governing boards are managed by civil servants and, hewing close to regulations, are not efficiency-driven. Moreover, public TVET directors are given neither clear-cut policy directives nor the authority to work directly with employers even if the opportunity were to arise. They are often appointed through political connections rather than experience in training.

With more than a dozen ministries engaged in TVET, there is a desperate need to ensure that all TVET activities are working together to meet national development targets. The Human Resource Council has yet to fulfill this function. However, public providers seem to be guided by goals that the TVEC sets with the supervising ministry. For example, over the last 10 years the TVEC has prepared 18 vocational education and training plans for industry subsectors. Thus, its efforts look beyond the short term. However, the very limited public and private exchange of information inhibits development of a truly agile TVET sector that is responsive to a dynamic economy.

The Future

TVET could have a bright financial future in Sri Lanka if the resources available were ramped up and linked to demand, if delivery were more efficient, and if there were a culture of governance leading to greater institutional autonomy and accountability.

The forecasted 8 percent GDP growth should lead to a 19 percent increase in public revenues. For such optimistic projections to materialize, though, the economy needs a steady stream of skilled labor. However, employers in Sri Lanka consistently complain that a lack of skilled workers is the major impediment to expanding their businesses.

The situation is not unique to Sri Lanka. According to the latest Talent Shortage Survey by the ManpowerGroup (2012), skilled workers and technicians—the two categories that would benefit most from TVET—are the first and the fourth kinds of jobs employers globally have the most difficulty filling. In 23 of 41 countries surveyed, these two categories are among the 10 most difficult jobs to fill. According to another survey of 25 countries, from the United States to India, 36 percent of employers mention skills shortage as the leading cause of entry-level vacancies (McKinsey 2012).

Because quality TVET services are vital for building and sustaining a pool of skilled workers responsive to employer needs, it is logical that TVET should have an expanded share of the public spending that can be expected in Sri Lanka. However, public resources will always be constrained, and private employers are the main source of demand for skilled labor. Hence, public funding will have to be increasingly complemented by other sources of funds, mainly from employers themselves.

The real challenge is to align the incentives for both demand and supply of training. The challenge is somewhat different for on-the-job training (OJT) than for training provided externally. With OJT, employers are the source of both demand and supply, which logically makes them the chief decision makers. With external training, employers are only on the demand side, but they could still be a source of funding.

From the workers' perspective, the main obstacles to attending and completing a TVET program are financial: not having enough resources to pay fees and daily subsistence costs, and the opportunity cost of not being gainfully employed while being trained. Both employers and workers also find it difficult to access full information about TVET and its benefits. These are all market failures that justify state regulation and financing.

Across the world, since the early 2000s there has emerged a broad consensus about funding TVET activities (table 5.26), based on a few general principles: diversification of funding sources through cost-sharing, income generation, training levies on enterprises, and decentralization. National training funds, vouchers,

Table 5.26 Emerging Policy Consensus on Financing Vocational Training

Funding diversification	Diversification of sources of funding; greater cost recovery and cost-sharing
Cost-sharing	More realistic training fees, with scholarships and possibly state-backed loans for needy trainees
Training levies	Levied on enterprises
Income generation	Public training institutions generate, and keep, income from their own activities
Decentralization	Greater institutional autonomy for public sector providers
Private sector	Public support to private provision of training
Consumer choice	Vouchers made available to trainees in order to develop demand side
Levy-grant system	Introduction of levy-grant system in case of formal sector underinvestment in training
Training funds	Development of national training funds to promote long-term view of training expenditures

Source: Adapted from Ziderman 2003.

and various kinds of stimuli to private provision are the main mechanisms advocated.

Most of these principles could apply to Sri Lanka. However, with additional experience from a more diversified sample of countries, emphasis has shifted to the "right" incentives and the "right" governance of a scheme. Providing incentives to stimulate both demand for and supply of effective training has particular reverberation in Sri Lanka.

A foundational point is that, regardless of their source, revenues should be allocated at least in part on the basis of performance. Consider what is happening in tertiary education. Concerned about the lack of alignment between what colleges and universities offer and what employers need, the National Governors Association in the United States recommends:

> Use performance–based funding for institutions of higher education to get—and reward—outcomes aligned with state strategic goals. Plus, award funds on a competitive basis to develop industry-oriented curricula and create new efforts to meet the workforce needs of specific key sectors (NGA 2011).

These concerns and recommendations are even more relevant for TVET institutions, whose raison d'être is precisely to ready individuals for the labor market, especially in sectors that have strategic priority.

Opportunities to make the system more responsive to the real needs of the economy and the expectations of labor do exist. These can be clustered in terms of public funding at the central level, institutional financing, and governance. Several of the policy options presented here are already in effect or on trial in Sri Lanka, and many others are being considered. The following menu links proposed actions both with problems identified here and with lessons learned in other countries.

Public Funding

Rather than a specific increase in the amount or rate of public monies allocated to TVET, what would serve the sector better is action in the short and medium term to make service provision more efficient and strike the right balance in allocating funds to training institutions and trainees to boost demand and improve supply.

Funding Providers (Supply Side). Financial support for the MYASD and the other ministries that manage their own centers comes from the general budget and from donor support. Although the share of foreign funding had been sinking until 2011, recent forecasts suggest it may be bouncing back. It would be in the interests of the entire TVET sector if MYASD were to manage its relationship with its foreign counterparts to reduce unevenness and uncertainty and align their support with the national skills development strategy.

When public providers use funds to finance training for their own staff, the state is at once financer, provider, and employer. This may appear to be an optimal situation, allowing a community of interests and facilitating decisions. However, it also raises the risk of conflicts of interest, or at least a confusion of roles. This is not necessarily conducive to efficiency or accountability. Therefore, it is advisable that funding decisions be made separately from allocation and provision decisions.

What generally happens, however, is that central budget funds buffer institutions (for example, VTA, NYSC) that manage training centers or subsidize schools, colleges, or centers. Because of this blanket financing, these institutions and centers need not be particularly concerned about the demand for training services; nor do they have to maximize their efficiency. It could be beneficial for Sri Lanka to link funding more tightly to national priorities; performance (as measured, for example, by graduation, retention, or employment rates); and targeted groups (such as school leavers or women). It is also conceivable to channel monies to public providers through a national training fund.

Block grants can be used to fund either public or private providers of occupational skills, but they are more common in general education than in TVET, where the nature of the product (skills) can change quickly, and trainees and trainers are both heterogeneous. The Indonesian experience, the *Kursus Para Profesi* (KPP), has had mixed results. The KPP was expected to address access, equity, and quality issues, with equity the main objective. It provided block grants on a per-trainee basis to private providers that met specified criteria. The KPP evaluation concluded that "conditional block grants by themselves are unlikely to incentivize training providers to improve quality or change targeting mechanisms" (World Bank 2010). Block grants, particularly those with equity objectives, need to be carefully regulated and accompanied by demand-side interventions.

Contracting with private partners to operate services in public training centers could improve the quality of delivery. Public-private partnerships (PPPs) have been tried in both general and professional education globally, with positive results. Activities that governments can contract out to private companies are (1) management, professional, and support services (including meals and transportation, teacher training, and quality assurance) and facility availability;

Table 5.27 Options for PPPs in Infrastructure

Design and build	The government contracts with a private partner to design and build a facility to specific requirements.
Operations and maintenance	The government contracts with a private partner to operate a publicly owned facility.
Turnkey operations	The government provides financing; the private partner designs, builds, and operates a facility for a specified time period; but the public partner retains ownership of the facility.
Lease-purchase	The private partner leases a facility to the government for a specified period, after which ownership is vested in the government.
Lease- or own-develop-operate	The private partner leases or buys a facility from the government and develops and operates the facility under contract with the government for a specified period.
Build-operate-transfer	The private partner has an exclusive contract to finance, build, operate, maintain, manage, and collect user fees for a facility for a fixed period to amortize its investment; afterwards it transfers title to the government.
Build-own-operate	The government contracts with a private partner to build, own, and operate a new facility in perpetuity.

Source: Adapted from Patrinos, Barrera-Osorio, and Guáqueta 2009.

(2) operational services (processes); (3) education and training services with specific outcome goals; and (4) a combination of these.[23] Although facility availability is the most common PPP model (table 5.27), those focused on training are likely to be most useful for TVET, since quality, a major weakness currently, can be addressed by well-designed arrangements with reliable firms. The government might identify areas where PPPs could be most efficient, the public providers most likely to benefit from PPPs, and the private partners most likely to add value.

Public support to private providers is also a serious option, given the important role they already play. With support, however, comes the need to regulate a still disorganized market and to protect consumers; establishment of the National Vocational Qualification (NVQ) was a critical step in that direction. Registration, accreditation, certification, and quality assurance are mechanisms to regulate a market where for-profit organizations, local and international NGOs, informal training boutiques, and established training centers can coexist, either competing with each other or operating in protected niches. Supporting such a heterogeneous group of suppliers is not easy, and there are real risks of not doing it efficiently and equitably, especially if support is in the form of direct funding for specific centers. One of the most promising alternatives is organization of national competitive funds for all registered centers.

As long as conditions are in place to make them credible and efficient, budget-financed competitive funds could promote quality delivery by both private and public providers. Such funds have proved effective in promoting quality higher education, though the conditions for their success may be more difficult to fulfill in TVET, which is far more heterogeneous. The most critical conditions are absolute transparency, clarity, and objectivity in selection criteria and processes. Such funds also require that competition be organized so that the strongest players do not always win and the weakest do not inevitably lose, which would defeat the purpose. The field of competition needs to be organized in tiers of institutions of similar experience, size, or trade. Other requirements are training for potential applicants and an effective monitoring system to periodically assess the performance of awardees. Finally, competitive funds have to be financially sustainable over the long run so that there is mobility among providers and confidence in the merits of the scheme.

Funding Employers (Demand Side). A training fund could be piloted, provided that a careful feasibility study is completed, full partnership with employers is enforced, full-fledged capacity-building is undertaken, and there is a rigorous tax collection system in place. Employers have an interest in hiring employees whose skills will make them more productive. Finding workers with technical skills at an intermediate level (upper secondary and postsecondary) is not easy, whether a country is developed or developing. It is good public policy to encourage enterprises to invest in such skills for both internal and external training. As training funds have begun to proliferate around the globe, some general principles are emerging about the conditions in which they are likely to meet their objectives (see, for instance: Adams 2008; Almeida, Behrman, and Robalino 2012; Dar 2004; Dar, Canagarajah, and Murphy 2003; Johanson 2009).

Regardless of whether they primarily target pre-employment or enterprise training, training funds are customarily categorized on the basis of how they are funded: revenue-raising or revenue-generating schemes and levy disbursement (incentive) schemes. The former are usually run by government entities; the latter, which are more common, are often administered as PPPs. Levy disbursement schemes use three main types of financing:

- *Cost reimbursement*: all firms pay the tax, but firms that invest in training are reimbursed, partially or in full, for training expenses.
- *Levy grant*: all firms pay the tax, but firms that invest in training receive a grant (conditional on some criteria but not strictly linked with specific training that the firms have invested in).
- *Levy exemption* (payroll tax exemption): only firms that do not invest in training pay the tax. This mode is based on a simple principle: train or pay.

Each of these modalities has benefits and disadvantages, depending on the country (especially its fiscal regime). What matters for both, however, is how the fund is managed and the capacity of the governing body to collect the funds, channel them efficiently, and translate priorities into concrete programs. Other issues relate to the buy-in of the partner enterprises, which may divert the schemes to purposes other than what was intended. Training funds are usually fed through financing mechanisms outside the regular budget. Usually an advantage, this can become a problem during an economic downturn. One common problem of levy-financed funds, too, is that they seem to be unable to benefit small firms. Some general principles have been identified to avoid the main problems (box 5.1).

Box 5.1 General Principles for Payroll Levy Schemes

- Levies should be subject to periodic review.
- Levies should vary by sector or industry to reflect the differing skills composition of the labor force and training needs.
- The system should be designed and administered in a way that encourages small as well as large employers to participate.
- Training authorities should not venture into extraneous activities.
- The range of training services and courses provided should reflect employer needs.
- Levies should be used to promote training by enterprises.

Source: Dar 2004.

Box 5.2 Redistribution of the Vocational Training Tax in Tunisia

- **A tax credit system**: Spending on vocational training is considered as an advance deductible from the VTT (up to 60 percent of the VTT paid in the previous year). Beneficiaries are companies subject to the VTT that have paid a tax amount above a fixed threshold.
- **A drawing rights system**: Businesses participating in apprenticeship programs benefit from subsidies to finance lifelong-learning programs for their employees. Beneficiaries are (1) companies exempted from the VTT; (2) companies subject to the VTT that did not use the tax credit system; and (3) companies that have used up all their tax credit rights.
- **Investment incentives**: Companies financing technological investments benefit from a subsidy covering up to 50 percent of personnel training expenses.

Source: World Bank 2011b.

Perhaps the most debated issue of training funds is how they should be financed. The underlying principle is to build a tax system that rewards investment in training. Usually the financing source is payroll taxes. In Tunisia, for instance, the Vocational Training Tax (VTT) is a compulsory tax on company payrolls that accounts for 13 percent of total public spending on vocational training. The VTT feeds into the Vocational Training and Apprenticeship Promotion Fund, which redistributes the proceeds of the tax through three different channels (box 5.2).

Regardless of how levy schemes are organized, payroll taxes are likely to act as a deterrent to hiring, which would defeat the employment-linked function of training; therefore, it seems preferable to finance the scheme from taxes on sales or profits. The performance of such funds is chiefly a matter of proper targeting so that they do not benefit large firms only[24]—a particular concern in Sri Lanka, where small firms and the informal sector predominate. It is also critical to carefully monitor what kind of training has been reimbursed or has led to a grant or a tax exemption so that the scheme is not distorted by a large pool of noncompliers and free-riders.

Funding Trainees (Demand Side). In helping trainees to defray the costs of attending TVET courses, mechanisms that allow a broad choice of institutions could be given priority. Encouraging firms to invest in training is important, but it will not be effective if individuals are reluctant to be trained. Although money is not the only obstacle, it has an obvious role. Financial incentives to potential trainees differ depending on the stage on their life path (for example, school graduates, pre-employment, in-service, mid-career) and their exposure to financial risks.

Generally, scholarships, fee exemptions, grants, and loans are used to attract youngsters to training centers. However, these mechanisms have to be adjusted to the specific needs of the students based on the direct cost of training and the opportunity cost of attending. Conversely, there are limitations on raising individual subsidies: (1) in the aggregate the costs can become a problem; (2) targeting the most vulnerable beneficiaries (especially through fee exemptions and scholarships) is complex and prone to errors (exclusion or mistaken inclusion); and (3) subsidies associated with a specific provider do not necessarily resolve the issue. It is mainly to overcome this last problem that voucher schemes have been launched to allow a choice of providers.[25]

An interesting finding of the voucher scheme targeting young adults in Kenya (Hicks *et al.* 2011) was that unrestricted vouchers, usable for either public or private programs, were associated with higher enrollments and lower dropout rates than public-program-only vouchers. In Tunisia, vouchers covering 65–85 percent of training costs target underprivileged students, are limited to priority sectors, and subsidize initial training provided by accredited private operators. Sri Lanka might consider such models to increase the participation of low-income youth.

Similarly, in India, the Pratham Institute for Literacy, Education and Vocational Training provides courses to get trainees employment-ready at very low cost. For the most expensive fields, such as hospitality, trainees pay only a portion of the tuition upfront and the rest in monthly installments or even after securing a job (which most do almost immediately on graduating). The Pratham program also gives a stipend to trainees who successfully complete the construction course, which helps them to transition from the school environment to the world of work (Pratham 2012).

Individual Learning Accounts (ILAs) are a special version of vouchers. Mostly found in Europe, ILA schemes are based on lifelong savings by employees, matched by the state's contribution in the form of a tax deduction or increasing interest payments. The proceeds of the savings are used exclusively for training purposes (Cedefop 2009).

Apprenticeship incorporates a contract that includes remuneration for the trainee. Even though it is usually less than the legal minimum wage, it nevertheless gives the apprentice hands-on training at no cost. Apprenticeship also provides cheap labor for the enterprise, practical skills acquisition for the apprentice, and usually good employment prospects. Apprenticeship is particularly well-adapted to the case of small and medium enterprises because it reduces the risk for both parties of a mismatch when the trainee gets a job at the end of the apprenticeship period. Apprenticeship is also well adapted to informal economies, where it bonds a usually very small entrepreneur, often self-employed, with one or two apprentices, often relatives.[26]

However, apprenticeships are increasingly being used to tackle large-scale youth unemployment.[27] Apprenticeships are common in Switzerland, which has record low unemployment and a highly flexible labor market and where employers realize that the costs are largely outweighed by the benefits (Muehlemann *et al.* 2007). "Apprenticeship 2000" is a special cross-country partnership scheme set up by branches of two German companies operating in the United States in order to secure a pipeline of employees with specialized skills. Companies commit themselves to cover the costs of the training for up to five years, but to preserve the return on the investment all members of the program are required to sign a non-poaching agreement (McKinsey 2012).

Several countries have engaged in schemes mirroring apprenticeship in a systematic way that may be of interest to Sri Lanka. The experience of community colleges may be particularly relevant, despite the different context, because they address both the economic demand for skills and the equity issues. Harper College in Illinois, for example, offers an 18-month program that includes internships in local companies.[28] Students start with six months of classroom study and earn an industry certificate; move on to an internship, earning a specialized certificate; and return for theoretical studies, after which they graduate with an associate degree. In addition to the benefits of exposure to both theory and practice, the students earn a stipend during their internship. The program was inspired by the German Fraunhofer model.[29]

Financing at the Institution Level

Tapping sources of inefficiency and generating revenues from the sale of byproducts of training activities are strategies with substantial potential in Sri Lanka. Given the financial constraints, for training institutions to be able to deliver quality and relevant training services they must be efficient in the use of resources and diversify the sources of their funds.

Maximizing efficiency should be an absolute objective of any institution regardless of the goods or services it supplies; institutions should not use more inputs than are required to produce a given amount and level of training. In Sri Lanka, resources are used suboptimally mainly in the management of staff; in particular, too many instructors get very low salaries. Exacerbating this problem is the fact that promotion is independent of performance, so that accountability is here a rather amorphous concept. Many training centers might therefore contemplate reviewing the staff mix and making performance a criterion for promotion, rather than simply seniority. Basing part of their remuneration on performance (e.g., bonuses) would give staff incentive to focus more on training center activities, spend more time with trainees, and improve the quality of instruction.

Although diversifying sources of revenue is already the practice in a few Sri Lankan TVET agencies (e.g., SLITHM), most are still exclusively resourced through the government budget, which reduces their agility and puts them at risk should priorities change or the fiscal space shrink. Diversification can be accomplished mainly in two ways. The obvious one is to share training costs with trainees by charging fees. The fee has to be rationally devised so that it conforms to the financing strategy of the training institution (this assumes that training centers are free to determine fees). However, fees place the financial burden on the trainees, so it is important that they are not so high that they prevent low-income students from enrolling. A reasonable policy would be to differentiate fee levels according to trainee capacity to pay, and combine fees with scholarships or grants on the same basis.

The other main avenue for diversifying sources of revenues is for training centers to generate their own income. One approach is to sell the goods or services produced. This fits well with the situation of training centers, which are designed to teach skills through practice and are in a position to manufacture marketable products; price them (generally low, because the costs of production are low); and open up markets for them. However, there is a risk that the sale of products might become a center's main objective with training coming second, so that the quality of training suffers. More critical is that a center be able to retain the income generated and use it to improve the quality of training, rather than returning it to the general budget or deducting it from the center's budgetary allocation. Otherwise, income-generating activities will neither help diversify resources nor improve the quality of the training (or the products). Other approaches are to tailor courses for mid-career workers and rent out facilities. Finally, consulting by teaching staff is also an option, although not as promising as it can be in tertiary education.

Sector Governance

Virtually none of the options suggested is likely to produce significant and durable effects if governance issues are not tackled first. Four issues stand out as most pressing: coordination, budget processes, status of public centers, and information.

Coordination

Because TVET is so fragmented in Sri Lanka, tighter coordination is needed—MYASD needs to become both more effective and more visible. The fragmentation of the sector can be observed in the MYASD centers themselves; between these and centers run by other ministries; and between public and private institutions. If not well-coordinated, donor financing and activities may be another source of distortion. Although it is neither realistic nor necessarily desirable to centralize all TVET activities under a single agency, it would be logical to give the TVEC the mandate to coordinate these activities. The TVEC should be supported by a consultative body of employers, providers, the private sector, NGOs, and donors to help make TVET more responsive to the needs of the economy.

Finally, as seen in Singapore, the Republic of Korea, or Malaysia, if it is to contribute fully to economic growth, TVET must be integrated into the national economic strategy rather than treated as a separate activity exclusively focused on employment issues.

One possible short-term measure is to consolidate the less viable small centers operated by various MYASD agencies. Although equity concerns may justify continuing to run some small centers, others should be clustered to eliminate duplication, benefit from economies of scale, and avoid waste. Any strategic redeployment plan could be designed in close consultation with local stakeholders.

Budget Processes

Aligning budget allocations with the performance of training agencies and centers could promote innovation, efficiency, and accountability. Sri Lankan budget processes for TVET, especially allocations, lack rigor and transparency; how the MYASD budget is determined and its resources are allocated is quite arbitrary at the moment. Rather than simply making the same allocations year after year, the government could adopt formulas that base allocations on previous progress toward specified goals. Incorporating performance elements, such as dropout rates or employability of graduates, in the funding formula would be an incentive for MYASD centers[30] to improve the quality of their services and would help instill a culture of accountability in public providers.

Institutional Status

The gradual devolution of administrative and financial powers from central agencies to training centers—along with an increase in their accountability—is likely to promote higher quality in the services centers provide. Training centers are where demand and supply can best be matched because they are more aware than centralized agencies of local realities. There is growing evidence worldwide that institutions that deliver these services perform better if they are autonomous, provided they are held strictly accountable.[31] Several training centers, under the MYASD and other ministries, already benefit from some degree of autonomy, but generally it is not enough. Allocations to the centers could be based on a set formula. They could retain self-generated revenues; set their own fees, perhaps based on centrally determined criteria; set salaries for permanent staff and remuneration for contractual staff based on performance criteria; and move resources from one budget line to another without having to request authorization from agency headquarters. Since setting up an entirely new financial management system is complex, it might be reasonable to pilot the idea and evaluate its impact before going full-scale.

Information

If supply of and demand for TVET services are to match both quantitatively and qualitatively, information has to flow freely in both directions. Making information more available and more timely would be highly beneficial for everyone; at the root of many of Sri Lanka's TVET issues is a deficit in information felt by training providers, funding providers, trainees,[32] and employers. Information about future skills requirements is not easy to obtain because the requirements are conditioned by general and local economic forecasts, which in turn are susceptible to many exogenous factors. Employers themselves often have only a short-term appreciation of what their needs will be. TVEC's biannual *Labour Market Information Bulletin* provides valuable information on the labor market (especially on unemployment), as does the *Education Guide* published by the JobsNet Project on the supply of services. However, there is not enough information available to guide either national policy or specific investments at the local or trade level.

A better match between TVET supply and demand requires better alignment between the expectations of trainees and employers, which in turn requires closer consultation between these groups and with service providers. TVET is still socially stigmatized even while employers actively seek it. If a voucher system were put in place progressively, better information would allow trainees to make good choices among diverse providers.[33] Particularly relevant here is one aspect of Mexico's 2007 TVET reform[34]: how to respond to the needs of the booming tourism sector in the Mayan Riviera. A strategy for gathering information was considered a precondition to addressing rapid changes in the sector (box 5.3).

Box 5.3 Mexico: An Information Collection Strategy

Mexico's TVET reform in 2007 attempted to respond to the needs of the booming tourism sector in the Mayan Riviera by developing a strategy for gathering information.

Macro Level
- Consult international benchmarks and knowledge bases, such as the OECD, the EU (for example, competence-based learning, European Qualification Framework), UNESCO data, and qualitative information on TVET systems.
- Engage stakeholders.
- Make a macro forecast (for example, number of jobs per room, number of indirect jobs per direct job created with each room).

Micro Level (Mayan Riviera)
- Forecast sector growth (from 35,000 rooms in 2007 to 80,000 rooms in 2020).
- Form the Association of the Hospitality Sector in the Mayan Region.
- Formulate sector needs as determined by the association by developing baseline statistical information about size and composition of different occupations.
- Gather information from hotel human resource managers about qualifications needed in the sector.
- Survey customer satisfaction, targeting specific hotels (to fine-tune the profile of skills needed in the longer term).
- Pilot new courses and programs.

Source: OECD 2009b.

The expected rapid growth of the hospitality sector in Sri Lanka, and the challenges and opportunities this growth entails, may warrant consideration of designing a similar comprehensive strategy to collect the information needed to tailor the skills supply and analyze the associated costs and financing elements.

Conclusion and Policy Options

Although no direct international comparisons are available as benchmarks, a tentative conclusion is that TVET in Sri Lanka is under-resourced compared to neighboring countries or other MICs. However, while it is certainly necessary to increase total funding for TVET if Sri Lanka is to keep up with the rising social and economic demand for training, improvements in its governance and in the use of available resources is a *sine qua non* to make TVET a genuine engine of productivity and competitiveness. Another prerequisite for making the sector more agile and fully productive of the skills a dynamic economy requires is deeper engagement with the private sector. Truly demand-driven TVET cannot flourish without the full participation of employers.

There is a major governance element in most TVET financial problems: The budgeting process is arbitrary, delinked from performance, not transparent, and generally inefficient. Because of tight central control, public centers are not fully accountable for their performance and have little incentive to respond to—let alone anticipate—potential demand. The activities of the numerous public TVET providers are not well coordinated. Timely and accurate information about the current demand for skills and training opportunities is lacking, as are reliable forecasts of potential needs. The private sector is associated only tenuously with the activities of public institutions and centers and with strategic planning for the sector.

Because the private sector is rapidly becoming the main source of demand for the skills that TVET providers supply, it must be more active in planning, management, provision, and funding of technical and vocational education. The Korea lesson is particularly relevant because that country's earlier ambition to accelerate on the growth path was similar to Sri Lanka's ambition now. When Korea was just starting to industrialize, the state-led TVET system was sufficient and efficient, but when technological changes began to escalate, it was unable to adapt. Full involvement of the private sector is what gave vocational training and education there the capacity to respond to change (Lee 2009). As its economy scales up, Sri Lanka confronts similar challenges; its TVET system cannot remain where it was when the country was still producing only low-value-added goods and services.

Improving the quality, relevance, and efficiency of the TVET sector will require that Sri Lanka harnesses physical and financial resources and the experiences of all the actors involved in supply of, and demand for, job-related skills. Experiences from countries as varied as Germany, Austria, Switzerland, the United States, Korea, and Malaysia[35] have demonstrated the power of bringing together all stakeholders to make TVET dynamic and responsive. Tripartite partnership arrangements of the sort found in Switzerland and Malaysia in particular demonstrate that the benefits of consultation outweigh the transaction costs. While remaining mindful of its own economic and social fabric, Sri Lanka could carve out a similar path to making TVET a viable engine of growth and prosperity. The following policy options might be considered:

- More effective coordination is needed to deal with the fragmentation of TVET activities in Sri Lanka, with the TVEC playing a more effective and visible role. If TVET supply and demand are to match both quantitatively and qualitatively, information has to flow readily in both directions.
- The most powerful driver of change for TVET would come from tripartite management of the sector by public authorities, employers, and all types of providers. In particular, employers should thoroughly participate at every stage, from vocational training centers up through the UNIVOTEC, and in every aspect, from forecasting skill needs to designing curricula, offering courses, exchanging staff, hosting interns, controlling quality, and financing.
- Public funding should be linked to national priorities and based on institutional performance, as measured, for example, by graduation, retention, and employment rates; and to inclusion of underrepresented groups, such as school leavers and women.
- It would also be advisable that, for public TVET, (1) funding decisions be made separately from allocation and provision decisions; (2) remuneration packages and career development of instructors be upgraded and good performance rewarded; and (3) support from donor agencies be made more predictable to ensure that successful programs are sustainable.
- Public training centers and technical colleges have many options for relieving inefficiencies. Allowing the centers to retain revenues generated from the sale of the byproducts of training or from other nongovernmental sources would stimulate their creativity and flexibility. It would also be advisable to eliminate the duplication caused by the multiplicity of public programs.
- The gradual devolution of administrative and financial powers from central agencies to training centers and colleges, together with increasing their accountability, would both promote quality and allow centers to be more responsive to changing needs.
- A training fund of the type that has proved successful in many countries could be activated, provided that careful feasibility studies are completed, full partnership with employers is enforced, capacity building is comprehensive, and a rigorous tax collection system is in place. It might be piloted in the tourism sector, where rapid development has the potential to transform the entire economy and where skills requirements, though massive, are relatively easy to forecast.

Building the Skills for Economic Growth and Competitiveness in Sri Lanka
http://dx.doi.org/10.1596/978-1-4648-0158-7

- Contracts with private partners to operate some services in public training centers have the potential to improve the quality of service delivery and lighten the burden on public finances.
- As evidenced in several countries at a variety of economic stages, facilitated by public authorities apprenticeship can greatly benefit both employers and trainees and deserves attention not just, as currently, in the informal sector but also from firms of all sizes.
- Among mechanisms to help trainees defray the costs of TVET courses, those that allow trainees more choice of institutions could be made a priority. Vouchers would be privileged instruments to help both private and public institutions exploit their own comparative advantages.

Notes

1. The National Human Resources and Employment Policy (SSM 2012) is silent about the costs of the sector.
2. Ministry of Industry and Commerce, Ministry of Ports and Highways, and so on.
3. The nine provinces also channel funds to 18 municipal councils, 42 urban councils, and 270 *Pradeshhiya Sabhas*.
4. About 52 percent of private sector providers are concentrated in the Western Province.
5. Calculations made from data collected from Sri Lanka's Ministry of Finance and Planning produce an even lower figure, 0.7 percent. This huge disparity illustrates the challenges in comparing data.
6. Again, estimates made directly from MFP sources provide a much lower figure (4 percent) than UIS (8.1 percent).
7. The coefficient of correlation between the two aggregates is $R^2 = 0.24$.
8. The huge increase in MYASD spending on welfare programs and retirement benefits in 2012 started from an almost zero base in 2009, thus accounting for a very minute share for these budget items.
9. The gap between forecasts and actual recurrent expenditures was less than 3 percent of the former for the same years.
10. While the SDFL is shown as a full-blown MYASD institute, it is not financially dependent on the ministry but is provisioned by the Treasury, which is the main investor in the company.
11. This category corresponds to International Standard Classification of Education (ISCED) Levels 5 and 6.
12. The ratio in SLITHM is 27 to1, in ATIs 14 to 1, and in the NGO Don Bosco Technical College, 11 to 1.
13. For ATIs, 35 staff members are permanent, 22 are visiting, and 3 are under contract.
14. Vocational qualification is very diverse. Usually it is characterized by a diploma or a graduation certificate, often earned by attending one of the MYASD institutions but in some cases granted by a private firm.
15. About 38 percent of all teaching staff in both NYSC and NAITA who responded to the DTET survey have more than 10 years of teaching experience.
16. In some cases, salary is not even the largest factor in remuneration.

17. However, civil servants fare better if retirement benefits are taken into account.

18. The minimum remuneration comprises the wage proper (SL Rs 380), attendance bonus (SL Rs 105), and productivity incentive (SL Rs 30).

19. Training centers run by the Department of Agriculture in the Western Province draw about 5 percent of their income from selling farm products.

20. The Finance Act (No. 25 of 2003), establishing the levy, does not provide detail on where the tax goes.

21. The law that established the tax (No. 32 of 1976) does not specify such use.

22. The rationale for control by the Treasury is its current supremacy as a shareholder.

23. See, for instance, Wang 2000 on PPPs in social sectors, LaRocque and Patrinos 2006 for PPPs in general education.

24. Small firms are often exempt because of the high administrative costs of compliance. See Adams 2008.

25. There are also many cases where vouchers are channeled to training institutions. Despite the positive impact on the latter to boost supply, this mechanism obviously does not open up choices for trainees; nor does it promote competition among training institutions.

26. It has been estimated that more than two-thirds of urban informal sector workers in Africa have been trained through this system (Adams 2008).

27. Germany is still the model par excellence of apprenticeship, even though it is based on a specific economic structure (with a backbone of small and medium size enterprises) and an even more specific form of industrial relations that cannot necessarily be replicated to other countries.

28. *The Chronicle of Higher Education*, February 13, 2013.

29. The Fraunhofer Model emphasizes articulation between formal and theoretical learning, concrete experience on the job, and the working processes. See Mattauch *et al.* 2001 for an example related to advanced vocational training.

30. The funding formula used to allocate resources from the center to the agencies could be replicated, with the necessary adjustments, in the allocation from agencies to their centers.

31. Though most of the evidence is drawn from primary or secondary schools (see Hanushek and Wößmann 2008), it is highly likely that training centers might benefit even more from additional autonomy.

32. A recent survey in nine countries found that "some 40 percent of youth also report that they were not familiar with the market conditions and requirements even for well-known professions." (McKinsey 2012, 31).

33. In Switzerland, the "apprenticeship barometer" monitors the match between apprenticeship supply and demand. It is based on a biannual survey of businesses and of youths aged 14–20. The barometer is complemented by monthly surveys carried out by canton. Similarly, the *Arbeitsmarktservice* in Austria monitors movement of job supply and demand on a real-time basis.

34. See OECD 2009b for a brief description of the RIEMS (*Reforma Integral de la Educación Media Superior*).

35. The Penang experience (see box 7.2 for a full description) has become a showcase of integration between universities and vocational education, and industry and public authorities.

Bibliography

Adams, A. 2008. *Skills Development in the Informal Sector of Sub-Saharan Africa.* Washington, DC: World Bank.

ADB (Asian Development Bank). 2011. *Innovative Strategies in Technical and Vocational Education and Training for Accelerated Human Resource Development in South Asia: Sri Lanka Country Report.* Unpublished draft, Manila.

Almeida, R., J. Berhman, and R. Robalino. 2012. *The Right Skills for the Job? Rethinking Effective Training Policies for Workers.* Washington, DC: World Bank.

Cedefop. 2009. "Individual Learning Accounts." Panorama Series 163, European Center for the Development of Vocational Training, Luxembourg.

Dar, A. 2004. "Training Levies: Evidence from Evaluations." Employment Policy Primer 6, World Bank, Washington, DC.

Dar, A., S. Canagarajah, and P. Murphy. 2003. "Training Levies: Rationale and Evidence from Evaluations." Human Development Network Social Protection Working Paper, World Bank, Washington, DC.

Finance Commission, Sri Lanka. 2009. *Annual Report.* Colombo.

Hanushek, E., and L. Wößmann. 2008. "The Role of Cognitive Skills in Economic Development." *Journal of Economic Literature* 46 (3): 607–68.

Hicks, J. H., M. Kremer, I. Mbiti, and E. Miguel. 2011. *Vocational Education Voucher Delivery and Labor Market Returns: A Randomized Evaluation among Kenyan Youth.* Report for the Spanish Impact Evaluation Fund (SIEF). Washington, DC: World Bank.

Johanson, R. 2009. "A Review of National Training Funds." Social Protection Discussion Paper 0922, World Bank, Washington, DC.

LaRocque, N., and H. Patrinos. 2006. *Choice and Contracting Mechanisms in the Education Sector.* Washington, DC: World Bank.

Lee, Y. H. 2009. *Vocational Education and Training in the Process of Industrialization.* Seoul: Korean Educational Development Institute.

ManpowerGroup. 2012. *Talent Shortage Survey.* http:www.manpowergroup.us /talent-shortage.

Mattauch, W., M. Rohs, S. Grunwald, and R. Walter. 2001. "A Workflow Oriented Model for Advanced Vocational Training in Information Technology." *Integrated Design and Process Technology* 1: 28–33.

McKinsey. 2012. *Education to Employment: Designing a System that Works.* McKinsey Center for Government. http://mckinseyonsociety.com/downloads/reports /Education/Education-to-Employment_FINAL.pdf.

MFP (Ministry of Finance and Planning). 2012. *Medium Term Public Investment Outlook for Skills Education Sector (2012–2016).* Draft. MFP, Department of National Planning, Colombo.

Muehlemann, S., J. Schweri, R. Winkelmann, and S. Wolter. 2007. "An Empirical Analysis of the Decision to Train Apprentices." *Labour* 21 (3): 419–41.

MYASD (Ministry of Youth Affairs and Skills Development). 2012. *Institutional Training Information, Year 2012.* Unofficial document, Colombo.

NGA (National Governors Association). 2011. *Degrees for What Jobs? Raising Expectations for Universities and Colleges in a Global Economy.* Washington, DC: National Governors Association Center for Best Practices.

OECD (Organisation for Economic Co-operation and Development). 2009a. *Switzerland. Learning for Jobs. Review of Vocational Education and Training.* Paris: OECD.

———. 2009b. *Systemic Innovation in the Mexican VET System. Country Case Study Report.* Paris: OECD/CERI.

———. 2012. *Education at a Glance.* Paris: OECD.

Patrinos, H., F. Barrera-Osorio, and J. Guáqueta. 2009. *The Role and Impact of Public-Private Partnerships in Education.* Washington, DC: World Bank.

Pratham. 2012. Institute for Literacy, Education and Vocational Training, Pratham. http://www.pratham.org/Default.aspx?id=1.

SSM (Secretariat for Senior Ministers). 2012. *The National Human Resources and Employment Policy for Sri Lanka.* Secretariat for Senior Ministers. Colombo: Government of Sri Lanka.

Tsang, M. 1997. "The Cost of Vocational Training." *International Journal of Manpower* 18 (1): 63–89.

Vegas, E., and C. Coffin. 2012. *SABER-Finance: What Makes an Education Finance System Effective?* Education Unit, Human Development Network. Washington, DC: World Bank.

Wang, Y. 2000. *Public-Private Partnerships in the Social Sector. Issues and Country Experiences in Asia and the Pacific.* Tokyo: Asian Development Bank Institute.

World Bank. 2007. "Learning for Job Opportunities: An Assessment of the Vocational Education and Training in Bangladesh." Bangladesh Development Series Paper 16, World Bank, Washington, DC.

———. 2009. *The Towers of Learning: Performance, Peril and Promise of Higher Education in Sri Lanka.* Washington, DC: World Bank.

———. 2010. "Education, Training and Labor Market for Youth in Indonesia." Human Development Department, East Asia and Pacific Region, Report 54170-ID, World Bank, Washington, DC.

———. 2011a. *Transforming School Education in Sri Lanka. From Cut Stones to Polished Jewels.* Washington, DC: World Bank.

———. 2011b. *Tunisia Profile.* Washington, DC: World Bank.

———. 2012. "Are Countries' Investments in Tertiary Education Making a Difference?" South Asia Human Development Sector Report 53. World Bank, Washington, DC.

Ziderman, A. 2003. *Financing Vocational Training in Sub-Saharan Africa.* Washington, DC: World Bank.

CHAPTER 6

Private Provision of Technical and Vocational Education and Training

Introduction

Private technical and vocational education and training (TVET) in Sri Lanka dates back to the first half of the 20th century, when training consisted of apprenticeships in private and public entities and specialized training was verified by the City and Guilds of London examinations. To satisfy their skills needs, companies that installed and maintained factory machinery, repaired and maintained ships, and transported export produce to harbors trained two types of apprentices, trade and special. Trade apprentices were equipped to become skilled workers and special apprentices to become foremen, supervisors, or workshop managers. Because the City and Guilds of London conducted examinations in Sri Lanka that would qualify workers to serve elsewhere in the British Empire, private institutions and individuals offered preparatory classes.

After Sri Lanka's 1977 trade liberalization, private training institutions mushroomed. Free market economic policies triggered the speedy and massive growth of the service sector, and the country saw employment opportunities emerge in accounting, marketing, management, computing, automobile repair, and the apparel industry. Numerous students enrolled with private providers to prepare for professional examinations in accounting, marketing, and management. From the 1980s on, as computer use and information technology (IT) became intrinsic to all businesses, private providers of computer literacy and IT courses also burgeoned.

This chapter complements the discussions in chapter 2 on public sector provision of TVET and chapter 5 on factors contributing to skills supply by describing private sector provision of TVET. It answers the following questions: (1) How active is the private sector in TVET in Sri Lanka? (2) What skills do private TVET institutions provide? (3) How successful in the labor market are students who graduate from private institutions? (4) How are private TVET institutions regulated and financed? and (5) What might enhance the contribution of the private sector to the quality and relevance of TVET? The chapter draws on multiple sources, such as information from the Tertiary and Vocational Education Commission (TVEC), focus groups, private sector representatives, and nongovernmental organizations (NGOs).

The chapter first describes the different types of private TVET providers operating in Sri Lanka and introduces institutions that took part in the study through focus groups. It then discusses types of skills provided by private institutions, how the institutions interact with industry, and how graduates fare in the labor market. It next describes how private TVET institutions are regulated and financed. The chapter concludes with a discussion of how to increase private participation in TVET and offers policy recommendations to help achieve this.

Types of Private Sector Engagement

About 70 percent of TVET graduates are trained in public institutions and 30 percent in private. In 2011 about 98,000 students were enrolled in public TVET institutions and about 53,000 in TVEC-registered private institutions (table 6.1). The gender distribution of students was quite similar: women constitute 43 percent of students in public institutions and 45 percent in private.

Private providers in Sri Lanka can be categorized into five groups: (1) for-profit providers of institution-based individual training; (2) NGO providers; (3) fee-based training provided by companies in their fields of expertise; (4) professional or paraprofessional institutions, local or foreign, training potential members; and (5) chambers of commerce and industry.

Of the 926 private and NGO institutions registered with the TVEC[1] in 2010 (table 6.2), private for-profit trainers constituted about 77 percent, NGOs about 16 percent, and companies and chambers of commerce, 7 percent. The Western Province has the largest share of all types (table 6.3), though NGO institutions are spread throughout the country; 20 are in the conflict-affected Northern Province. Professional institutions are found only in the Western Province, mostly in and around Colombo.

Private For-profit Providers

These trainers are either registered as a business with the Company Registrar or as a sole proprietorship with the Divisional Secretariat. To stay in business,

Table 6.1 TVET Enrollment and Completion, Public and Private Institutions, by Gender

	Public		Private	
	Enrolled	Completed	Enrolled	Completed
Men	56,177	33,544	28,737	18,586
Women	41,747	24,916	24,122	13,450
Total	97,924	58,460	52,859	32,036

Source: TVEC 2011a.

Table 6.2 Private Training Providers Registered with TVEC, 2010

Provider category	Number
Institution-based providers of individual training for profit	714
NGO nonprofit training providers	148
Fee-based training by companies in their fields of expertise	36
Professional or paraprofessional institutions, local or foreign, training potential members	12
Chambers of commerce and industry training	16
Total	926

Source: TVEC Registration Database.

Table 6.3 Distribution of Private Training Providers by Province, 2011

Province	Private institutes	NGO	Company	Professional	Chambers of commerce
Southern	60	28	2	—	2
Western	416	35	15	12	2
Eastern	29	16	4	—	7
Sabaragamuwa	38	4	5	—	—
Central	68	10	4	—	1
Uva	14	19	1	—	—
North Western	56	8	2	—	1
North Central	16	8	2	—	1
Northern	17	20	1	—	2

Source: TVEC Registration Database.
Note: — = not available.

private providers need to attract enough students to reap a profit, so they offer courses in areas for which social demand is high. However, high social demand does not always equate to high labor market demand. Courses offered by for-profit providers are mainly in computing and IT, finance and management, personal development (for example, beauty culture and hairdressing), hotels and tourism, garment production, health care, preschool teaching, and light engineering occupations, such as electrician, automobile mechanic, and construction machinery operator. Many training providers are in the Western Province, where economic activity and population density are high. Most operate only one center, but some have several in different parts of the country.

Private institutions may offer National Vocational Qualification (NVQ)-accredited courses or their own diploma or certificate. Often, they also teach preparatory courses for examinations conducted by others. Certificate courses tend to be short or offered as a series, each with a separate certificate, to make the fees affordable. However, 12-month or even longer courses are offered either in areas where there is high demand locally and overseas or to prepare students for external examinations. Courses leading to NVQ 4 certification (see table 2.2) have an on-the-job training (OJT) component, which the institutions arrange with private establishments.

Building the Skills for Economic Growth and Competitiveness in Sri Lanka
http://dx.doi.org/10.1596/978-1-4648-0158-7

NGO Providers

Temple and church-based training centers have traditionally operated in Sri Lanka with funds donated by charities and philanthropists. The courses they offer are mostly in construction (masonry, carpentry, electrical work, plumbing, aluminum fabrication, etc.) and light engineering (welding, machining, automobile mechanics, motorcycle mechanics, refrigeration and air-conditioning, etc.). These occupations are not of interest to most for-profit trainers because social demand for blue-collar jobs is low. However, personnel skilled in construction and light engineering are in great demand not only in Sri Lanka but also abroad. Since the NVQ was introduced, some NGO institutes have diversified their offerings to, among other areas, computing, baking, cooking, and motorcycle mechanics.

Some NGO institutes and networks are exclusively concerned with the rural and urban poor, such as the Don Bosco network, which has centers in several areas. Some also provide room and board for trainees. NGO institutions depend primarily on funding from charities to meet capital and operational costs. Organizations like the World University Service of Canada (WUSC) help NGO providers in specified geographical areas to improve the relevance and quality of vocational courses. In both individual interviews and focus group discussions, NGO providers spoke of finding it difficult to cover operational costs because of the rise in the cost of living.

A few training institutions are registered as charities and funded by companies as part of their corporate social responsibility portfolio. One that was studied conducts construction courses successfully.

Fee-Based Training Provided by Companies

Many manufacturing and service companies contribute to the training coordinated by the National Apprentice and Industrial Training Authority (NAITA). Although NAITA trainees receive a maintenance allowance, many companies augment this with an additional allowance or payment for extra hours of work. Apprentices pay no fees.

A handful of companies offer training for a fee when there is a demand for specialized skills, such as the center operated jointly by Diesel and Motor Engineering Company (the agent for Mercedes Benz) and Tata Motors or the baking school operated by Prima Flour Milling Company, a leading processor and distributor. Good training in an up-to-date industry is extremely conducive to learning.

Professional or Paraprofessional Training of Potential Members

Among professional organizations offering skills-based training are the Institution of Engineers, Institute of Architects, Institute of Chemistry, and Chartered Institute of Accountants. Similarly, paraprofessional organizations offer less than degree-equivalent qualifications. Some professional organizations conduct courses themselves; some for-profit providers offer preparatory courses for examinations to become a member of a professional organization.

The Chartered Institute of Accountants and the Association of Accounting Technicians have the largest enrollments among Sri Lankan organizations, and the Chartered Institute of Management Accountants (CIMA) has the largest enrollment among international organizations.

Chambers of Commerce and Industry

The training offered by chambers of commerce covers issues that impact business operators, from business and strategic planning to daily operational concerns—such as customer care, basic labor law essentials, and taxation—to support entrepreneurs, employees, and unemployed youth. Some institutions train only in skills in areas of their interest. The Construction Chamber, for instance, operates several centers to train craftspeople in areas affected by civil conflict where infrastructure is being rebuilt. While some courses offered by the chambers are fee-based, most are funded by donors, both local and foreign.

Skills and Labor Market Outcomes of Graduates

Skills Provided by Private Training Institutions

Private TVET institutions offer courses in a variety of fields. Table 6.4 provides information on the number of students enrolled by TVEC-registered training providers and the number that graduated in 2011. Typically, students enroll in these courses directly after general education.

The three most popular fields of study are information, communication, and multimedia technology (ICT); finance, banking, and management; and personal and community development. In 2011, total enrollment in ICT courses was about 18,000 students. However, this course has a high dropout rate (about 63 percent of the 2011 enrollment completed the course). One explanation may

Table 6.4 Students and Graduates, TVEC-Registered Private Providers, 2011

	Number enrolled			Number completed		
Field of study	Male	Female	Total	Male	Female	Total
Information communication and multimedia technology	8,699	9,707	18,406	5,517	6,101	11,618
Finance, banking, and management	3,606	4,361	7,967	243	230	473
Personal and community development	1,449	3,294	4,743	1,389	2,359	3,748
Building and construction	3,570	133	3,703	3,098	74	3,172
Medical and health science	280	1,680	1,960	242	1,171	1,413
Textiles and garments	334	1,248	1,582	201	950	1,151
Hotels and tourism	1,053	468	1,521	865	389	1,254
Electrical, electronics, and telecommunication	1,320	60	1,380	871	32	903
Metal and light engineering	1,188	15	1,203	916	11	927
Automobile repair and maintenance	1,112	7	1,119	673	26	699
Other fields	6,126	3,149	9,275	4,571	2,107	6,678
Total	28,737	24,122	52,859	18,586	13,450	32,036

Source: TVEC 2011a.

Building the Skills for Economic Growth and Competitiveness in Sri Lanka
http://dx.doi.org/10.1596/978-1-4648-0158-7

be the general education examination cycle. After taking the GCE O-level examination, students often enroll in vocational courses as a stopgap but return to general education after they get their examination results. One-third of the registered private providers offer ICT courses (table 6.5).

Social demand is also high for finance, banking, and management. Because these courses typically prepare students for professional and paraprofessional work and no NVQ courses are offered in this field, very few students stay on to earn a certificate. Personal and community development, which includes hairdressing and beauty culture, is especially popular among women (about 70 percent of total enrollment in 2011) and has a low dropout rate (about 20 percent in 2011). On average each of the 48 institutions that offer this specialization hold more than three courses a year (table 6.5).

Building and construction, which had the fourth-highest enrollment (about 3,700 students in 2011), was offered by 70 institutions. Although the field has very high labor market demand, because social demand for it is low it does not easily attract students. Most courses are offered by NGOs and industrial

Table 6.5 Number of Private Courses and Providers, by Field, 2011

Field	Number of providers	Number of courses
Information technology	299	716
Personal and community development	48	172
Building and construction	70	123
Finance and management	48	99
Textiles and garments	32	93
Teacher training	51	59
Office management	23	51
Food and beverages	37	49
Metal and light engineering	36	48
Aviation, aeronautics, and navigation	6	45
Medical and health sciences	42	43
Hotels and tourism	23	37
Electrical	50	31
Mechanical	30	30
Automobile repair and maintenance	46	25
Electronics and communication	26	22
Refrigeration and air conditioning	18	20
Art and media	15	20
Marine shipping and fisheries	7	13
Gems and jewelry	7	12
Carpentry	29	6
Printing and packaging	7	5
Rubber and plastic	2	4
Agriculture and livestock	5	2
Total	957	1,031

Source: TVEC database 2011.

chambers of commerce. To encourage enrollment, students are given financial or logistical assistance. Courses in drafting, quantity surveying, and construction management are related areas in which private for-profit institutes offer courses.

Private providers not only serve students leaving general education, they also offer skills upgrading for employed workers (mid-career trainees). Unfortunately, no data are collected systematically with which to assess skills upgrading services. Rough estimates suggest that most students are still school-leavers. Comments in focus groups suggest that the percentage of mid-career trainees in total student enrollment depends on the course (table 6.6). Mid-career trainees are mainly interested in courses that prepare them for City and Guilds certification examinations; school-leavers prefer NVQ courses. Another preferred option for skills upgrading is short, specialized ICT courses; these are mainly geared to learning about specific software.

Private providers have more flexibility in curriculum and course design than public providers. They are free to use NVQ curricula, the curricula of foreign institutions, or their own. (Company-based training programs apply their industry expertise to curricula.) Since most private institutions are profit-oriented, they respond faster than public agencies to changes in market demands for skills as well as to social demand for courses.

Since the courses offered by private providers are driven to a large extent by social demand, there is less emphasis on teaching English and other skills that enhance employability. Most private courses are conducted in Sinhala or Tamil. Of the 10 private institutions that participated in study focus groups, only one conducted courses in English. Generally only NGO-run and some company-based training centers teach English as a separate subject. Providers stated in focus groups that teaching English and other soft skills, such as teamwork, leadership, and interpersonal skills, is not a high priority because it adds to training costs. However, many private providers use technical English terms when teaching, some instructional materials are printed in English, and a number encourage student leadership, teamwork, and involvement in community service programs.

Table 6.6 TVET Participation of Midcareer Trainees

Institute	Sector	Course	% Mid-career trainees
Ranmali Associates	Hair and beauty	Regular NVQ	20–25
		City and Guilds	95
Prima Baking School	Baking	Regular NVQ	20–30
DIMO Automobile TC	Automobile	City & Guilds Certificate	20
		City & Guilds Diploma	60
Training Division of Federation of Chambers of Commerce and Industry of Sri Lanka (FCCISL)	Professional development	Certificate	10
Technology and Computer Training Institute (TCTI)	Computer & IT	Short, specialized courses	50–75

Source: Direct interviews with training providers.

Labor Market Outcomes of Graduates

Placement in practical training is a well-regulated process for public providers. It is administered by the NAITA, which puts students of public TVET institutions into both private and public businesses. Private providers place students in private firms through their own industry network (public firms do not accept private trainees). Placement is not difficult for occupational streams with high labor market demand, but students studying IT-related courses in the private sector find it difficult to secure internships.

Private providers do not systematically collect post-training employment information, and their graduates rely on informal contacts in their job search. For example, some Don Bosco affiliates have an alumni association, which is often tapped for employment purposes. Tables 6.7–6.9 describe transition to employment for graduates of different types of private providers that participated in focus groups. In general, almost all find employment within a year of graduation. By institution, 80 percent or more of graduates from Wayamba, DIMO, and Don Bosco find employment immediately. Students trained in certain institutions— DIMO, Prima Baking School, and Ranmali Associates—also find it easy to find jobs abroad.

The employment search time for graduates of private and public TVET providers is comparable (table 6.10). The TVEC conducted a tracer study of 628 graduates in the Southern Province employed in both the public and private sectors who held NVQ certificates as computer application assistants,

Table 6.7 Employment of Graduates, Private For-Profit Training Providers, 2012
Percent

	Ranmali Associates		Wayamba TC		TCTI	
	Employed, local	Employed, foreign	Employed, local	Employed, foreign	Employed, local	Employed, foreign
Immediately on completion	25	5	80	—	30	—
Within 6 months	27	2	13	—	70	—
Within 1 year	35	8	—	7	—	—

Source: Focus groups.
Note: — = not applicable.

Table 6.8 Employment of Graduates, NGO Training Providers, 2012
Percent

	Don Bosco		AGIO Sirilak	
	Employed, local	Employed, foreign	Employed, local	Employed, foreign
Immediately on completion	100	1	50	—
Within 6 months	—	2	30	—
Within 1 year	—	3	20	5

Source: Focus groups.
Note: — = not applicable.

Table 6.9 Employment of Graduates, Company-Based Training Providers, 2012
Percent

	DIMO Automobile		Prima Baking	
	Employed, local	*Employed, foreign*	*Employed, local*	*Employed, foreign*
Immediately on completion	100	—	60	10
Within 6 months	—	—	20	20
Within 1 year	—	40 (after 2 years of experience)	10–20	30

Source: Focus groups.
Note: — = not applicable.

Table 6.10 Time Elapsed between Graduation and Employment, Public TVET Graduates, 2011

Time elapsed	% Employed
Within 3 months	47.6
Within 3–6 months	23.8
Within 6–12 months	14.3
More than 12 months	14.3

Source: TVEC 2011b.

computer graphic designers, carpenters, masons, electricians, aluminum fabricators, machinists, or automobile mechanics. About 48 percent of graduates of public TVET providers found a job within three months and 86 percent within a year.

Private training institutions typically do not conduct tracer studies of their students to determine how much graduates earn. Focus group participants stated that employment opportunities and salaries in the private sector varied substantially and were dependent on both student trade specialization and the institution from which a student graduated. For example, the monthly salary of a beautician or hairdresser could be over SL Rs 15,000 in registered salons. Graduates of engineering crafts earn about SL Rs 12,000 in Colombo and SL Rs 7,000 in Kurunegala. Graduates of Prima Baking School start at about SL Rs 15,000–20,000, and experienced pastry chefs can earn about SL Rs 100,000–150,000 monthly.

A TVEC tracer study on NVQ certificate holders (Jayalath *et al.* 2011) shows wage employment of NVQ certificate holders by job type in both public and private sectors in all provinces. Over 50 percent of the jobs they hold are permanent (table 6.11).

About 50 percent of NVQ certificate holders earn a monthly salary of SL Rs 5,000–15,000; the starting salaries of graduates of private and public TVET institutions are comparable. Also notable is that a larger proportion of self-employed graduates earn less than SL Rs 5,000 or above SL Rs 25,000, highlighting the distribution of entrepreneurial ability.

Table 6.11 Job Types of Wage-Earners, 2011

Job type	Number	Percent
Permanent/monthly waged job	291	50.2
Contract/temporary monthly waged job	151	26.0
Daily payment job	50	8.6
Piece rate job	35	6.0
No response	53	9.1
Total	580	100.0

Source: Jayalath *et al.* 2011.

Regulation and Financing of Private Providers

Registration and Accreditation

The TVEC registers public and private training providers under the Tertiary and Vocational Education Act, No. 20 of 1990, as amended by Act No. 50 of 1999. The first list of registered trainers was published in 1992. A registration is valid for two to three years, depending on the institutional category assigned to it, and is then renewable. However, a number of institutions, mainly small-scale, do not register, while some register but do not renew. At any given point, then, there are more training providers operating than are registered.

Though institutional training is expanding briskly, the majority of employees still acquire skills at work and through informal apprenticeships. Department of Census and Statistics data show that 84 percent of working people have no formal training and are not certified.

The 1990 act regulates academic and training standards in all establishments that provide tertiary and vocational education. It specifies procedures for the registration of providers, specified courses, and examinations. It also provides for formulating the National Development Plan and gives TVEC the power to regulate admissions requirements, curricula, qualifications of trainers, and certification; require training performance reports and inspect institutions; and cancel registrations for breach of specified conditions.

The purposes of the act are to

- Improve content and training methods to make courses more responsive to the job skills the market requires.
- Establish nationally recognized standards in order to raise the quality of testing, evaluation, and certification.
- Improve the efficiency and effectiveness of provider management.
- Expand the employability of training graduates.
- Ensure optimal use of resources.
- Keep the curricula of similar courses uniform.

The TVEC has standard applications for initial and renewal registrations. The application must be supported by documents on the adequacy and relevance of infrastructure, training equipment, teacher qualifications, course curricula, and training delivery methods. Curricula are judged on their relevance to NVQ criteria, if applicable, or on the opinions of subject experts. During the registration evaluation, institutions are advised on how to improve areas where they fall short. Once an institution has satisfied all the criteria, staff makes a recommendation to the TVEC Board of Directors that the institute be registered. There are four categories of registration:

- Grade C: Marginally acceptable for provisional registration.
- Grade B: Fully acceptable for provisional registration.
- Grade A: Has been registered at Grade B or C and over 50 percent of the courses are accredited.
- Grade A+: Has obtained Grade A and established a Quality Management System.

Institutions may qualify to offer either certificate or diploma courses. Certificate courses must be comparable to similar NVQ courses in content and duration, or any deviations must be justified. Diploma programs, which do not offer NVQ courses, must offer curricula at levels comparable to diploma qualification descriptors, and students must have over 400 teaching contact hours. NVQ diploma courses are expected to satisfy criteria published in the *NVQ Operations Manual*.

Accreditation is designed to ensure that courses comply with National Competency Standards, curricula and equipment are adequate, teaching and learning systems are appropriate, and continuous and summative assessment systems are in place. Students of accredited courses are assessed for award of the relevant NVQ. The standard adopted for the NVQ Level 5 diploma, for instance, is 60 credits of the European Credit Transfer System, or about 1,500 hours of learning; and for the NVQ Level 6 diploma the standard is 120 credits. Competency standards and accreditation criteria are in place for 115 certificate and 16 diploma courses.

Private training providers offer accredited certificate-level courses in several fields but do not as yet offer NVQ diploma courses, mainly because those longer courses have higher capital and operating costs. In 2007, private institutions that conducted accredited courses formed the Accredited Training Providers Association (ATPA) to promote standards to ensure quality TVET. The TVEC helped to form the association, and it is considered a registered company. ATPA is active in propagating NVQ training, helps refine the NVQ framework, offers students career guidance, and works to further private sector involvement in TVET.

Financing of Private TVET Providers

How private training institutions are financed depends on the type. For-profit institutions depend on fees collected from trainees. To finance investment in buildings and equipment, they borrow from banks at commercial rates. For example, to date Wayamba Technical College has invested a total of SL Rs 50 million. It took out bank loans totaling SL Rs 8 million at 12 percent,

13 percent, and 16 percent interest and four- to five-year terms, and the TVEC granted it SL Rs 1.8 million in 2007 under its private sector assistance scheme. The college's monthly operational costs are about SL Rs 950,000, of which debt service is 30 percent, salaries are 40 percent, services and utilities take up 6 percent, rent is 7 percent, and consumables and training materials are 10 percent.

NGO providers, which do not charge students fees, mainly depend on donor funding. The TVEC has helped many of them by providing 70 percent of the funds required to procure equipment and tools to fulfill course accreditation requirements. However, Treasury funds are limited. NGO providers occasionally undertake external projects that generate income by producing items for sale as part of training, such as furniture or machinery components.

The training provided by DIMO Automobile Training School is funded by the company; in 2011 the total cost was SL Rs 24 million. Regular trainees do not pay fees, but part-time students preparing for external examinations do. Prima Baking School depends almost entirely on trainee fees. The Training Division of the Federation of Chambers of Commerce and Industry of Sri Lanka (FCCISL) charges fees for professional development courses and receives funding for construction-related training from partner organization in Germany.

Cost Efficiency of Private TVET Providers

Reliable figures relating to internal cost efficiency and graduate employability are difficult to obtain for many training centers. Treasury-funded public institutions receive annual grants to meet operational costs and for new capital developments and acquisition of equipment. Calculations of the cost of public courses do not consider capital costs; nor do they account for depreciation. The cost per student per course calculated by the Vocational Training Authority (VTA) is based on the assumption that each course has 15 students and one instructor. The estimate takes into account spending on training materials and the operational costs of the center.

Similar calculations are not available for the private sector. However, fees charged to students were obtained during interviews with fee-charging providers. Table 6.12 shows cost per student in selected courses in institutions supervised by the VTA and fees charged by private providers who were interviewed.

VTA costs per student are lower than those of the Department of Technical Education and Training, another Ministry of Youth Affairs and Skills Development (MYASD) public network where the staff-to-student ratio is high. Fees charged by Wayamba Technical College for engineering courses may be slightly higher or lower than the VTA cost estimate. Fees charged for private beautician and hairdresser courses are higher than the VTA cost. Courses offered by Prima Baking Schools are an exception: the fees charged are about five times higher than the VTA cost. Prima has very modern facilities and highly qualified staff. The brand name attracts students who can afford the fees.

The costs per student of *Agio Sirilak*, DIMO Automobile Training School, and the Training Division of FCCISL are higher than the VTA costs (table 6.13). None of the three charges trainees. All three have well-qualified instructors,

Table 6.12 Cost Per Student of Public and Private Courses, 2012

Course	Public institutes		Private institutes	
	Duration (months)	Cost[a] (SL Rs)	Duration (months)	Fee (SL Rs)
Automobile mechanic	12	57,890	6	36,000
AC and refrigeration mechanic	12	61,758	6	36,000
Electrician (domestic wiring)	6	37,880	6	36,000
Draftsman	12	52,025	12	72,000
Computer application assistant	12	56,758	8	36,000
Computer graphic designer	6	27,879	8	36,000
Beautician	6	15,606	6	35,000
Hairdresser	6	16,272	6	45,000
Baker	6	32,545	6	167,100

Source: VTA data and interviews.
a. Cost per student was calculated based on 15 students per course.

Table 6.13 Cost of Training, Institutes That Do Not Levy Fees, 2012

Institute	Field of training	Monthly cost per student (SL Rs)
Agio Sirilak Vocational Training Centre	Construction and light engineering	15,500
DIMO Automobile Training School	Automobile mechanic	31,750
Training Division of FCCISL	Construction skill upgrading	11,000

Source: Focus groups.

ample training materials, and a good training environment, and look after student welfare, such as offering free meals.

Discussion

The study team conducted focus group discussions with private training providers, the MYASD, the TVEC, and public providers on how to encourage the private sector to provide high-quality TVET, with special attention to access, relevance, demand for courses, and implementation. Several incentives were identified.

Strengthen career guidance. In Sri Lanka, school children and youth are generally unaware of TVET and its benefits. In general education, students aim to enter university and earn a degree. Even students who have not done well on lower secondary examinations are promoted to upper secondary in the hope of gaining entry to university. As a result, TVET is considered an option only when students are not admitted to a university.

The general education curriculum in Sri Lanka does not provide enough orientation to vocational education, though discussions are underway to introduce vocational orientation in secondary school. The experience of countries that have done this will be useful. The upper secondary technology stream introduced in 2005 has not been popular because it does not facilitate entry to university science or engineering courses.

Building the Skills for Economic Growth and Competitiveness in Sri Lanka
http://dx.doi.org/10.1596/978-1-4648-0158-7

MYASD operates 38 national career guidance centers and 17 more at the district level. However, these have not attracted many students to TVET. More labor market information should be disseminated to students, with career paths spelled out along with job titles and salary structures. Closer collaboration is desirable between the Ministry of Education (MoE) and the MYASD to push this through. Although the Policy Document on Higher Education and Technical and Vocational Education formulated by the National Education Commission (2009) proposed that a National Council for Career Guidance be established, this has not yet been done.

Finances for capacity building. Private providers can respond faster to changing social and labor market demands than the public sector. Increasing training capacity and diversifying courses to new and emerging fields requires capital investment. Similarly, equipment needs to be upgraded periodically to respond to current industry requirements. However, financing through commercial banks at prevailing interest rates is often limited. Opening up a facility for loans at concessionary interest rates is one option to promote investment in private training. However, commercial banks will not provide concessionary loans unless they are guaranteed by a third party. When the government launched the Self Employment Promotion Initiative (SEPI) in 2005, arrangements were made to provide loans to trainees who complete vocational training to start their own businesses. The Central Bank of Sri Lanka held a fund amounting to SL Rs 100 million, provided by the Asian Development Bank, and operated the scheme through commercial banks at lower interest rates. Commercial banks followed their own procedures for issuing loans, and for loans less than SL Rs 50,000 parents were allowed to provide a guarantee without collateral. Setting up a similar fund and making loans at concessionary rates for providers to expand training in areas of high labor market demand are worth considering. However, caution needs to be exercised so that funding does not go to vocations with low labor market demand but high social demand, such as white-collar jobs.

The TVEC provides government grants to private trainers in occupational areas identified in vocational education and training (VET) plans for the purchase of tools and equipment. The grants have helped enhance the quality and capacity of private training and are an encouragement for private providers to seek NVQ accreditation. Grants for specified equipment and tools are capped at SL Rs 1 million per course; the provider has to contribute 30 percent of the cost. The TVEC allocates an average of SL Rs 5 million a year to assist the private sector. The initiative has helped many NGO and other providers to get courses accredited, which means more trainees have access to quality training. Such targeted financial assistance should continue, but probably be expanded.

While public networks of training institutions might have resources, building space, and fully-equipped laboratories and workshops, they sometimes lack trainees. Public-private partnerships (PPPs) could help to get value out of these facilities and reduce both public and private training costs. PPPs can also avoid duplication of expensive equipment that is rarely used for training. Such partnerships have been attempted in the past, but the lack of PPP policy and procedures has meant there has been little progress. Formulating policies and procedures and devising a model PPP management structure will benefit all training providers.

Support to students. The success and sustainability of private for-profit providers of vocational training depends on whether students can afford the course fees. Since public institutions provide training charging at most nominal fees, it is natural that trainees from low-income groups would choose them for training. The problem of affordability arises particularly with lengthy courses of high labor market demand but that have high costs, such as nursing and marine engineering. The International Institute of Health Science and Colombo International Nautical and Engineering College have memoranda of understanding with banks to facilitate loans for their students. However, because this arrangement is only possible when demand and remuneration are such that high earnings are guaranteed, the experience of these two institutions cannot be generalized.

Because banks consider student loans to be high-risk, Malaysia, like some other countries, has established the Skills Development Fund corporation to provide low-interest loans to trainees. This has encouraged students to seek training in diverse fields and enhanced private capacity to deliver training. However, about 25 percent of the loans are not repaid. Other mechanisms, such as vouchers with a particular monetary value for students to seek training from either public or private institutions have been discussed in Sri Lanka but never actualized. The concept of free education provided by the government is so deeply rooted in Sri Lanka that alternate funding mechanisms need careful thought if a change is to be made.

Supporting the self-employment of TVET graduates is another possibility. SEPI, launched with an initial fund of SL Rs 100 million, helped graduates to broaden their understanding of entrepreneurship and financially supported and guided them as they started their own enterprises. SEPI has been a success. Now the model needs to guide and mentor more graduates.

State assistance to NGO trainers. NGOs operating as charities find it difficult to meet the costs of operating training centers when donor funding does not increase as fast as costs. When some NGO centers stopped receiving funds in the past, the VTA intervened to manage and bear the operational costs of some centers. NGO institutions target vulnerable groups and provide TVET in areas of high labor market demand—a worthy cause. They are known to enroll a steady stream of trainees in fields like construction and light engineering when public institutions in the same areas are unable to do so. The monthly cost per trainee is higher in many NGO centers than with the VTA because they give trainees more support, such as meals, a daily allowance, travel subsidies, and uniforms. After the Asian tsunami, using special relief funds public institutions in Sri Lanka opted to support NGOs in construction training.

NGO training centers are now seeking government assistance to meet operational costs, and the government should respond. Among proposed modes of assistance are for the government to pay the salaries of center staff or to buy trainee output. The first option would likely have to be a long-term government commitment and might lead to demands from NGO staff to become government employees. Purchasing training products in areas specified by the government might offer more flexibility to promote quality employment-relevant training while preserving the identity and objectives of NGO operations.

Tax concessions to import equipment for training. Private institutions pay taxes when they import training equipment; DIMO recently had to pay over SL Rs 23 million. This is true for all providers of training in fields where expensive equipment is necessary (taxes on computers and accessories are minimal but not on other equipment). Tax concessions for equipment imported for training purposes would help private providers expand their facilities and keep their equipment current with the labor market. Perhaps requests from private providers for importing equipment exceeding a particular value could be evaluated by the TVEC and MYASD and, with the approval of the Ministry of Finance, be given tax concessions.

Upgrading current worker skills. Private providers have not concerned themselves much with upgrading the skills of those already employed, as is evident from how few mid-career trainees there are in their training centers. Participants in the focus group were unable to comment on a suggestion to establish a training fund with contributions from employers. However, skills upgrading and building new skills in current workers is vital to increase productivity and keep companies competitive.

Strategies to upgrade workforce skills vary from country to country—in some, such as Germany, companies voluntarily take this upon themselves; in others, such as Malaysia, it is managed with government intervention. Both can be considered good examples. Centers set up and funded by chambers of industry in Germany systematically train employees of member companies. This voluntary system is not successful in all countries, mainly because companies are afraid they may lose workers whose skills they have upgraded. In some countries this has resulted in keeping the workforce less productive, disadvantaging not just the companies but the country as a whole. To counter this type of situation, some countries have established funds with compulsory contributions from companies for upgrading the skills of their employees. Companies in Malaysia contribute 1 percent of employee salaries to the Skills Development Fund Ltd. (SDFL), and the amount contributed by each company can be claimed for SDFL-approved skills upgrading programs. The SDFL is managed by a private governing board and the money collected is held separately and not credited to a consolidated fund. This model has worked well both in upgrading workforce skills and generating new opportunities for private providers. However, a training levy program must carefully specify what is to be achieved and how levies will support industry involvement in TVET. The system must help increase not only training capacity but also training relevance.

Public assistance to vocational teacher training. The private sector cannot train TVET instructors without government teacher training facilities and without regular assistance with pedagogy and training delivery. Currently, TVEC provides ad hoc training in specific areas, such as course accreditation. This is not sufficient. With the introduction of the NVQ system, training has to be competency-based and there is a need to set qualifications for training craft teachers and those instructing in diploma courses. Training of instructors must be delivered flexibly and should reach out to both public and private instructional staff. Once the teacher training system becomes established, it can be made mandatory for all instructional staff.

The Faculty of Training Technology of the University of Vocational Technology (UNIVOTEC) is responsible for training TVET teachers. The capacity of this faculty must be built up not only to ensure that both public and private teacher training and upgrading programs are adequate but also to conduct research. Several programs to improve technical knowledge and upgrade skills for public trainers have been held in Malaysia and Singapore. Private providers believe they should also have overseas training opportunities.

Improved assistance for quality assurance. Private providers also believe that TVEC assistance in ensuring the quality of courses is not adequate. They expect more accreditation visits. TVEC assistance to training providers in course accreditation and then assessing for compliance with accreditation regulations may seem like a conflict of interest; the two functions need to be separated so that evaluation is truly independent. Perhaps some of the work could be outsourced to TVEC regional institutions staffed by people trained by UNIVOTEC. There should be considerable discussion before mechanisms for ensuring the quality of courses are settled.

Training providers have stated a need for regular updating of course syllabi and other materials. It has been accepted in principle that the National Competency Standards (NCS) will be revised every two or three years, with curricula and training materials updated accordingly. However, this has not happened as yet. While the NCS should be revised regularly because industry needs are evolving faster than TVET responses, it is necessary to rethink the entire process to speed up responses. One option is to outsource the work to resource persons, institutes, or trade associations, with training where necessary. The present process of National Information Technology Advisory Committees working with industry to draft the NCS, and then UNIVOTEC again conferring with industry to draft curricula, is expensive and time-consuming. Although the NVQ on Basic Competencies to Work (BCW) addresses some areas of employable skills, the skills must be incorporated into other NVQ packages and assessed accordingly. Incorporating the BCW employable skills module into all NVQ courses will be a valuable step forward, as will assessment of students on those competencies. Assessors need to be trained for this express purpose. However, basic employable skills are embedded in all NCS—assessment is perhaps difficult because they are not separated out. Australia and the United Kingdom are grappling with the same problem.

The concept of Sector Skills Councils (SSCs) to manage training by sector was discussed earlier. SSCs established for each industry sector would be mainly responsible for setting standards for and promoting and facilitating training. There are different ways to fund SSCs, the most usual being a levy on employers. SSCs are different from the training funds previously described. Sri Lanka needs to think about what will best suit its needs.

Building the Skills for Economic Growth and Competitiveness in Sri Lanka
http://dx.doi.org/10.1596/978-1-4648-0158-7

Strengthening competency-based assessment. Private providers are not satisfied with the technical competence and work ethics of NVQ assessors. This needs to be addressed promptly. Assessors are currently selected based on nominal qualifications rather than skills and experience. Although over 1,000 assessors have been trained, only about 150 have applied for a license after conducting more than 25 assessments. Apparently a few assessors have all the work. TVEC approval is mandated for those who assess trainees in the private sector, but in public institutions, there is no such control. Thus, the assessment concept and the systems that can roll it out effectively need to be rethought so that competency-based assessments are meaningful, effective, and cover both public and private trainees.

System improvements to NVQ. After the National Vocational Qualifications Framework (NVQF) was introduced in 2004, in the first phase certificate-level courses and supporting systems were drafted. In the second phase, in 2007/08, diploma and degree-level courses were put in place. While the NVQ system has brought Sri Lanka many good TVET practices, it is time for critical analysis to support improvements based on similar systems in other countries. Sri Lanka's NVQ system and procedures tend to have rigid requirements for how competency-based training is done. That was necessary to make the required change in training, introduce quality assurance measures, and overcome initial resistance to change. Now, providers see a need for more flexibility. For example, the Advance Construction Training Academy offers a course in waterproofing that is very popular with industry, but NVQ makes no provision for a certificate. This has forced the academy to award its own certificate. Now that the NVQ transition period is coming to an end, the time is ripe to identify how a more flexible system could increase the quantity of both private and public training while maintaining quality standards.

Conclusion and Policy Options

The public sector is the major provider of TVET in Sri Lanka, but private participation is fairly substantial. Public institutions train about 70 percent of TVET students; the private sector makes up the shortfall. Courses provided by for-profit institutions are oriented to social demand and are typically of shorter duration than public courses. Private providers run by NGOs usually serve students from disadvantaged backgrounds and teach skills that have high labor market demand.

About 77 percent of private providers are for-profit, for which student fees represent the major source of financing. NGO training courses (16 percent), which are free, mostly rely on donor funding. Some private companies have their own training institutions, where training may be free (NAITA apprenticeships) or for a fee (e.g., Prima Baking School). Chamber of commerce and industry training is typically financed by a mixture of fee collecting, donors, and treasury funding, though some courses are free. Professional and paraprofessional trainers rely on student fees. In terms of time to find a job after graduation and monthly earnings, labor market outcomes are similar for graduates of both private and public training.

Given the government goal of providing skills for all youth and its sector capacity constraints, the private sector can complement public services by broadening the coverage of resources invested in TVET. Possible policy options include the following:

- The government should consider revising its secondary education curriculum to provide an orientation to vocational education so that students realize the benefits of the TVET opportunities available. The MYASD and the MoE should make a concerted effort to coordinate on career guidance.
- A guaranteed fund operated through commercial banks should be launched to provide loans at concessionary interest rates for private providers to expand training in areas of high labor market demand. Targeted financial assistance from the TVEC for specific quality improvements in private training must continue and be expanded. PPPs should be established to ensure full utilization of public facilities and reduce the costs of training for both public and private institutions.
- Options for supporting students with financial assistance to pursue TVET in private institutions could be explored and supportive systems established.
- The government could make a policy decision to contribute to the operational costs of NGO centers that provide labor-market-responsive training. One option is to purchase training from them in job areas the government has identified as priorities while preserving the identity and objectives of NGO operations.
- Import duties on high-value training equipment are slowing expansion of private training. The government could make it a policy to allow approved training equipment to be imported on tax concessionary terms.
- Skills acquisition and upgrading for the current workforce is necessary to increase productivity and promote company competitiveness. Legislation to promote skill upgrading is essential. One route to make this a reality is to levy funds from employers that they can then claim back to fund approved training programs for their employees.
- Public training of vocational teachers could be expanded to cover training private teachers. Teacher training methods should be made flexible.
- The regulatory process for assuring quality and helping private training providers comply with quality assurance should be revisited and better methods adopted. Speedier and more efficient mechanisms are necessary for the drafting and periodic revision of competency standards and course curricula.
- Competency-based assessment should be reinforced by ensuring that assessors are more professional and expanding the assessor pool to cover more occupational areas and provide regional reach. This mission would be furthered by close coordination to overcome the present shortcomings.

- Critical analysis of the NVQ system is needed. By learning from its own experience and from similar systems and improvements in other countries, the government could move forcefully to make the system more flexible so as to increase the quantity of training, both public and private, while maintaining relevance and quality.

Note

1. The numbers presented most likely underestimate the actual number of private training providers because some of them do not renew their registration with TVEC, and many do not register at all. Training providers that do not renew their registration are generally small-scale.

Bibliography

Jayalath, Laksara, Damayanthi, Chammika, Nirodha, Anura, Samanmalie, and Kalpage. 2011. "A Tracer Study on NVQ Certificate Holders." Colombo: TVEC.

National Education Commission. 2009. *Policy Document on Higher Education and Technical and Vocational Education.* Colombo: National Education Commission.

TVEC (Tertiary and Vocational Education Commission). 2011a. *Labor Market Information Bulletin.* Colombo: TVEC.

————. 2011b. *Southern Province Vocational Education and Training Plan.* Colombo: TVEC.

CHAPTER 7

Firm-Based Training in Sri Lanka: A Brief Overview

Introduction

Firm-based (on-the job) training (OJT) is prevalent throughout the world. Both employers and employees have incentives to engage in training—employers, because a trained workforce is more productive; workers, because higher productivity translates into higher earnings (Becker 2009; Mincer 1974). In Sri Lanka, the empirical evidence supports this as well (Dutz and O'Connell 2013; Riboud, Savchenko, and Tan 2007; Tan 2012). Since employers may be able to extract some of the increased productivity due to their monopsony power, they would seem to have even greater incentive to invest in training than may first appear (Acemoglu and Pischke 1998).

Firm-based training should form part of the policy discussions as a potentially useful vehicle for upgrading skills, especially for youth, who comprise a significant segment of unskilled labor. If Sri Lanka is to realize the Five Hub Strategy, it is important to consider all alternatives for maximizing labor force productivity. This is especially true because every year—despite the vision and intermediate realization of sections of the *Mahinda Chintana* (MC)—about 140,000 young people enter the labor market without job-specific skills, creating substantial untapped potential (MFP 2010). While the MC explicitly considers youth to be the prime target for specific training and skills development programs, in-service training could be useful for bringing especially the unskilled youth up to speed productivity-wise so that they can find their rightful place in the Sri Lankan labor market.

Firm-based training refers to training provided by employers to employees, whether as informal mentoring, organized training in-house, or organized external training provided, for example, by universities, technical vocational education and training (TVET) institutions, private companies, and industry associations.

To keep the labor market at peak efficiency, it is important for policy makers to determine how prevalent firm-based training is; what types of firms and workers engage in it; the possible consequences of providing or not providing it; and whether employers are satisfied with training by outside providers. This chapter contributes to the supply side of the skills conceptual framework outlined in chapter 1 (figure 1.6) by analyzing recent employer surveys that detail information on in-service training and related issues. The chapter first examines the incidence of firm-based training in Sri Lanka and compares it to other countries and regions. Next, it explores the types and sources of in-service training and the types of providers. It then examines the results of in-service training in terms of firm productivity and worker wages and then assesses what Sri Lankan employers think of in-service training by outside providers. The chapter concludes by presenting the policy implications of in-service training based on the analysis.

Firm-Based Training in South Asia and Other Regions

Although firm-based training is widespread, there are large differences by region and country. Based on evidence from the World Bank Enterprise Survey,[1] 14.6 percent of firms in South Asia (the least) provide firm-based training compared with 44.1 percent of East Asian and Pacific firms (the most). Within South Asia, firm-based training covers a wide range: from 6.7 percent of firms in Pakistan to 18.4 percent in Sri Lanka (figure 7.1), with Indian firms second at 15.9 percent. Although Sri Lanka appears to be doing well for the region, its firms provide less than half the training of firms in East Asia and the Pacific, high-income OECD countries, or Latin America and the Caribbean. Since firm-based training heightens worker productivity and therefore growth in the economy (Dutz and O'Connell 2013; Riboud, Savchenko, and Tan 2007; Tan 2012), making the environment conducive to firms providing more training should be a policy priority.

Figure 7.1 Firm-Based Training in Sri Lanka and Selected Countries and Regions (Various Years)

Percent

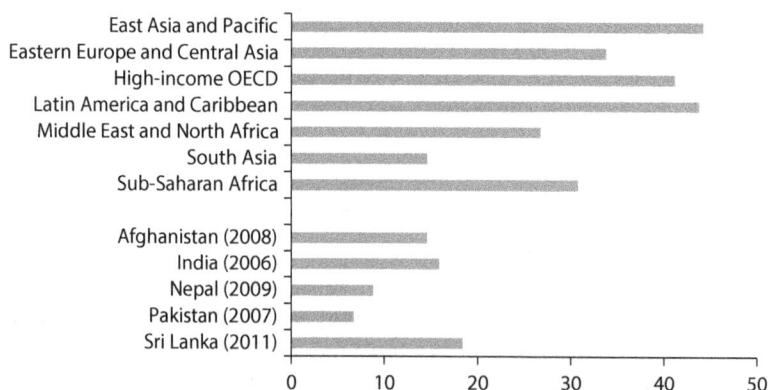

Source: Enterprise Surveys, various years (http://www.enterprisesurveys.org/).

Firm-Based Training in Sri Lanka

As evidenced by the recent Skills Toward Employment and Productivity (STEP) Employer Survey (figure 7.2), in Sri Lanka about 40 percent of high-skilled workers and about 58 percent of low-skilled workers received some training on premises. For external training and in-service training by outside providers, the numbers were substantially lower and the difference by worker type was minimal. The percentages are quite high compared, for example, to India, where no more than 16 percent of firms provide any worker training (World Bank 2008), and Bangladesh, where only about 22 percent do so formally (World Bank 2008); the track record of both countries is low compared to the rest of the world, including fast-growing economies like Malaysia.

Firms are more likely to provide internal training for low-skilled workers and external training for high-skilled workers (figures 7.3 and 7.4) Firms with international business contacts abroad ("international firms") train substantially more than domestic, innovative firms far more than non-innovative, public firms more than private, and larger firms more than smaller. Though this is true for all types of training, the differences are even more obvious for external and in-service training by outside providers (figures 7.3–7.5). This underlines how globalization and innovation drive demand. International firms and innovative firms are the primary growth engines of the Sri Lankan economy, and now it is clear that some of that additional productivity comes from better-trained workers.

For both high- and low-skilled workers (figure 7.6), most internal training was OJT (learning as they work, with help from more experienced workers), followed by training conducted by the firm's managers, technical persons, and peers. Training by dedicated trainers was the third most common type of

Figure 7.2 Incidence of On-the-Job Training, by Type
Percent

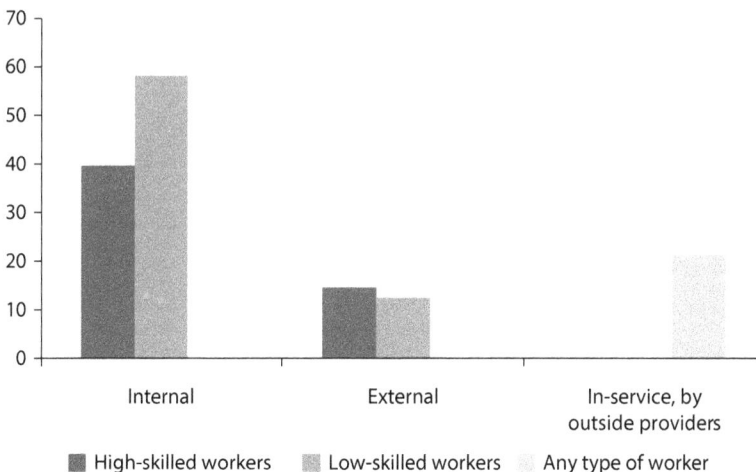

Source: World Bank Employer STEP Survey 2012.

Building the Skills for Economic Growth and Competitiveness in Sri Lanka
http://dx.doi.org/10.1596/978-1-4648-0158-7

Figure 7.3 Firm-Based Training Incidence, by Firm Level and Type
Percent

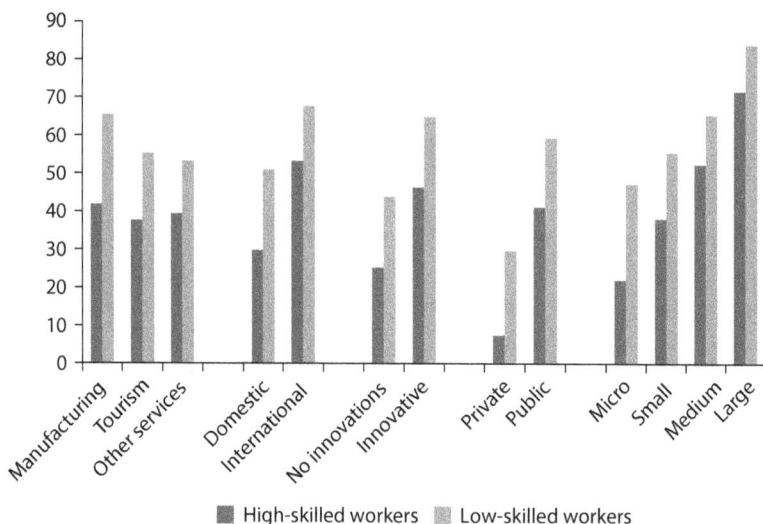

Source: STEP Employer Survey 2012.

Figure 7.4 External Training Incidence, by Firm Level and Type
Percent

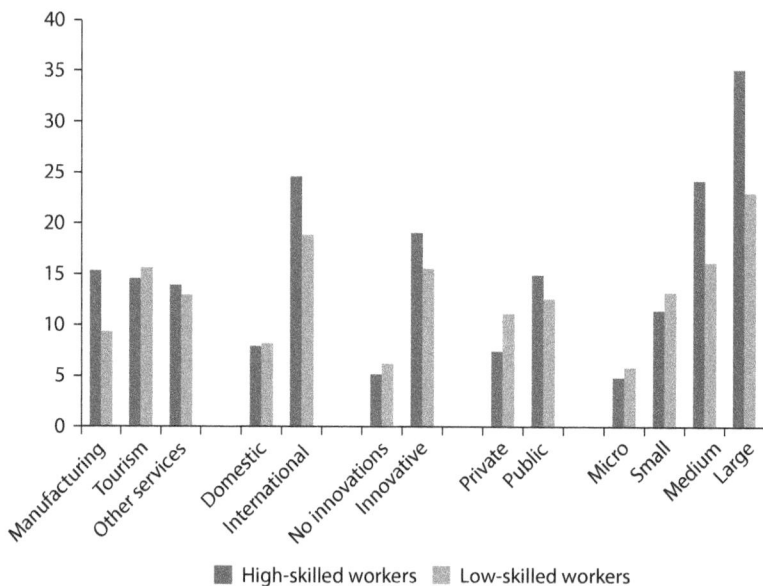

Source: STEP Employer Survey 2012.

Figure 7.5 Firm-Based Training Using Outside Providers, by Type

Percent

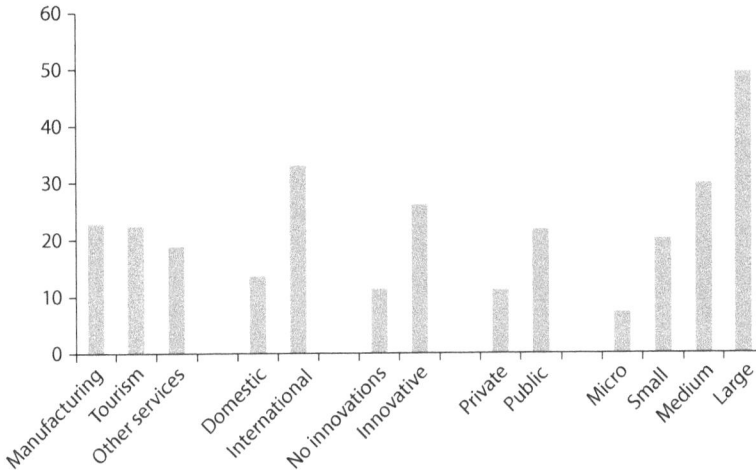

Source: STEP Employer Survey 2012.

Figure 7.6 Share of Employees Receiving Firm-Based Training, by Source

Percent

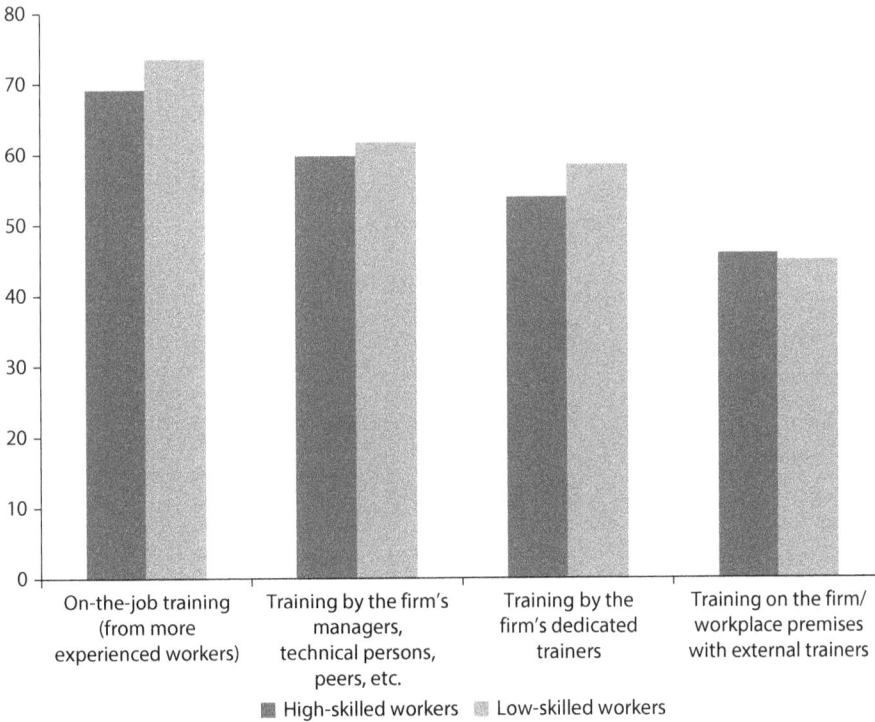

Source: STEP Employer Survey 2012.

internal training, followed by on-premises training by external consultants, private training companies, or government institutions.

The average number of days trained was fairly similar for both high- and low-skilled workers, though the latter received slightly more, averaging as much as 60 days a year for training by the firm's managers, technical persons, and peers; 20–30 days from dedicated trainers; and 15–20 days on-premise by external trainers.

The most popular source of external training is private providers (figure 7.7), followed by technical or vocational education and public training providers, NGOs or international organizations, and finally equipment suppliers (for example, training on software).

The distribution of outside providers of firm-based training varies greatly. The most popular source at 67.7 percent is "other" (which includes, for example, private companies, industry associations, and tertiary non-university institutions), followed by TVET at 41.4 percent, and universities at 15 percent. TVET and university training providers are mainly public, "other" providers are mainly private.

Consequences of Firm-Based Training

In Sri Lanka, as in the rest of the world, firm-based training seems to have substantial impact on both firm and worker outcomes. While it may be another way to compensate for skills shortages (see chapter 3), it is also important in its own right. It can equip workers with skills that go beyond merely formal general or even technical and vocational training because they are better prepared for a specific industry or occupation. In Sri Lanka, on-premises training has been found to be associated with higher wages; though external training was not

Figure 7.7 Employees Receiving External Training, by Source[2]
Percent

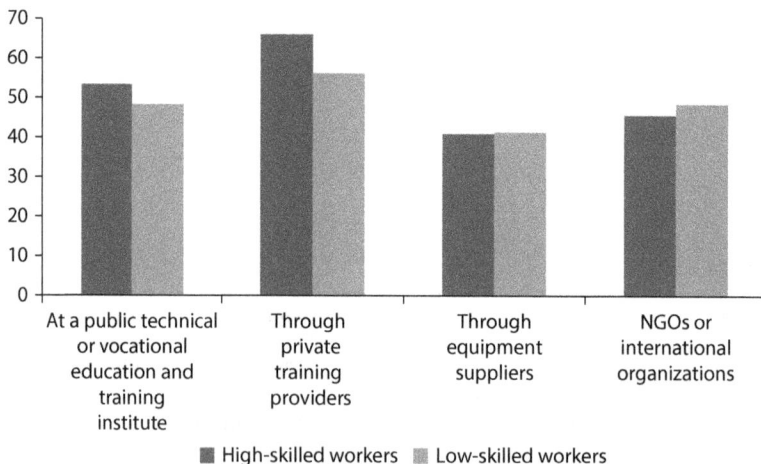

Source: STEP Employer Survey 2012.

Building the Skills for Economic Growth and Competitiveness in Sri Lanka
http://dx.doi.org/10.1596/978-1-4648-0158-7

(Riboud, Savchenko, and Tan 2007). Both internal and external firm-provided training, especially on-site, has also been found to have substantial impact on firm performance in Sri Lanka (Dutz and O'Connell 2013; Riboud, Savchenko, and Tan 2007; Tan 2012).

The STEP Employer Survey results show a positive and substantively large direct association between total firm production and internal, external, and in-service training by outside providers (Blunch 2013), though taking into account other factors—such as firm size, material inputs, region, and sector—weakens the relationship in terms of both statistical precision and estimated magnitude. Firm-based training by outside sources other than TVET and university (such as private companies, industry associations, and tertiary non-university institutions), however, still has a sizable, though somewhat imprecisely measured, association with firm productivity: if a firm offers in-service training by providers other than TVET and university, productivity is about 73 percent higher than firms that do not offer such training. While the number of firms in this analysis of the STEP survey is small, which introduces imprecision into the estimated results, the analysis still suggests that in Sri Lanka more firm-based training could boost productivity.

Employer Perceptions of the Quality of Firm-Based Training

Employers perceive in-service training to be fairly successful in terms of the quality of providers, though there are variations in the assessment (figure 7.8). It appears that while employers are generally not very critical of in-service training, they are somewhat less positive about TVET and university than about other providers.

Though satisfaction is relatively high, utilization of in-service training by outside providers is comparatively low relative to fast-growing economies (though high relative to other countries in South Asia), which suggests that employers may have issues with in-service training costs or with the incentives

Figure 7.8 Employer Perceptions of In-Service Training, by Outside Providers[3]
Percent

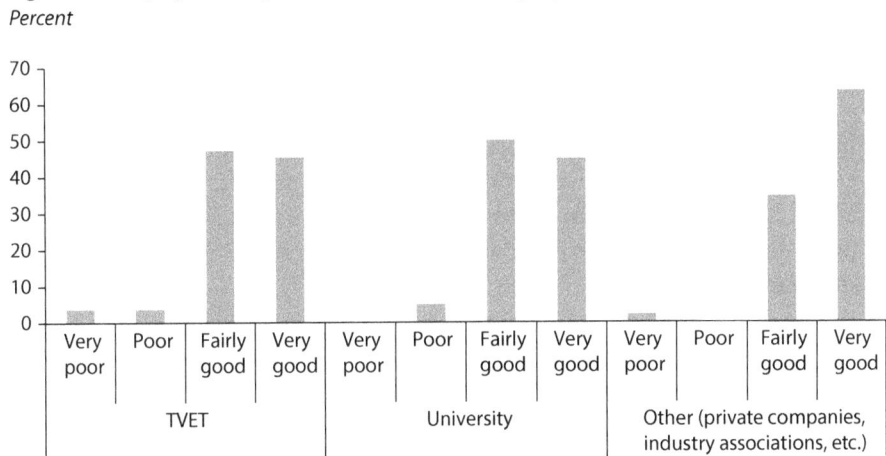

Source: STEP Employer Survey 2012.

for providing in-service training. It would therefore seem important for policy makers to examine why few employers call upon outside providers. If cost is indeed an issue, they might consider ways to subsidize this type of training because of the productivity potential.

An active skills development fund (SDF) might be a particularly useful vehicle in this regard. While officially Sri Lanka already has an SDF, established under the Tertiary and Vocational Education Commission (TVEC) Act, it has never become functional. Sri Lanka may want to look to the experience of other countries; the Singapore SDF may be a promising example (box 7.1), as is the Penang Skills Development Centre (PSDC) in Malaysia.

Conclusion and Policy Options

Demand in Sri Lanka for firm-based training is above that of other countries in the region, though still below international levels. Most firm-based training is internal, though there is also external training and in-service training by outside providers. OJT is the main source of internal training, and private providers are the main source of external training; in-service training by outside providers mainly originates from sources other than TVET and university, such as private companies or industry associations.

Demand for training and the sources differ widely by both firm and worker type. Internationally oriented, innovative, public, and large firms do more of all types of firm-based training than other firms. Firms are more likely to train low-skilled workers in-house and send high-skilled workers for external training.

Firm-based training, in Sri Lanka and throughout the world, is associated with favorable outcomes for both workers (better employment and wages) and firms (higher productivity).

The relatively low rates of firm-based training by international standards, despite the high rates of return to both firms and workers, merit attention. More firm-based training may both help realize the MC vision of Skills for All and promote growth of the entire economy through higher productivity and wages. To accelerate reform and help increase the provision of firm-based training, the findings of this chapter lead to a number of specific policy observations:

• Involving industry and employers more directly in firm-based training, for example by advising TVET institutions about the specific needs of industry and employers so they can better design their training programs, should be a policy priority. Ultimately, employers need to be more active in every phase of the training system.

• To help motivate employers to provide more firm-based training it will be necessary to set up an incentive-based scheme, such as an SDF. Sri Lanka can benefit from the experience of other countries (boxes 7.1 and 7.2). It is important that employers perceive a training fund financed through levies as a genuine instrument to build staff skills, not just an additional fiscal burden.

Box 7.1 Singapore and Malaysia: Skills Development Funds

The Singapore Skills Development Fund (SDF) has been operating since 1979. All employers, including those in the public sector, pay a levy of 1 percent of the wages of all employees earning up to S$2,000 a month. The intent is to motivate employers to train workers by reimbursing some or all of their training expenses. SDF reimbursement is not restricted to contributing companies—any enterprise that undertakes training may apply. Applicants for grants must demonstrate the need for training. Grants can be used for direct training costs—for example, fees for external training—or to establish training infrastructure, including paying trainers. There must be some cost-sharing; SDF grants cover 30–70 percent of training costs. Trainees must be employees of the firms receiving the grants. The present policy is to encourage training for services firms, small and medium-sized enterprises, less-educated and less-skilled workers, and older workers. Skills training for certification is emphasized. The SDF has been responsible for massive growth in company training. In fiscal year 2003, for instance, the SDF reached 100 percent of all companies with 10 and more workers and 41 percent of those with fewer than 10. The 578,000 training places created represented a ratio of one for every four workers. Total company investment in training reached the target of 4 percent of payroll some years ago (ADB 2008).

The Malaysia Human Resource Development Fund (HRDF) is a levy reimbursement scheme established under the legal requirements of the Human Resources Development Act of 1992. The enabling act created the Human Resource Development Council, with representatives from the private sector and government agencies responsible for training and a secretariat to administer the scheme. Employers make a payroll contribution of 1 percent to the HRDF and are eligible to claim a portion of allowable training expenditures up to the limit of their total levy for any given year. Reimbursement rates vary by sector and type of training. The HRDF is considered to be one of the best-run schemes administratively and is extremely efficient in reimbursing claims and making application procedures easy to comply with. As of 2012, 12,953 employers in 44 subsectors were registered with HRDF. Early impact evaluations have shown that while HRDF did not increase training by small firms, it did increase training by medium and large firms (HRDF 2012; Tan 2005; Tan and Gill 2000).

It is therefore imperative that employers are explicitly involved in reviving the Sri Lankan SDF from the very beginning. Experience also suggests that taxes to finance training funds should not be imposed on payrolls, since that tends to make employers reluctant to recruit new staff.

- More responsive regulation and innovative public-private partnerships (PPPs) would help leverage private provision of both pre-employment training and OJT. Currently training by private providers is of uneven quality, but those who meet high standards can be encouraged to prosper along with public providers. Regulation and quality assurance for both public and private institutions need to be adapted to that end. It might also be advantageous to adapt to Sri Lanka innovative training PPPs that have worked well in Malaysia and other countries (box 7.2).

Box 7.2 A Public-Private Partnership: The Malaysia Penang Skills Development Centre

The Penang Skills Development Centre (PSDC) was the first industry-led training center to be set up in Malaysia. It was conceptualized in 1989 out of an urgent sense that if Penang was to continue to attract foreign direct investment, its human capital must keep pace with changes in technology. Although the initiative, land, and some financial support came from the state and federal governments, the lead role—with initial support from U.S. electronics firms already operating in the state—was taken by private industry, which not only provided the initial trainers and equipment but also designed programs that met their needs.

The government acts as a facilitator, supporting PSDC through cash grants and subsidized training materials, equipment, and trainers, and helps evaluate the impact of the training. It is represented on the PSDC management council by an ex officio member.

PSDC, which now has 140 members, operates as a nonprofit association. Its mission is to pool resources to provide up-to-date training and education programs that support current operational requirements and to keep current with technological advances. Companies pay to send employees to the center for training. To ensure that the training meets industry needs, programs are continually adapted as skill needs evolve.

The PSDC now caters to the firms in the free industrial zones and industrial parks in Penang, which as of late 2007 had 1,277 factories employing about 220,000 workers. The center has trained more than 150,000 workers in more than 7,000 courses, pioneered local industry development initiatives, advised on national policies for building human capital, and contributed directly to Malaysian workforce transformation initiatives. The PSDC recently set up a new Shared Services Centre to house Malaysia's largest Electromagnetic Compatibility Lab, which will provide training in partnership with member companies to fast-track the work readiness of university graduates and bridge the competency gap between what they know and what industry needs. The unique PSDC model has since been adopted throughout the country; 11 of 13 states in Malaysia now have skills development centers.

Source: World Bank 2011 (based on Penang Skills Development Centre 2010).

Notes

1. More details can be found in chapter 3.
2. Three firms reported "other" as a source of external training—this category has been omitted here to simplify the graph.
3. Two firms reported "don't know" and four firms reported "other" for the sector for one of the three sources of providers. These have been omitted here to simplify the graph.

Bibliography

Acemoglu, D., and J-S. Pischke. 1998. "Why Do Firms Train? Theory and Evidence." *The Quarterly Journal of Economics* 113 (1): 79–119.

ADB (Asian Development Bank). 2008. *Education and Skills: Strategies for Accelerated Development in Asia and the Pacific*. Manila: ADB.

Becker, G. S. 2009. *Human Capital: A Theoretical and Empirical Analysis, with Special Reference to Education*. Chicago, IL: University of Chicago Press.

Blunch, N-H. 2013. "Skills Demand of Employers in Sri Lanka." Background Paper, Human Development Division, South Asia Region World Bank, Washington, DC.

Dutz, M. A., and S. D. O'Connell. 2013. "Productivity, Innovation and Growth in Sri Lanka: An Empirical Investigation." World Bank Policy Research Working Paper 6354, World Bank, Washington, DC.

HRDF (Human Resource Development Fund). 2012. "Human Resource Development Fund presentation to Australian Trade Commission." Kuala Lumpur, Malaysia: HRDF.

Mincer, J. 1974. *Schooling, Experience and Earnings*. New York, NY: Columbia University Press.

MFP (Ministry of Finance and Planning). 2010. *Mahinda Chintana*. http://www.treasury.gov.lk/publications/mahindaChintanaVision-2010full-eng.pdfc.

Riboud, M., Y. Savchenko, and H. Tan. 2007. *The Knowledge Economy and Education and Training in South Asia*. Washington, DC: World Bank.

Tan, H. 2005. *The Skills Challenge of New Technology: Training, Technology and Productivity Growth in Malaysian Manufacturing in the 1990s*. Washington, DC: World Bank Institute.

———. 2012. "Sri Lanka: Education, Training and Labor Market Outcomes." Background Paper for Sri Lanka Skills Development Report, World Bank, Washington, DC.

———. and I. S. Gill. 2000. "Malaysia." In *Vocational Education and Training Reform*, edited by I. S. Gill, F. Fluitman, and A. Dar, 218–60. New York, NY: Oxford University Press.

World Bank. 2006. *The Bangladesh Vocational Education and Training System: An Assessment*. Human Development Unit, South Asia Region, World Bank, Washington, DC.

———. 2008. *Skill Development in India—The Vocational Education and Training System*. Report 22, Human Development Sector, South Asia Region Washington, DC.

———. 2011. *Special Economic Zones in Africa: Comparing Performance and Learning from Global Experience*. Washington, DC.

———. 2012. STEP Employer Survey. World Bank, Washington DC.

CHAPTER 8

An Assessment of Workforce Development Policies

Introduction

The purpose of this chapter is to document and assess national policies and institutions that guide workforce development (WfD) in Sri Lanka and discuss their implications for skills supply and demand, focusing on technical and vocational education and training (TVET). It complements the discussion of the factors contributing to skills supply (figure 1.6) by analyzing related policies, examining these questions: (1) How are Sri Lanka's WfD policies aligned to its economic and social priorities? (2) How effective is the system for governing WfD? And (3) How effective is service delivery in terms of results?

The first section briefly summarizes the Systems Approach for Better Education Results–Workforce Development (SABER-WfD) framework and diagnostic tool. The second provides country and sector context. The third summarizes the SABER-WfD, benchmarking results in terms of the strategic framework, system oversight, and service delivery. The chapter concludes with brief findings and recommendations.

The SABER-WfD Framework and Diagnostic Tool

The diagnostic tool used here is a product of the World Bank SABER initiative, which looks at several policy domains, one of which is WfD.[1] The three broad functional dimensions of WfD are the *strategic framework*, which pertains to policies that set the direction for WfD; *system oversight*, which relates to the rules (including those related to funding) that guide how the system functions; and *service delivery*, which concerns provision of training to equip individuals with market- and job-relevant skills (figure 8.1).

From the perspective of the line ministries, strategy typically involves sensing, influencing, and responding to the external environment for WfD; oversight governs the activities of all stakeholders with a direct interest in WfD; and delivery is about managing the activities of those providing training.

Figure 8.1 Functional Dimensions of Workforce Development Policies

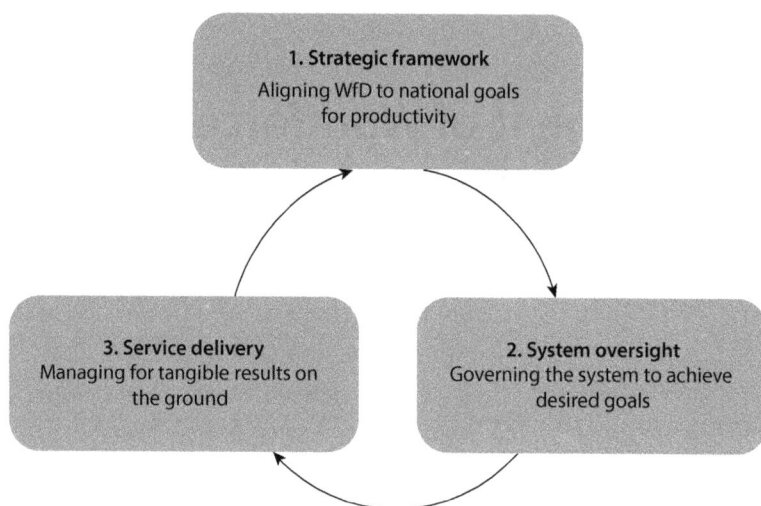

Source: Tan *et al.* 2012.

These three dimensions constitute a closed policy-making loop. Together they make it possible to analyze how a WfD system functions as a whole. Each functional dimension is composed of *policy goals* that span the three broad areas of governance, finance, and information. Each goal is defined by three *policy actions*, for a total of 9 goals and 27 actions (see annex 8A for details).

Data collection, processing, and scoring. For each of the 27 policy actions, the Data Collection Instrument poses questions related to the corresponding aspect of the WfD system. Each question is answered by choosing from a list of closed options corresponding to stages of development. The choice is substantiated either by documentary evidence or by information supplied and corroborated by knowledgeable and credible informants.

The information gathered is scored according to standard rubrics, which correspond to four stages of maturity in WfD policy and institutional development: (1) *latent* (limited engagement); (2) *emerging* (some instances of good practice); (3) *established* (systematic good practice); and (4) *advanced* (systematic good practice meeting global standards). The scores on the 27 policy actions form the basis for analysis of the 9 policy goals. The scores awarded to the four levels are 1, 2, 3, and 4 for each policy action (integer values and policy actions scores are averaged out to form the score for the policy goal).

Simple weights are applied to aggregate scores on the actions that relate to each policy goal, typically one-third for information related to policy concepts and design and two-thirds for information related to implementation. Finally, scores for the policy goals that relate to each dimension are aggregated with equal weights in order to obtain scores for the three functional dimensions of the SABER-WfD framework. The SABER-WfD assessment, led by a principal investigator,[2] is based, as noted, on information from credible informants (box 8.1).

Box 8.1 Documentary Sources for the Sri Lanka SABER-WfD Assessment

The Sri Lanka SABER-WfD assessment is based primarily on data collected by a desk review of documents produced between 1990 and 2010 and information gathered from discussions with informants who have TVET experience and knowledge. The documents are categorized as

- National policy and planning documents of the Ministry of Finance and Planning, the Ministry of Youth Affairs and Skills Development (MYASD), and the Central Bank.
- MYASD TVET documents related to public budgetary allocations, performance data, project initiatives, and related survey reports.
- Acts of public training institutions, corporate plans, performance reports, and partnership agreements.
- Unified National Qualifications Framework information with quality assurance directives and processes, labor market information, and sector-related research information.
- Documents pertaining to private training provision and workforce skills upgrading for and by industry.

Sector Context

Workforce Development Priorities

Economic development, especially when fuelled by the rapid growth of the service sector, creates employment opportunities that require specialized competencies. Recognizing the expected growth of industry in the medium term, the government is focusing on certain strategic sectors that will make increasing demands on the country's workforce. It has already initiated action in some segments:

- The number of employees in the information and communication technology (ICT) sector, for instance, is expected to increase from 50,000 in 2010 to 186,000 by 2016, especially in the areas of database management, digital media and animation, business analysis and systems integration, network administration, programming and software engineering, and related applications.
- Since the civil war ended, tourism has been growing fast; Sri Lanka expects to receive 2.5 million tourists in 2016. Expansion will require rapid growth in the areas of food and beverages, construction, furniture making, transport, and hotel and tourism-related management, which together are expected to open up 700,000 jobs.
- The two seaport development projects and construction of an international airport have generated employment in engineering, skilled crafts, and service-related activity. Similar employment is expected to be generated in the commercial, road and transport, urban development, irrigation, and knowledge segments of the economy.

Building the Skills for Economic Growth and Competitiveness in Sri Lanka
http://dx.doi.org/10.1596/978-1-4648-0158-7

- It is estimated that in the health sector additional 2,500 nurses and 600 radiographers, pharmacists, medical laboratory technicians, and so on, are likely to be needed annually to serve domestic and overseas demands.

Current and Proposed Reforms

The Presidential Task Force on TVET, established in 1998, provides guidance on WfD and has been guiding TVET to be more industry-relevant and quality-conscious. A major recommendation was to transform training in public centers to competency-based training (CBT) aligned with industry-identified standards and quality assurance mechanisms, such as course accreditation and quality management. This process was facilitated by the creation of a ministry dedicated to TVET and bringing most of the public training centers within its purview by 2004.

The reforms were further reinforced by the National Vocational Qualification (NVQ) framework, which offers competency-based qualifications through accredited public and private training programs. Competencies are acquired through work practices using the recognition of prior learning (RPL) methodology. The NVQ framework set pathways for upgrading qualifications, and institutions were established to offer mid-level technical courses and bachelor's degree TVET programs. The government proposes extending training in priority sectors by using networks of training institutions and apprenticeship-based training, and by encouraging the private sector to provide more training. Simultaneously, mid-level technical education is to be expanded in areas experiencing high labor market demand. Providing more access to students who have completed upper secondary education should encourage them to enter the programs in significant numbers. To achieve a competitive edge in the national and international labor markets, the relevance and quality of programs are slated for improvement.

Benchmarking of WfD Policies and Institutions

Strategic Framework Dimension

The strategic framework dimension of the SABER-WfD analysis looks at three policy goals: setting a strategic direction for WfD; fostering a demand-driven approach; and better coordinating implementation. Each of these leads to one or more policy actions—e.g., information, issues, good practices, and level of consolidation—that are identified for closer examination by collecting diagnostic data. In Sri Lanka this dimension is scored at the *established* level (2.6). The score reflects the commitment of Sri Lanka's political leaders and policy makers to enhancing the skills of the labor force (scored at 3.0), but there is less concern for a demand-driven approach (2.2) and poor coordination of implementation (2.7).

With respect to setting a strategic direction for WfD, Sri Lanka's political leaders have been doing so for the past two decades, focusing mainly on industry and services. With the creation of the Tertiary and Vocational Education Commission (TVEC), the planning and regulatory body, in the 1990s, WfD became systematized. Government economic development policy documents emphasized WfD and in 1998 and 2009, TVET policy documents set out specific strategic directions for a competent and labor market–relevant workforce. Some of the major reforms were the introduction of CBT and of the NVQ framework. The National Human Resources and Employment Policy (2012), though yet to be implemented, takes a comprehensive inter-sectoral approach.

Fostering a Demand-Driven Approach

WfD has so far concentrated on providing initial vocational education and training (VET) for postsecondary students. In 2011, 98,000 students were reportedly enrolled in public training institutions and 53,000 in private institutions. How to incorporate VET into secondary education (to guide students to consider TVET as a viable career path) is not well-elucidated in policy documents. While pathways and institutions have been established for diploma- and degree-level learning, access to continuing VET that integrates the current workforce into both formal and informal industry has not been accorded priority. Even though the 2004 creation of a separate ministry for skills development facilitated TVET coordination, without clear milestones and benchmarks and institutionalized stakeholder engagement, progress is difficult to monitor.

The Central Bank of Sri Lanka and the Department of National Planning have analyzed what changes in different economic sectors imply for WfD. The Department of Census and Statistics (DCS) provides data on labor force education and training and labor market outcomes, and TVEC collects and analyzes some data to examine trends in skills demand and supply. However, TVEC does not yet regularly ascertain the skills various business sectors are demanding nationally and regionally, and coordination between the Department of National Planning, TVEC, and the DCS has not been institutionalized. To date, the government has engaged employers in setting WfD priorities only ad hoc. Employers themselves have had to upgrade employee skills and train the school leavers they hire. Moreover, there are no official mechanisms to encourage employers to upgrade the skills of their employees, such as training levy systems, and there are no comprehensive incentives for employee training, skills testing, and certification. Meaningful dialogue on WfD between the government and employers is rare.

Promoting Critical Coordination

What has greatly improved, however, is the coordination and implementation of WfD programs. This has been achieved by bringing most of the training institutes under MYASD supervision. However, other ministries operate specialized areas of TVET, so inter-ministerial coordination will be vital if the government is to attain its WfD objectives. Closer coordination between MYASD and its training institutions through effective regulation and monitoring will also make it easier to reach training targets. Currently, coordination with private trainers to improve the quality and relevance of their programs is mostly limited to registering institutes and accrediting courses. Employer participation in the governing boards of training institutions could ensure that TVET addresses employer skills needs.

Reflections on the Findings

- Visible "policy champions," such as the comprehensive National Human Resources and Employment Policy (SSM 2012), provide sustained advocacy and strategic direction for WfD. Routine monitoring and review processes will help Sri Lanka realize its WfD goals.
- Introducing VET within secondary education will help more students to recognize TVET career development opportunities. This has potential not only to contribute to systematic WfD but also to reduce youth unemployment.
- Continuing VET by integrating the workforce into both formal and informal industry (with employer participation) will both promote productivity and fulfill the career development aspirations of the workforce.
- A TVEC process to regularly ascertain national and regional skills demands and institutionalize cooperation with the Department of National Planning will help meet employer WfD needs.
- Mechanisms that stimulate employers to upgrade employee skills, such as a training levy system, have served many countries well.
- Mechanisms for coordinating, and reviewing WfD at various levels (institutional, ministerial, inter-ministerial, and nongovernmental) will help to mainstream successful WfD features.

System Oversight Dimension

The SABER-WfD system oversight dimension focuses on (1) ensuring efficiency and equity in funding; (2) assuring relevant and reliable standards; and (3) diversifying pathways for skills acquisition. Each of these leads to one or more policy actions, such as information and good practices, that are identified for closer examination by collecting diagnostic data. For Sri Lanka, the overall rating for this dimension, 2.4, hits the emerging level. This score reflects a well-established system of accreditation, registration, skills testing, and certification (2.8), but relatively poor funding strategy; lack of clear linkages between funding, performance, and accountability; flimsy partnership arrangements between WfD authorities and other stakeholders (2.3); insufficient diversity of programs and ease of movement between them; and few lifelong learning opportunities, though procedures to renew programs are quite well-established (2.2).

Ensuring Efficiency and Equity in Funding

As summarized in chapter 5, public TVET is primarily funded through general taxation. Some institutions do not charge course fees; some, like the Vocational Training Authority (VTA), charge fees at subsidized rates. Recurrent funding for initial VET (IVET) and continuing VET (CVET) are mainly based on the previous year's financial outlay, and only government officials take part in the budgeting process. IVET commands maximum funding and CVET very little. Entrepreneurship training and loans for self-employment for TVET graduates, having proved successful, are now better funded. Thus, recurrent budgeting is at the emerging level.

The most recent review of the impact of funding for IVET was in 2008. The review examined (1) the efficiency of public and private TVET; (2) quantification of its economic and social benefits; and (3) costing methodology and cost recovery mechanisms to ensure that public programs are financially sustainable. The review incorporated a tracer study of the employment status of students who had completed vocational education. The MYASD is implementing some review recommendations. Reviews of active labor market policies have been limited to entrepreneurship training and self-employment loans. Most partnerships between training providers and employers are in the National Apprentice and Industrial Training Authority (NAITA) and VTA networks, where head office initiatives and different models of partnerships are benefiting both parties. Thus both monitoring and enhanced equity in funding for training are below the *established* level.

Assuring Relevant and Reliable Standards

Sri Lanka formally launched the NVQ Framework and CBT in 2004. The NVQ Framework consists of four certificate and two diploma levels and a bachelor's degree. In keeping with international best practice, with active industry participation the country has put in place 114 competency standards at the certificate level and 17 at the diploma level, all of which are to be reviewed every three years. The certificate standards are based on occupation, e.g., electricians, machinists, and beauticians and the diploma standards on fields of study, such as automotive or construction technology. Competency standards identify units and elements of competence, together with performance criteria, range statement, assessment guide, and knowledge foundation. They are drafted by National Industry Training Advisory Committees appointed for each business subsector with representation from the subsector, professional or trade bodies, training providers, and the labor ministry. Sri Lanka is at the *established level* in broadening the scope of competency standards.

Most MYASD institutions base their training on competency standards and curricula. A significant proportion of private and other public institutes also offer voluntary courses aligned with national certificate competency standards. Trainee skills are assessed by certified assessors; in 2011, 16,572 trainees were awarded NVQ certificates. While the government recognizes NVQ certificate for recruitment to different grades in the public service, the certificate is not as yet highly valued by private employers.

TVEC has established a system of course accreditation to ensure compliance with competency standards and the quality of course delivery and assessments. At the end of 2011 TVEC had accredited 652 public and 303 private courses. TVEC provides technical assistance and limited funding targeted to course accreditation to both public and private institutes. It appears, therefore, that enforcing accreditation standards for maintaining the quality of training is at the *established* level.

Building the Skills for Economic Growth and Competitiveness in Sri Lanka
http://dx.doi.org/10.1596/978-1-4648-0158-7

Diversifying Pathways for Acquiring Skills

Postsecondary students have limited TVET learning pathways through government networks and private institutions. Mid-level technical qualifications are offered by the Colleges of Technology, the Sri Lanka Institute of Advanced Technological Education (SLIATE) network, and such individual institutions as the new University of Vocational Technology (UNIVOTEC).

The NVQ framework also gives trainees an opportunity to advance their career prospects by moving up to the diploma and degree levels (figure 8.2). Means are provided to non-NVQ holders whose qualifications have been assessed against NVQ to enter these pathways. Unfortunately, there are few public career development services and progression through multiple pathways is only now emerging.

RPL allows employees who have acquired competencies at work to have them assessed and certified and provides avenues for further learning. In 2011 RPL issued 1,996 certificates but the system suffers from lack of awareness among the general public, inadequate competency assessment facilities and coordinating mechanisms, and the inability or lack of willingness of individuals to pay assessment fees. However, enhancing support for skills acquisition by workers, job seekers, and the disadvantaged is above the *emerging* level.

Reflections on the Findings

- Expanding TVET access to more trainees and enhancing program quality will require both substantial capital and recurrent funding and more efficient budgeting.
- Because TVET graduates have had great success with self-employment, entrepreneurship training, enhanced funding for loans, and institutionalizing coordination and mentoring processes are likely to promote enterprise growth.
- Sri Lanka is at an advanced stage with its NVQ framework and in setting competency standards, but continuous improvement of both to keep up with global best practices will move WfD forward and enhance public and employer confidence.
- Having certified assessors available island-wide—covering the complete range of trades and occupations—will speed timely assessment of trainees and employees.
- Trained instructors and fully equipped workshops are essential to quality training and retaining course accreditation. Policy intervention may be required to ensure these essentials in both the public and private sectors.
- Currently, course accreditation is voluntary for private providers and public providers other than those under the MYASD purview, but the situation might be reviewed to ensure course quality across the board.
- The public has little understanding of TVET or awareness of how to progressively gain skills. Career guidance and social marketing targeting secondary school students, teachers, parents, workers, and employers might be useful to raise the awareness.

Figure 8.2 Pathways for Upgrading Qualifications through NVQ

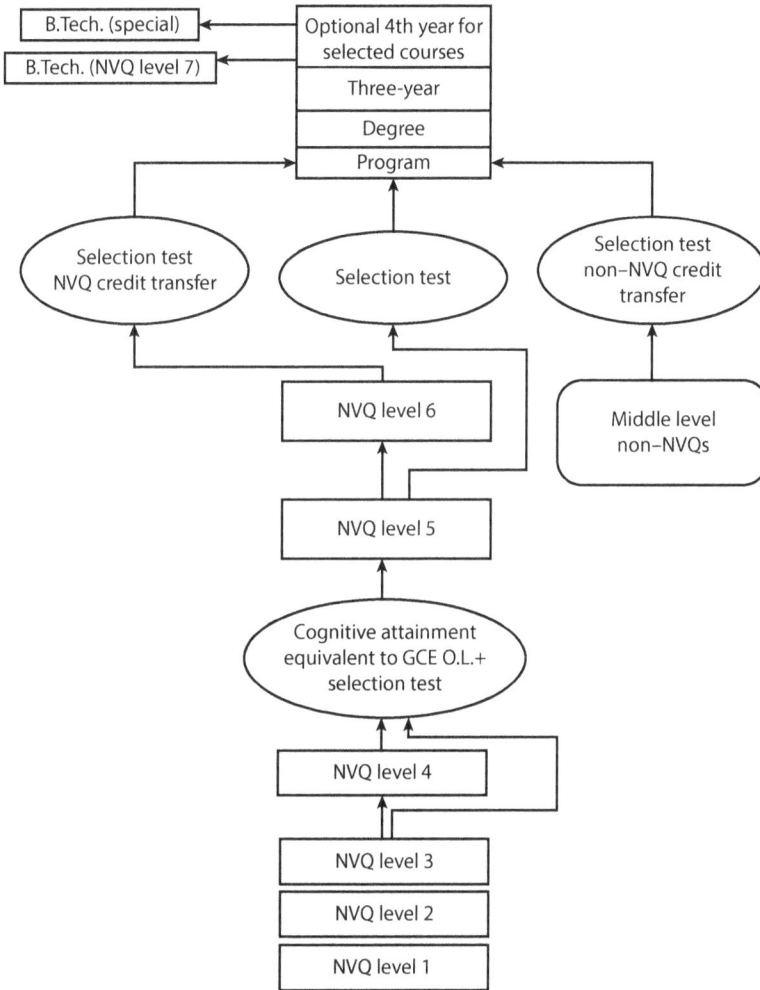

• Support for workers to acquire skills by making RPL testing and career advancement services widespread will not only help upgrade worker skills but also improve their satisfaction and productivity.

Service Delivery Dimension

The service delivery dimension of the SABER-WfD analysis focuses on (1) promoting diversity and excellence in training; (2) keeping public training programs relevant; and (3) enhancing accountability for results. Each of these leads to policy actions that are identified for closer examination by collecting diagnostic data. The rating for this **emerging** dimension is 2.2.

Building the Skills for Economic Growth and Competitiveness in Sri Lanka
http://dx.doi.org/10.1596/978-1-4648-0158-7

Promoting Diversity and Excellence in Training

The Tertiary and Vocational Education Act established mechanisms to register private institutes and assure their quality. However, because it has no enforcement provisions, only about 80 percent of training providers have registered with TVEC.[3] During the registration process, the TVEC gives them technical guidance on physical facilities, course curricula, instructor qualifications, competency assessments, and record-keeping. It also offers technical assistance and small-scale financial support for buying any equipment necessary for course accreditation and NVQ issuance. However, incentives for all types of private providers are below par, and the government has yet to make it a priority to facilitate expansion of private training.

Sri Lanka has been giving precedence to expanding public training. Public providers are issued enrollment targets and approximate numbers to be trained in particular fields of study or occupations. Trainee output targets are not generally available, but the dropout rate for all trainees seems to be about 25 percent. Examination pass rates, job placement rates, and employer and trainee satisfaction are not regularly considered in performance assessments, although they are sometimes reviewed in ad hoc surveys. There are no rewards for better-performing public institutions, although individual officers and instructors are commended. There is no formal mechanism for closing training programs that fail to achieve targets, although some have been forced to shut down based on ad hoc reviews.

Public institutions have the authority to spend the budgets allocated except for determining the number of positions (teaching and nonteaching) and their remuneration, both of which require Ministry of Finance and Planning (MFP) approval. Except for the Department of Technical Education and Training (DTET), they may generate funds from regular courses or part-time extension courses and use them to pay staff for work beyond their assigned duties. Thus, though staff can receive additional income, the institution cannot retain net income. How incentives and autonomy in management of public training institutions are combined is assessed at the *emerging* level.

Fostering Relevance

Links between training institutions and industry have been forged to improve course quality and relevance through competency standards, employer endorsement of course curricula, employer representation on governing boards and advisory bodies, assessment of labor market needs, industry training for instructors and trainees, collaborative training programs, and business provision of part-time trainers. However, these links do not operate well in practice, and there is as yet no significant industry role in setting facility standards for training providers and no formal links with independent research institutes. Research on improving provider and course operational efficiency is coordinated by the TVEC research unit, which presents its findings at an annual seminar.

Enhancing Accountability

All statutory bodies are expected to have rolling five-year corporate plans, updated every year. A detailed activity plan is prepared before each year begins and is forwarded to the MFP. Results are monitored against the annual activity plan. At the end of each year an annual report is presented to the Parliament and then becomes a public document. DTET produces a performance report. All MYASD training agencies report to the ministry and the TVEC on enrollments and completions. Registered private institutions report enrollments and completions to the TVEC; in 2011, 286 submitted reports—about 30 percent of those registered. Trainee competency assessments are submitted online by head offices of training agencies to TVEC as the basis for issuance of NVQ certificates.

Public provider heads and instructors are recruited based on criteria approved by the MFP Department of Management Services that cover academic and vocational qualifications and industry and teaching experience. However, the lower salaries in the public sector do not attract the best-qualified staff. Orientation for new hires and further professional development is ad hoc.

Public provider reporting of training-related data is mainly confined to enrollments and completion of training; client feedback, job placements, and earnings of graduates are rarely reported. However, the annual reports that statutory bodies send to Parliament contain more information on, for example, staffing, capacity improvement, and how allocated budgets have been spent. Although there is a computer-based public management information system (MIS), data feeds are irregular. Because of the lack of electronic information, the TVEC has conducted special surveys to collect accurate data from MYASD providers. Training institutions and donor-funded projects have also conducted surveys on special topics to support requests for policy interventions. Use of data to monitor and improve programs and systems is limited; in the recent past, no significant improvements have been made based on data collected. Thus, use of policy-relevant data to focus provider attention on training outcomes, efficiency, and innovation is at the *latent level*.

Reflections on the Findings

- A well-functioning and comprehensive registration process for private providers will enhance quality assurance.
- Even though private providers have been given some incentives and technical assistance, major WfD policy interventions could facilitate capacity growth and diversity in private training.
- Giving public training institutions more management and financial autonomy will enhance their operational flexibility and efficiency.
- Links between training providers and employers for setting competency standards and curriculum development are still emerging and need reinforcement. Employers should be more involved in setting facility standards, and links with research institutes need to be closer.

• Systematic professional development of instructors and training center managers is vital to improve training quality and efficiency. It might be useful to set up dedicated institutions and programs for those purposes.
• Reporting of public-training-related data is incomplete and cannot effectively contribute to analysis of training operations, which makes informed decision making difficult. MIS operations should be upgraded to gather more reliable and comprehensive data, which would certainly enhance the planning process.
• Links between public providers and reputable research institutions should be established so that strategic decisions on WfD are based on well-founded research findings.

Key Findings

Figure 8.3 shows the results for Sri Lanka for the nine SABER-WfD policy goals. Simple aggregation of the scores for each functional dimension yields the following results: scores for strategic framework and system oversight are at the established (2.6) and service delivery is at the low emerging level (2.3).

Assessment of the strategic framework as being at the established level reflects several findings: (1) for over two decades Sri Lanka's political leaders and policy makers have demonstrated their commitment to putting in place a TVET system to support the building of a competent workforce; (2) the government is addressing WfD as part of its strategy for economic development; (3) it has articulated explicit policies and strategies to build up the WfD system; (4) Sri Lanka has already made progress in increasing access to training for disadvantaged groups and improving training relevance and quality; and (5) despite major initiatives in the last 10 years in making Sri Lanka a regional leader in undertaking some reforms, a well-functioning WfD system is still a distant goal.

Figure 8.3 Sri Lanka WfD Benchmarking Results, 2011

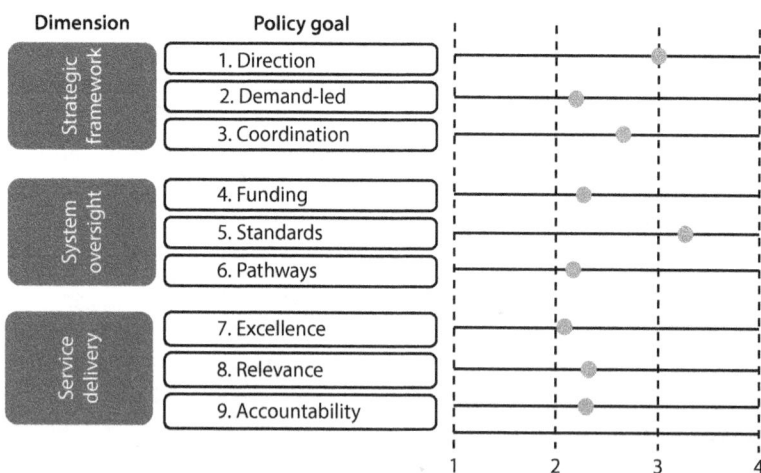

System oversight is also assessed at the established level: (1) funding for TVET is not based on explicit criteria with performance indicators; (2) partnerships with WfD authorities and other stakeholders are ad hoc; (3) training providers lack incentives to seek and retain accreditation; and (4) the drafting of occupational standards for competency-based testing and certification is not yet complete.

Service delivery is assessed at the emerging level: (1) the quality of training is still low; (2) a formal monitoring and evaluation system is not yet in place; and (3) TVET institutions have few incentives to respond directly to the market demand for skills.

In the last two decades, Sri Lanka has issued a number of documents to direct the transformation of education and training systems, and successive governments have supported the process. As a result, it has made significant progress in WfD over the past decade. However, its WfD system is not yet fully effective because it faces difficulties in moving from policy conceptualization to actual production of skills the labor market is demanding.

WfD Priorities
TVET institutions are mostly financed by public funds, which has enabled both urban and rural youth to access TVET, although public networks need to build their capacity to accommodate far more secondary school leavers. The government is mainly focused on IVET and on facilitating the transition of students from school to vocational training. It intends to increase its IVET share from the current 28 percent of the 350,000 annual school admissions to 40 percent in the short term, with special attention to attracting General Certificate of Education (GCE) A-level holders. Because upgrading the skills of the current workforce through CVET has been accorded lower priority, there are few mechanisms to support it.

Remittances from Sri Lankans working abroad are the second-largest foreign exchange earner but the country cannot fully meet external demand for skilled workers. Currently, training targeting foreign employment is acquired through informal work practices.

To build employer confidence, it is vital to both improve TVET quality and ensure that graduates are competent to perform tasks in identified occupations. The TVEC registers both public and private training. Standards have been established for assessing facilities, course curricula, and qualifications of instructors, and the TVEC offers technical guidance. However, the TVEC estimates that about 20 percent of providers operating in the private sector are not registered; it is working on mechanisms to counter that.

WfD Institutes: Strengths and Weaknesses
By bringing most public providers under the MYASD, the government is building coordination between WfD programs, although inter-ministerial coordination has not improved.

Four major public networks—DTET, VTA, NAITA, and NYSC—have training centers throughout the country, making it easy for trainees to access centers close to where they live. Moreover, most centers cater to vulnerable groups, including the disabled. Most public centers offer courses leading at least to NVQ certification, operated in the CBT mode. Course accreditation and quality management systems further improve the training experience. While most public courses are accredited, expansion of coverage will need more funding and more professional and fully committed staff. Some private providers also operate NVQ qualification courses and have formed the Accredited Training Providers Association (ATPA) to coordinate their activities and ensure course quality.

Placement of trainees for on-the-job training (OJT) is an important component of the programs; there is legal provision for trainee placement in businesses, which can accept them without any obligation to provide employment. Private institutions provide OJT through arrangements with businesses. Public-private partnerships (PPPs) have improved the relevance and quality of training and enhanced operational efficiency. Industry-based apprenticeships and entrepreneurship training, coupled with micro loans for self-employment, have been modeled successfully and could be brought into the mainstream.

Policies and Processes

The report of the Presidential Task Force on TVET Reforms (1997) certainly led to TVET improvements, such as adoption of CBT and launch of the NVQ system. The National Policy on Higher Education and Technical and Vocational Education (2009) reinforced the NVQ framework and quality assurance. The latest National Human Resource and Employment Policy (2012) takes an economy-wide approach, but its realization has suffered because of inadequate coordination and monitoring. Thus far, policies and implementation have tended to address issues connected with public training and done little to incentivize private providers.

By definition, WfD caters to the staffing requirements of an economy. The Departments of National Planning (NPD) and Census and Statistics (DCS) and the TVEC analyses of development trends and identification of priority areas provide direction for labor-market-oriented development. However, labor market assessment results are not yet used much in planning public training.

The 2004 NVQ framework provides diverse pathways for acquiring skills and upgrading qualifications, which are further enhanced by mapping NVQ framework to the Sri Lanka National Qualification Framework (SLQF). Competency standards for a number of occupations and fields have been established with industry participation, but they need to be more widely used in all types of training programs. A rigid qualifications framework may have been a necessity as Sri Lanka was transitioning to CBT, but after nearly a decade of experience with the NVQ framework, a more flexible approach that promotes WfD diversification might work to expand NVQ training faster. Design, review, and application of competency standards and curricula, taking into account feedback from the private sector, will encourage the drafting of standards and curricula that meet business needs; it will also require a continuous upgrade of institutional managers and teaching staff.

Training and administrative data gathered from public and private providers have many gaps. Although regular studies coordinated by the TVEC Research Cell have advanced processes, there are few if any studies of policy improvements or collaborations with independent research institutions. Without reliable data from survey results and impact evaluations, designing policy and system improvements is a huge challenge.

Conclusion and Policy Options

Sri Lanka's WfD policies were assessed in terms of strategic framework, system oversight, and service delivery using the World Bank's SABER diagnostic tool. The strategic framework and system oversight were found to be at the established level, but service delivery is weaker.

Sri Lanka's political leaders are thoroughly committed to WfD and have worked for the last two decades to establish a TVET system to support development of a competent workforce. Several policy documents have provided direction for transforming the education and training systems, and successive governments have supported the process. But although there has been significant progress, capacity still does not seem adequate in terms of delivering results.

The Government of Sri Lanka is aware of the difficulties confronting its skills development system as it responds to the needs of a rapidly growing economy; it has already drafted strategies and policies to address access and equity and improve the quality and relevance of TVET programs. Further reforms in the following areas could better align Sri Lanka's WfD policies with its economic and social priorities and make governance and service delivery more effective.

Strategic Framework
- Mechanisms to coordinate the activities of the institutions that provide direction for WfD (NPD, TVEC, and DCS) could make TVET more labor market–oriented and hone the government's ability to deploy resources appropriately.
- Businesses and other stakeholders should have a more active role in planning, oversight, and delivery of training. WfD could be better synchronized—within training institutions and the MYASD and between ministries tasked with skills development, non-state training providers, and businesses—to model and mainstream a coherent approach to WfD.

System Oversight
- TVET financing needs more diverse funding sources, and funding mechanisms could create incentives for better performance. Public funding should be used to promote both internal and external operational efficiency.
- Employers have not as yet made it a priority to upgrade employee skills. Systems that stimulate continuous skills upgrading, such as training levies, could improve employee productivity.

- How the NVQ framework is operationalized, including quality assurance, should be reviewed to make the system more flexible and advance training quality and quantity.
- Obtaining an RPL certification should be made easier to maximize the advantage of continuing education.

Service Delivery
- Policy interventions to promote properly regulated private training could offer private trainers an incentive to bring excellence and diversity into their programs.
- To advance labor market–oriented training and increase operational efficiency, training centers should have more autonomy.
- Steps should be taken to build capacity for monitoring and evaluation, which is essential for planning and evidence-based policy making. Collaborations with independent research institutes could generate reliable data on which to base policy and system improvements.
- Because TVET staff development currently tends to be ad hoc, systematic training for instructors and training center managers could enhance both the quality of the training imparted and the operational efficiency of training centers.
- Expanding initial vocational education and training (IVET) is necessary, especially focusing on diploma and degree levels to meet the growing demand for skills; it is also important to provide skills development opportunities for both the unskilled and those working in the informal sector.

TVET is not the preferred option of many school leavers mainly because they are not aware of the employment and career progression opportunities it offers. Because career guidance services are scattered and uncoordinated, institutionalizing a coordinating mechanism could address this problem.

Annex 8A: Analytical Framework of SABER-WfD

Policy dimensions	Policy goals	Policy actions
Strategic framework	Setting a strategic direction for WfD	Advocate for WfD as a priority for economic development
		Evaluate economic prospects and their skills implications
		Develop policies to align skills demand and skills supply
	Prioritizing a demand-led approach	Promote a demand-driven approach to WfD
		Strengthen company demand for skills to improve productivity
		Address critical challenges in the future supply of skills
	Strengthening critical coordination	Ensure that strategic WfD priorities are coherent
		Institutionalize the structure of WfD roles and responsibilities
		Facilitate communication and interaction among all WfD stakeholders

table continues next page

Policy dimensions	Policy goals	Policy actions
System oversight	Diversifying pathways for skills acquisition	Foster articulation across levels of instruction and types of programs
		Promote lifelong learning through recognition of prior learning
		Set policies and procedures for introducing, adjusting, or closing publicly funded programs
	Ensuring efficiency and equity in funding	Articulate a strategy for funding WfD
		Allocate public funds for WfD to achieve results with efficiency
		Foster partnership between WfD authorities and stakeholders
	Assuring standards are relevant and reliable	Specify accreditation and skills certification
		Strengthen skills testing and certification
		Assure the credibility of accreditation and skills certification
Service delivery	Fostering relevance in training programs	Strengthen linkages between training institutions, industry, and research institutions
		Integrate industry inputs into the design of training programs
		Enhance the competence of WfD administrators and instructors
	Incentivizing excellence in training	Promote diversity in training
		Incentivize private providers to meet WfD standards
		Motivate public training institutions to respond to demand for skills
	Enhancing accountability for results	Strengthen WfD monitoring and evaluation
		Specify reporting requirements for training institutions
		Increase focus on outcomes, efficiency, and innovation in service delivery

Notes

1. For details on SABER, see http://www.worldbank.org/education/saber.
2. For Sri Lanka, the principal investigator was Dr. Tilkaratne A. Piyasiri.
3. This is the TVEC estimate.

Bibliography

SSM (Secretariat for Senior Ministers). 2012. *The National Human Resources and Employment Policy for Sri Lanka*. Secretariat for Senior Ministers. Colombo: Government of Sri Lanka.

Tan, J-P., K. H. Lee, A. Valerio, and R. McGough. 2012. *What Matters in Workforce Development: An Analytical Framework for the Pilot Phase*. World Bank, Washington, DC. http://siteresources.worldbank.org/EDUCATION/Resources/278200-1290520949227/7575842-1336502112143/SABER_WfD_Framework_Paper_9-07-12.pdf.

TVEC (Tertiary and Vocational Education Commission). 2009. *National Vocational Qualification Framework of Sri Lanka: Operations Manual*. Colombo.

CHAPTER 9

Main Findings and the Way Forward

Skills development is an important component of national development strategies in both developed and developing nations. The demand for job-specific technical skills in Sri Lanka is high due to structural changes in the economy and sustained economic growth over the past decade. The demand for skills is intensified as the country transforms itself into an efficiency-driven middle-income economy following the *Mahinda Chintana* strategy (MFP 2010) of becoming a regional hub in key economic area as population growth slows. Recognizing the importance of skills and the implications of skills constraints for the country's economic development, the MC highlights the significance of skills for raising national competitiveness and reducing poverty.

This book contributes to the understanding of skills demand and supply in Sri Lanka, with a focus on technical and vocational education and training (TVET). It analyzes the demand drivers and employer needs for skills, studies the skills supply of the workforce and how skills are formed by education and training systems, and examines the strategic directions in skills development and how the system is managed and financed. It also offers suggestions on how to improve skills development so that the country is in a better position to achieve economic growth and reduce poverty.

Main Findings

While recent studies looked at general and higher education systems in Sri Lanka (World Bank 2009, 2011), this is the first attempt at a comprehensive assessment of Sri Lanka's skills development sector, focusing on technical and vocational education and training by considering skills supply and demand, skills gaps and mismatches, and system management, governance, and financing. The analysis is based on original surveys and data from multiple sources; it goes beyond the standard measures of skills in terms of enrollment and completion rates by looking at skills in three broad categories: cognitive, technical, and noncognitive ("soft"). The main findings emerging from the study are as follows:

- Although the Sri Lankan labor force is the most educated in South Asia, with the highest literacy rates and the highest pre-tertiary enrollment and completion rates, the job-specific skills supply is trailing. Self-reported reading and writing skills are lower than in the other countries that participated in the World Bank Skills Toward Employment and Productivity (STEP) survey. Few workers have the technical skills a modern competitive economy requires, such as computer knowledge and English. Moreover, the education and training system does not do much to shape soft skills, which are also in high demand for a wide range of occupations.

- The returns to higher levels of education (GCE A-levels and above) have been rising and remained sizeable between 2000 and 2012. But even after accounting for educational attainment, there are also returns to both job-specific and soft skills. Sri Lankans with certain technical skills, such as technology, computer knowledge, and English, and such soft skills as openness, extraversion, and emotional stability, earn more than those without them.

- The major drivers of skills demand in Sri Lanka, including economic growth, labor migration, urbanization, the expansion of primary and secondary education, and demographic change, increasingly call for a better educated and trained labor force, upgraded skills, and workers equipped with higher-order competencies that can use new technologies and perform complex tasks efficiently. Firms in Sri Lanka complain more often about the lack of adequately educated labor force than in other South Asian countries. Sri Lankan employers also point out that TVET is not relevant to their needs and question the quality of its curricula. There are mismatches between the skills produced by the education and training systems and the skills employers demand. The mismatch is especially severe in higher levels of education (GCE A-levels and above and TVET) and job-specific and soft skills.

- Every year an estimated 140,000 students complete general education without having acquired job-related skills. Since the capacity of the Sri Lankan higher education system is limited, the government sees the TVET system as the main means to close the gap. However, serious deficiencies in the system prevent TVET from playing this role, thus jeopardizing Sri Lanka's goal of becoming a competitive middle-income economy. Along with skills shortages in a number of fields and occupations, Sri Lanka is also experiencing both underemployment and youth unemployment.

- The study found that the current skills development system faces challenges in such areas as organization and management (e.g., excessive centralization, responsibility overlaps, few accountability mechanisms); access and equity (e.g., regional disparities); internal efficiency and effectiveness (low quality of instruction, inadequate qualification of instructors); resource allocation and utilization (e.g., lack of incentives, absence of links between resources and performance); relevance or external efficiency (e.g., quantitative and qualitative skills mismatches and shortages); and information (e.g., lack of visibility of skills needs, social stigma attached to technical training).

- As the absorptive capacity of the public sector is shrinking, the private sector is becoming the main source of job creation. Yet employers are not fully integrated into the planning, provision, and regulation of the skills they need to make job creation a reality. Skills development in Sri Lanka is yet to become a truly demand-driven activity aligned with the ever-changing needs of the economy.

The Way Forward

While a skilled workforce is necessary for growth and poverty alleviation, skills do not automatically lead to jobs and growth. Skills development needs to be part of a comprehensive economic development strategy, and job creation and skills development should be pursued together as part of that strategy. Furthermore, skills development should be part of a comprehensive lifelong education and training strategy because it is a cumulative life cycle process. The Government of Sri Lanka has identified skills development, including TVET, as an important part of the MC.

Sustaining economic growth and achieving the government's development goals require investment in skills development, including pre-employment training. The current quantitative and qualitative mismatch between supply of and demand for skilled labor threatens a critical source of growth. In particular, current TVET is not responsive to changes in employer demand for skilled labor. TVET, if well-designed and implemented, could stimulate workforce acquisition of the type of skills required for an innovative, service-based economy.

This book has identified challenges in Sri Lanka's skills development sector and possible reforms to make the workforce development system more responsive to the labor market. The government commitment to skills development outlined in the MC and the NHREP policy documents created great momentum to foster skills development in Sri Lanka and improve the TVET system. Building on the vision and strategic directions of the MC, the government has recently adopted a sector-wide, medium-term program (2014–2020) to transform Sri Lanka's TVET sector into an effective skills development system. Yet much remains to be done if the potential of a skilled labor force is to be fully unleashed. The following reforms should be strategic priorities:

- Implementation of the skills sector development strategy is essential to develop a coherent framework conducive to focused and realistic measures to equip workers with relevant skills.

Building the Skills for Economic Growth and Competitiveness in Sri Lanka
http://dx.doi.org/10.1596/978-1-4648-0158-7

- The quality of current TVET services needs to become both more attractive for youths and more relevant for employers—implying better training and more experience in industry for instructors.
- As the economy moves forward, the TVET system will need to become more diversified; active engagement with employers (from upstream involvement in curriculum development to involvement in teaching, regulation, financing, and provision) would make the system truly demand-driven.
- The effectiveness of the TVET system will depend on whether it is adequately resourced, whether resources are linked to performance, and whether the funds allocated are used efficiently.
- Flexible and accountable governance mechanisms are needed at all TVET levels, with their components coordinated not only with each other but also with all system stakeholders—which implies, in particular, rationalization of the responsibilities of the various agencies under the Ministry of Youth Affairs and Skills Development (MYASD) umbrella.
- Given the importance of the informal sector, its skills development needs should be specifically targeted, with incentives to boost the skills of informal workers.
- It would be beneficial to evaluate and specifically address the needs of companies related to enterprise-based training, which remains the training instrument privileged by many firms.

Because the reform agenda is so comprehensive, all the reforms cannot be implemented immediately; priorities must be identified. Once they are sequenced as a package designed to establish a demand-driven TVET sector, Sri Lanka should be well on its way to building a skilled workforce that will promote economic growth and competitiveness. Annex 9A summarizes challenges, possible strategic directions, and priorities that the government can consider in addressing Sri Lanka's skills challenge.

Annex 9A: Sri Lanka: Matrix of Main Issues and Strategic Priorities and Policy Options

Issues/Findings	Options/Recommendations		Timing
	Strategic directions of reforms	Policy actions	
The quality of primary and secondary education[a]			
• High enrollment in primary and secondary education but relatively low basic knowledge and skills, which affects student learning and ultimately labor market outcomes	• Improve the quality of primary and secondary education.	• Apply strategic directions and policy actions (identified in the general and higher education studies) supported by World Bank-financed education projects.	Continuing
The quality and relevance of TVET—skills shortages and mismatches			
• Poor-quality and irrelevant TVET programs • Little participation by employers in TVET curricula, delivery, and assessment	• Enhance the quality and relevance of TVET by making it demand-driven.	• Encourage private sector participation in managing TVET institutions to ensure greater responsiveness to demand.	Medium-term
		• Establish Sector Skills Councils in priority sectors to advise the government on sectoral skills needs and standards.	Medium-term
		• Revise curricula to respond directly to labor market needs; explicitly incorporate soft skills in curricula.	Medium-term
		• Recruit teachers with industry experience and provide them with professional development opportunities.	Medium-term
		• Analyze how the National Vocational Qualification (NVQ) Framework operates to improve course accreditation, quality assurance, and the NVQ certification process.	Medium-term
		• Give public institutions more autonomy in the design and delivery of training programs, hiring or firing of teachers, and revenue generation and utilization.	Short-term
		• Adopt public–private partnership (PPP) models.	Short-term
• Inadequate supply of skills, especially in emerging economic sectors	• Expand the supply of skills, especially advanced skills in emerging economic sectors, with the active participation of private sector providers.	• Expand the capacity of selected institutions gradually, based on inputs from Sector Skills Councils with employer representation.	Medium-term

table continues next page

| | | Options/Recommendations | |
Issues/Findings	Strategic directions of reforms	Policy actions	Timing
• Inadequate supply of private training	• Leverage the contribution of the private sector to both pre-employment and on-the-job training, while improving quality.	• Introduce incentives for private providers to take a more active role.	Short-term
		• More vigorously enforce registration and accreditation requirements for private institutions.	Short-term
• Inefficient delivery of TVET (for example, under-utilization, high dropout rates in some programs)	• Improve the efficiency of public training institutions.	• Involve the private sector in institutional management.	Short-term
		• Rationalize the delivery of public training institutions and programs based on inputs from employers.	Medium-term
		• Link resource allocation to performance.	Medium-term
• Limited opportunities for lifelong learning, resulting in low student demand for some TVET programs and high dropout rates in the TVET system	• Build pathways to enable lifelong learning through more vertical and horizontal mobility within the education and training system.	• Implement the Sri Lanka Vocational Qualifications Framework (SLQF), which encourages flexibility and mobility within the education and training system.	Medium-term
		• Introduce career guidance into school curricula.	Medium-term
Management and governance			
• A complex and fragmented skills development sector that lacks accountability and incentives for good performance	• Improve management, governance, and accountability arrangements.	• Review, clarify, and streamline assignment of the responsibilities of national institutions for TVET.	Short-term
		• Increase coordination among the relevant ministries (for example, education, youth affairs and skills development, higher education, finance and national planning, and ministries responsible for specialized skills development programs) to reinforce national coordination of skills development and ensure that programs are consistent with the national economic development plan.	Short-term
		• Build MYASD and Tertiary and Vocational Education Commission (TVEC) capacity for strategic planning, policy implementation, and monitoring and evaluation.	Medium-term
		• Tighten coordination between skills providers and the private sector to ensure that the system is responsive to demand.	Short-term

table continues next page

Issues/Findings	Options/Recommendations		Timing
	Strategic directions of reforms	Policy actions	
• Inadequate information on what the labor market needs to guide skills development policy	• Build up labor market information systems.	• Improve labor market information through regular surveys and studies to assess demand for skills.	Medium-term
		• Collect and make available quality data on institutions (for example, enrollments, courses, staff, financial data, etc.) to assess the skills supply.	Medium-term
		• Improve coordination between public and private training providers, industry partners, and ministries and agencies.	Medium-term
		• Build up the management information system capacity of TVEC as the central unit for collection, analysis (including tracer studies), and reporting of data on labor market and institutional performance.	Medium-term
		• Analyze and report information on the status of skills development at regular intervals (for example, an annual report) to increase accountability to clients; inform preparation of budgets; and strengthen governance of the TVET system.	Medium-term

Use of public resources for TVET: scope for improved efficiency and effectiveness

Issues/Findings	Strategic directions of reforms	Policy actions	Timing
• Ad hoc financing of the TVET sector that is not linked to performance, creating inefficiencies	• Improve sector planning, budget formulation, and implementation to achieve sector priorities.	• Draft a medium-term skills development plan, together with a Medium Term Expenditure Framework (MTEF) coordinated at the national level. Consider using this plan for allocating budgetary resources.	Short-term
	• Use financing as a tool to make TVET spending more efficient by providing incentives for better training quality and relevance; and by reinforcing accountability to promote performance for results.	• Allocate resources based on the performance of TVET institutions (for example, link budgeting to enrollment, graduation, and employment rates) in terms of achieving national priorities.	Short-term
		• Mobilize additional resources by broadening the financial resource base: give institutions incentives to generate and use nonbudgetary resources (for example, student fees, training fees for firms, sale of services).	Medium-term

table continues next page

Issues/Findings	Options/Recommendations		Timing
	Strategic directions of reforms	Policy actions	
	• Mobilize additional resources by establishing a training fund for allocation of resources.	• Restructure the Skills Development Fund to manage mobilization of resources and allocate the resources competitively to both public and private institutions that are performing well, starting with a pilot in selected trades before scaling up.	Medium-term
Inequities in access to TVET: reducing disparities by gender, income, and location			
• Inequities in access to TVET by gender, income, and location	• Improve access to TVET by gender, especially for girls and the poor, and address regional disparities.	• Review how existing financial aid programs are operating.	Short-term
		• Implement a targeted, need-based scholarship program to address critical skills shortages and ensure access for disadvantaged groups.	Medium-term
		• Initiate a program of vouchers that allows potential trainees to opt for training institutions of their choice.	Medium-term
Skills for the unskilled workers in the informal sector			
• Inadequate training opportunities for workers in the informal sector	• Program and plan skills development for informal workers.	• Formulate policies for increasing training programs for the informal sector.	Short-term
		• Pilot proposed interventions, such as better-structured apprenticeship programs, and assess their effectiveness before scaling them up.	Medium-term
Upgrading skills—firm-based training			
• A shortage of firm-based training, which is a barrier to labor force skills upgrading	• Evaluate and address the needs of firms related to enterprise-based training.	• Restructure the Skills Development Fund and pilot the restructured program.	Short-term
		• Offer firms incentives to build their in-house training capabilities.	Short-term

a. This is a summary of strategic directions and policy actions extracted from a recent World Bank education sector review.

Environmental Benefits Statement

The World Bank Group is committed to reducing its environmental footprint. In support of this commitment, the Publishing and Knowledge Division leverages electronic publishing options and print-on-demand technology, which is located in regional hubs worldwide. Together, these initiatives enable print runs to be lowered and shipping distances decreased, resulting in reduced paper consumption, chemical use, greenhouse gas emissions, and waste.

The Publishing and Knowledge Division follows the recommended standards for paper use set by the Green Press Initiative. Whenever possible, books are printed on 50 percent to 100 percent postconsumer recycled paper, and at least 50 percent of the fiber in our book paper is either unbleached or bleached using totally chlorine free (TCF), processed chlorine free (PCF), or enhanced elemental chlorine free (EECF) processes.

More information about the Bank's environmental philosophy can be found at http://crinfo.worldbank.org/wbcrinfo/node/4.

green press INITIATIVE

Bibliography

MFP (Ministry of Finance and Planning). 2010. *Mahinda Chintana.* http://www.treasury .gov.lk/publications/mahindaChintanaVision-2010full-eng.pdfc.

SSM (Secretariat for Senior Ministers). 2012. *The National Human Resources and Employment Policy for Sri Lanka.* Secretariat for Senior Ministers. Colombo: Government of Sri Lanka.

World Bank. 2009. *The Towers of Learning: Higher Education in Sri Lanka.* Human Development Unit, South Asia Region, World Bank, Washington, DC.

———. 2011. *Transforming School Education in Sri Lanka: From Cut Stones to Polished Jewels.* Washington, DC: Human Development Unit, South Asia Region, World Bank.